POLITICS AND PUBLIC ADMINISTRATION

POLITICS AND PUBLIC ADMINISTRATION

P. R. DUBHASHI

KALPAZ

First Published, 2020
Published by
Kalpaz Publications
C-30, Satyawati Nagar,
Delhi – 110052
Ph.: 011-47034999, 9811692060
www.kalpazpublications.com
E-mail: kalpaz@hotmail.com
Printed at: G. Print Process, Delhi

Cataloging in Publication Data—DK
Courtesy: D.K. Agencies (P) Ltd. <docinfo@dkagencies.com>

Dubhashi, P. R., author.
Politics and public administration / by P.R. Dubhashi.
pages cm
ISBN 9789353240035

1. India—Politics and government. 2. Public administration—India. 3. India—Economic conditions. 4. India—Social conditions. I. Title.

LCC DS407.D83 2019 | DDC 954 23

Contents

POLITICS - I

SOCIAL - II

CO-OPERATIVES - III

ECONOMICS - IV

ADMINISTRATION -V

EDUCATION - VI

INTERNATIONAL RELATIONS - VII

POLITICS - I

Chapter - 1

Reflections on the Indian Polity and Some Suggestions for its Reconstitution

Indian democracy is passing through a period of crisis. The 1989 elections led to the situation where no party had a majority in the Parliament to form government, The Congress, through still the largest, declined the invitation; the next largest combine viz. the National Front came to power with the outside support of B.J.P. and the Leftist parties. The goodwill for the non-Congress combine in the country was such that it was felt that the National Front Government would be able to carry on for a full period of five years, However, within a few months of assumption of office, bickerings started within the Janata Dal and in the attempt to counter his deputy and to capture vote banks through populist and radical postures, the Prime Minister Shri. V. P. Singh, lost the 'outside support' of the B.J.P. This led to a greater anomaly in that a party which had no more than 54 MPs and which was in fact a breakaway group of Janata Dal formed government with the support of the Congress party. As was only to be expected, the government could not last long. General elections had to be held in less than one and half years. To prevent the agony of a general election so soon after the 1989 elections, the President of India himself explored the possibility of forming of National government but that proved to be a non-starter and fresh elections had to be gone through.

In 1991 elections turned out to be the most violent involving, on a large scale, gun battles, booth capturing and rigging especially in Bihar and U.P. The violence ultimately culminated in the dastardly assassination of Shri Rajiv Gandhi in the midst of the election process itself. The Election Commission postponed the remaining part of the election by three weeks. This virtually turned the 1991 election into two elections and led to protest from several parties to the Election Commission. As was expected there was a definite change in the election atmosphere following Mr. Rajiv Gandhi's assassination appropriately described as the 'sympathy wave', which doubtless affected the outcome of the election.

However, it was feared that despite all the expense and trouble of the general election, the nation would still be faced with a hung Parliament. The fear came true. The Congress and its allies failed to get the majority, though they came very near it, while the B.J.P. on the right and the National Front and its allies on the left won about 120 seats. The Leftist Party have promised 'Constructive support', whatever that might be and the B.J.P. also promised to support the Government in the 'National interest', depending, of course, on the policies of Government, thus putting the onus on the ruling party.

For sometime the choice of leadership of the Congress party in Parliament itself became a matter of tension and uncertainty with Shri Pawar staking his claim by insisting on the election of the leader through secret ballot. However, after some period of anxiety, the party unanimously resolved to elect Shri Narasimha Rao as the leader of the Congress party, who after being called upon by the President to be the Prime Minister, lost no time in forming a full-fledged government.

The manner in which Indian parliamentary democracy has survived a severe political crisis has once again proved wrong its worst critics who had spoken of dark days for the nation and the disintegration of its democratic institutions.

In a way the situation prevailing in Indian democracy as it stands today may well be considered to be the normal situation while what existed in the past, specially during the period of one party, one person domination, is bound to be considered, in the historical context as only an aberration. If charismatic leadership, the delusion of grandeur, the dynastic rule, the influence of a manipulating coterie and the palace intrigues give way to open compromises and consultations between politicians from different parts of the country and coalition of different sorts between the leftist and rightist parties (though the terms leftist and rightist may have changing connotations at different levels), it is bound to be considered a normal pattern of Parliamentary democracy in our country.

The singular contribution of the 1991 elections is the emergence of a non U.P. personality as the Prime Minister in India. Many had considered it nearly impossible for non U.P. politician ever to become the Prime Minister of India but the 1991 elections have proved them wrong. This development of having a Prime Minister from the South is bound to strengthen the stakes of the South in the Central Government. To add to this, the absence of a dominating charismatic personality imposing his or her political will on the Chief Ministers in different states in India is bound to increase the capacity of the states to bear responsibilities and promote healthy relations between the centre and states as envisaged in the Indian constitution. Again, in recent years, because of the dominating personality of the Prime Minister, cabinet government had virtually become the prime ministers government and this, in turn had an unhealthy impact on the working of the Central Government. The Prime Minister is expected to function as 'primus interpares', the first among equal's. With Shri. Narsimha Rao as Prime Minister, if this happens, as is likely the Cabinet Government will start functioning in a normal manner on the basis of individual and collective responsibility.

Another welcome outcome of the 1991 election which would go a long way to strengthen the India polity is the setback received by aggressive regionalism, in Assam, Tamil Nadu, Maharashtra, Haryana and Goa. Forces behind the regionalist tendencies would now have to relate themselves to a national perspective.

With a hold new industrial policy and budget and assured IMF assistance, and good agricultural crops because of good monsoons. India can look forward to uninterrupted growth of its economy on sound lines.

While India may breaths a sign of relief at these developments, the working of India's polity has also to be seen in the long term perspective. From time to time, Indian constitutional and political thinkers have thought of changing from Parliamentary democracy to Presidential democrary. The founding fathers of the constitution had favoured Parliamentary democracy because the Presidential democracy of the USA type was not familiar to Indian and the model of British democracy – the West minister model was considered to be the only choice for India. At the time of India emerging to independence, Indian politicians had the experience of running elected governments in provinces. They had also participated in the Central Legislative assembly. Independent India, with the availability of stalwarts familiar with Parliamentary democracy could, therefore, easily start working with the institutions of Parliamentary democracy. However, in the face of difficulties which the Indian polity has gone through in the recent years, many constitutional thinkers have proposed the replacement of Parliamentary democracy with Presidential democracy. With the outcome of 1991 election, the talk of switching to the Presidential form of democracy is likely to subside. However, this is precisely time when the comparative merits of the two systems should be considered in a calm atmosphere. Presidential democracy has its own difficulties. The Presidential system is based on the separation of the Executive from the legislature. Consequently, the President has to face constant difficulty in pushing his legislative programme and even in getting clearance for various high level appointments. Not too long in the past, the USA found itself in a situation where even the normal working of the federal government was jeopardized because Congress failed to sanction funds and the situation was saved only at the last moment. Separation of the Executive from the Legislature as envisaged in the Presidential system is not conducive to a smooth functioning of the government. Moreover, the concentration of power in the hands of the President as envisaged in the Presidential system may lead to dictatorial tendencies with unpredictable consequences. This tendency may not emerge or prevail in USA but cannot be ruled out in India.

The type of Presidential system working in France may not also have much to command itself. France had to go through an uncomfortable period when there was a tortuous 'co-habitation' of a socialist President and Gaullist Prime Minister. The right and proper course of action, therefore, would be to consider whether the short-comings of the Indian Parliamentary Democracy can be removed in the light of experience through suitable constitutional amendments.

Free and fair election constitute the foundation of Parliamentary Democracy. However, four factors have tended to destroy the very foundation viz. increase in use of money power and muscle power at the time of election, incitement to caste and communal prejudices of the voters and misuse of public machinery. Bribing the voters by offering them money or gifts has been an old phenomenon for quite sometime now. It is in order to prevent this, that the Representation of People's Act envisaged limits on expenditure by every candidate standing for election. Every candidate has to give a certificate after the elections to the effect that the statutory limits on expenditure have been observed. However, it has been widely acknowledged that these limits are hardly observed in practice. And the Election Commission itself had admitted that the rules laid down under the Representation of the People's Act for limiting election expenditure have been violated. The use of money power has enormously increased with the emergence of the phenomenon of black money. It was openly said during the last general election that Rs. 50 lakhs to one crore had to be spent by every candidate standing for Parliamentary elections. In order to prevent this abuse, it has been suggested many times that we should follow the example of the Scandinavian countries, where the state bears the election expenses for all candidates and hence no private expenditure by any candidate is allowed. However, in our country, the proposal has not been accepted so far. Mainly because of the enormous burden it is likely to throw on the public exchequer which will bear the burden, Private expenditure by the candidates themselves could not be ruled out.

Allied to money power is muscle power. Allied to the black economy and working in tendem with it, is the growing criminalisation of Indian politics which manifests itself at the time of elections in the form of booth capturing, rigging and gun battles between rivals gangs working on behalf of the candidates. It has been reported during the 1991 elections that all these were the orders of the day in many constituencies in Bihar and UP. Smt. Nalini

Singh shocked the audience by presenting on the television the actual process of booth capturing. The blatant use of muscle power makes a mockery of free and fair elections and though confined largely to Bihar and UP at present, the menace can spread to other parts of the country, if not vigourously handled at this stage itself.

Appealing to caste and communal prejudices at time of elections is again nothing new to Indian democracy. Caste and communal factors are always taken into account by all political parties (and not only the avowedly communal ones like the Muslim League, Hindu Maha sabha and Akali Dal) in the selection of candidates, having regard to the composition of the electorate. However, caste and communal appeals became particularly strident during the 1991 elections with the Mandir and Mandal issues getting overwhelming prominence., The audio cassettes of Sadhvi Ritambhara were the high water mark of communal propaganda at election time. Secularism, which had always been the first casualty at election times, was this time simply swept away under the deluge of communal and caste propaganda.

Money power, muscle power and caste and communal appeals constitute the three great challenges faced by Indian democracy. The only way to combat these challenges is by vigourously enforcing the provisions of the Representation of People's Act. What comes in the way of a strict enforcement of the Act is the fact that the Chief Election Commissioner who is responsible for enforcing the Act has to act through the agency of the State officials and these agencies are accountable to those very authorities of the State who are guilty of perpetuating these evils (of money power, muscle power and caste and communal appeals)

Over and above these evils, there is the gross abuse of state machinery by governments in power, who not only bestow illegitimate and out-of-turn benefits to their supporters but also use government servants for party purposes, although the latter is specifically banned, both, under the Representation of People's Act and under the Civil Servants Conduct Rules.

All the violations of law which come in the way of free and fair elections can be eliminated if from the time from which the electoral process starts till the results are declared, rule of the State Government is replaced by President's rule. This would then enable the Chief Election Commissioner to hold the Chief Election Officers and the Returning Officers to account for strict Act. It is also necessary to provide for constitutional safeguards against parties which get votes in the name of caste and community. The Constitution, at present has no article, relating to the most important participants in the political process viz. political parties. It is high time that the constitution bans all parties with communal denominations and required all parties to have regular internal elections and audit of its finance.

Another serious short-coming of the Indian Parliamentary Democracy is the persistent disparity between the percentage of votes received by various political parties and the percentage of seats captured by them in the Parliament under the 'first past the post system' of elections. As a result of this, with minority electoral support, parties have been able to get huge majority of seats in the Legislature. In the past, the Congress party was the main beneficiary of this phenomenon. There has been a long time demand, therefore, of the main opposition parties and their leaders, for some from of proportional representation based either on multi-member constituencies with single transferable vote or on the 'list system'. These systems are prevailing in Europe and can be examined by experts of election systems for adoption in India. A system which is easy to operate, can be adopted in India and could then become the basis of Parliamentary Democracy wherein Parliament, reflects more truly the popular will.

The purpose of Parliamentary elections is to form a co-herent and stable Government, accountable to Parliament. However, the phenomenon of hung Parliament makes it difficult for any party to form a government which could be viable and would last for five years. So long as one party, viz. The Congress enjoyed a dominant position in India politics, there was no difficulty at all in forming Government. However, one party dominance was not considered healthy and it was expected that in course of time a viable opposition party as an alternative to the Congress would evolve in the country; but that has not happened. No single party left or right of Congress, was able to develop as a strong nationwide alternative. Rajgopalachary started a new party of the Right viz. the Swantantra Party but, it soon ceased to be. Dr. Shayma Prasad Mukherjee brought into exisetence Bharatiya Jana Sangh which has now taken the form of the Bharatiya Janata Party. The 1977 elections saw the emergence of the Janata Party under the inspiration of Shri. Jai Prakash Narayan. After many transformations of this party we have now the Janata Dal and the Samajwadi Janata Party. In addition to these, there are a number of regional parties like the Telugu Desham, The D.M.K., Haryana Vikas Manch, Jharkhand Mukti Morcha etc. The existence of a number of parties has meant the absence of two party system of the sort existing in U.K., which makes the phenomenon of a hung Parliament impossible. In India, it is clear that we may have to live with multiplicity of parties and the consequent possibility, indeed probability of elections always bringing into existence a hung Parliament. In such a situation, coalition government would be a normal phenomenon. But, in India, instead of the coalition, both after the 1989 and 1991 general elections, what we have are minority governments which are much more vulnerable to no confidence motion than coalition governments. If minority government become short-lived, India would be faced with a a constant need for premature elections at short intervals. A country as desperately poor as India, can hardly afford the enormous expenses involved in such elections. Besides frequent elections would make sustained policies and approaches in government impossible.

The difficulties mentioned above, demand that we give serious thought to amending the Constitution in order to ensure that the country gets a stable government for a full period of five years between two general elections. One way for doing this, I suggest, is the introduction of German constitutional provisions of 'constructive voter of no confidence' which makes it impossible for the Parliament to pass a vote of no confidence without simultaneously electing another government with a majority support in Parliament. Till an alternative leader capable of gaining confidence of the Parliament is elected, government in power would not be disturbed. In case the Parliament is caught in an imbroglio, where no party or coalition of parties can form the government, the constitution must provide for the President's rule at the Centre till the Parliament is in a position to form a viable coalition. The President would carry on his rule with a council of ministers of his choice headed by the Vice President of India. This may appear to be serious departure from a system of Parliamentary Democracy, but taking into account the kind of situation in which we have found ourselves in recent times, this combination of Parliamentary government with Presidential government as a stand-by arrangement seems inevitable, and the only way by which we can escape the evils of hung Parliament and frequent elections.

The Indian Constitution was framed by Constituent Assembly in which legal luminaries had the benefit of experience of other countries but only a vague awareness of the problem that were likely to develop in the future. Now, more than forty years after independence, the time has come to set up a new Constituent Assembly consisting of both the elected representative of the people and experts and thinkers from various walks of national life who should have a close look at the working of the Indian polity and the constitutional machinery and introduce, in the light of experience of the last forty years, necessary amendments which would ensure stability and better government. The suggestions made in this brief article are some of those which such a Constituent Assembly might well consider.

Chapter - 2

The Federal Issues in Indian Polity

Discord on NCTC

The federal issues in the Indian polity have come to the fore in recent times. They came up prominently when the proposal of the Union Home Ministry to setup a national counter terrorism centre (NCTC) was placed before the meeting Chief Ministers convened by the Union Home Minister, Several Chief Ministers opposed the proposal to the tooth and nail. The Chief Ministers included not only Chief Ministers of the states where BJP the main opposition party at the centre is in power, especially Shri. Narendra Modi, Chief Minister of Gujarat and Chief Ministers who head regional parties in power like Smt. Jayalalita, ADAMK in Tamil Nadu and Naveen Patnaik, head of BJD in Orrisa but even the Chief Minister of alliance party in the UPA government at the centre viz. Trinmul Congress in West Bengal headed by Smt. Mamata Banerjee. All those Chief Ministers took exception to the Central Government taking a unilateral decision without consulting the State government even though law and order, according to the constitution, is a subject which falls in the state list as per seventh schedule of the Constitution. (It may be pointed out that the word that appears in the state list is 'public order' and not (Law and order). Also 'Police' are under the jurisdiction of the state and it is they who have tackle the violation of public order by the terrorists. The Home Ministry of the Union Government decided to convene a conference of the State Directors Generals of Police and later the Chief Ministers of the State only after strenuous objections raised by the Chief Ministers. What added fuel to the fire was remark alleged to have been made by the Union Home Secretary who reprimanded, the Director General of Police of State Governments 'not to behave like stenographers to the Chief Ministers and Home Minister of the State." The Chief Ministers also did not approve of the proposal to put the NCTC under the IB because the IB has been used by the Central Government to keep an eye on the Chief Ministers and Ministers of States Governments. They feared that the central counter terrorist agency will be used by the IB for the same purpose. The Union Home Minister agreed to make suitable amendments, including taking the NCTC out of the jurisdiction of the IB and including State Director Generals in the composition of NCTC. Both the Prime Minister who inaugurated the conference and the Home Minister who addressed it appealed to the State Chief Ministers to agree to their proposal pointing out terrorist threat is not confined to the jurisdiction of a single state, it spills across several states and therefore the central and state government should join hands to deal with the terrorist threats which pose serious challenges to the security of Indian republic. In spite of the fervent appeal, the conference of Chief Ministers could not arrive at a consensus, through the Home Minister insisted that a NCTC is a must for dealing with grave challenge of the terrorists who are determined to attack the authority of the state by their own armed forces in which men and women and even children mainly of the tribal community are enlisted and indulge at will in attacking police stations, public offices and panchayat etc. and recently abducting even high level officers like Collectors and elected MLA's.

Only united strategy and efforts by State and Central Government can effectively deal with the grave challenges posed by the terrorists. After abduction of collectors and MLAs, the terrorist outfits made demands for the release of several terrorists and their helpers including those guilty of murder held in prison by the state. Should the state governments deal with the situation as it arose by bargaining with the terrorists or should there be a nationally agreed strategy such as not conceding to any of the demands of the terrorists in return for the release of officers or other individuals abducted and held in custody by the terrorists? On the policy, there has been no agreed formulation. Reference was made to the 'no negotiation strategy' of a country like Israel though it was pointed out that even country like Israel had to bargain on many occasions. The position, as of now, in dealing with the terrorist threat seems to be nebulous and indecisive and does not inspire confidence. It is agreed that the problem of terrorists is not just of law and order; it is also of 'development of the tribal people and regions.

This development efforts has to be taken up by the State administration rather than the Centre administration. Centre can at best offer financial support. The challenges posed by the Maoists in large forest tracts extending over several states like MP, Maharashtra, AP, Odisha, West Bengal, Chattisgarh, Jharkhand and Bihar are so serious that a joint strategy by the Centre and States is necessary. Yet the Home Ministry is not able to bring around the states to accept the view. Not that the states do not realise the gravity of the terrorist challenge but clearly there is lack of trust generated by the tendency of the Centre to assume that it knows best and the states have to fall in line.

This, the Chief Ministers of States are not prepared to accept despite the gravity of the situation. The Chief Ministers have reminded the centre many times that they are nearer to field than the central ministers and their view must be taken account by them before formulating policies and programmes, whether in respect of law and order or development.

Terrorism as an organised threat whether in external and internal threat is a phenomenon which did not exist when the founding fathers framed the constitution nor could they have anticipated it in the then existing situation. Hence, it does not expressly figure in any of the three lists in seventh schedule of the constitution. Perhaps time has come for an amendment to the constitution to include the subject of terrorism expressly in the concurrent list. The full fledged discussion on the subject in the central and state legislatures and will provide opportunity for comprehensive discussion on nature of terrorism and strategy and organisation for dealing with the threat. This would remove ambiguities of provide a base and framework for joint action by the Union and State governments.

The Chief Ministers resent that they have go to Planning Commission to get funds due to them. Recently after a meeting in the Planning Commission to seek funds for his State, Shri. Prakash Singh Badal, Chief Minister of Punjab came out in a rage and told the waiting reporters that 'they were being treated like beggars by the Planning Commission and their governments like municipal corporations'. Similar views were expressed by Jaylalitha of Tamil Nadu and Naveen Patnaik of Odisha.

Arbitrary imposition of President rule on the States in the past has created deep distrust between Centre and the State. In today's political scenario, it is unlikely that such a arbitrary exercise of power by the Union government would be possible.

The idea that there are some national issues on which both the Union Government and State Government are under different political parties should work in unison that the national cleavages of caste, community and ideology must sink in the political psyche of the country is of paramount importance.

Bill on Lokpal and Lokayukta

Under the pressure of fast by Anna Hazare, the union government was forced to take up the legislation for setting up Lokpal to deal with corruption which has been pending for the last 42 years. The Hazare team insisted that the bill should include not only the appointment of Lokpal at the Centre but also Lokayukta in States to deal comprehensively with corruption. But the latter provision become a stumbling block. Several Chief Ministers like Naveen Patnaik, Jayalalita and Mamata Banerjee opposed the inclusion of Lok Ayukta in central legislation saying that this violated the federal character of the constitution. The Bill could not be passed in Rajya Sabha where the ruling Congress had no majority and the legislation is hanging fire.

Issues of External Affairs

Even on issued of external issues the opposition alliance partners in government deeply embarrassed the Union Government. Thus, just on the eve of departure of the Prime Minister Dr. Manmohan Singh for a long awaited visit to Bangladesh during which a historic treaty of co-operation between the two nations was to be signed, the Chief Minster of West Bengal Smt. Mamta Banerjee refused to join Prime Minister's delegation on the ground that she opposed the proposal for sharing the Teesta river water. At the last moment proposal had to be dropped.

This disappointed the Bangladesh Government and its Prime Minister Hasina who was trying to more closer to India and gave a point to the opposition parties to foment anti-India sentiments and help Bangladesh National Party led by Khalida Zia and her anti India party supporters to come back to power.

In yet another case, the External Affairs ministry succumbed to the pressure of a supporting regional party. The US, always assuming the role of protectors of civil rights in all the countries of the world introduced a resolution in the UN Committee on civil rights to condemn atrocities on Tamils in Sri Lanka and denial of civil rights to them. The US started pressuring India to support the resolution. The Minister of External Affairs Shri. S.M. Krishna issued a lofty statement that India does not support any country specific resolution on 'civil rights', fearing that its own treatment of minorities in cases like attacks on Sikhs in Delhi after assassination of Indira Gandhi by Sikh guards, attack on Muslims in Gujarat after burning of a bogey carrying Hindu *Karsevakas* and 'suppression' of the Muslim separatists in Kashmir, may also attract similar resolution against India's record of providing civil rights. However, soon India had to change its stand when DMK ally, through out of power in Tamil Nadu, pressurized the Union Government to support the resolution to uphold the cause of Tamils. The External Affairs Ministry supported the resolution though with some amendments as a fig leaf. The Sri Lankan Government immediately responded by raising objection to nuclear plant in Koodankulan and harmful effects of nuclear radiation on their people. The Government was hard put to it in mollifying Sri Lankan Government.

US ever eager to poke its nose in the affairs of other countries, saw the opportunity to meddle in Indian affairs. It saw that the Union Ministry of External Affairs succumbs to pressure of regional parties and above all from Mamta Banerjee head of Trinmool Congress. The US Secretary of States Hillary Clinton started her recent visit to India from Kolkata where she met fiery Chief Minister of West Bengal and heaped praise on her for seizing power from the communists after their uninterrupted rule over 34 years. She also promised liberal investments by US firms to West Bengal. The Chief Minister felt highly elated by the US largesse. This was a clear example of US interference in India's internal affairs and violation of the India constitution. Item 10 of the Seventh Schedule clearly state that 'foreign affairs' and 'relations with foreign countries fall in the Union list. And yet the Ministry of External Affairs could not muster the courage to take exception to Mamata's direct dealings with the US Secretary of states or the brazenness with which the latter dealt directly with a state government.

Assertion of autonomy by Chief Ministers of States

It is for the first time that Chief Ministers of States have joined to assert their autonomy in a federal polity and resist the Central government in what they consider as illegitimate encroachment on that autonomy, and forcing the central government to concede to the position taken by State Government. Why has this major change in Central State relationship come about? The constitution is the same but the working relationship between the centre and state under the constitution has radically altered. This requires careful consideration.

The Constitutional Features

The Indian Constitution does not mention anywhere that India is a 'federation'. The very first article says that India "shall be a union of states" yet the India Union does have the characteristic features of a federation as defined in text books of political science.

A federal state is distinguished from a Unitary state where only the Central Government exists. For example, in Britain, there are no other governments but the Central Government and only local authorities exist. Even there the assertion of local sentiment forced the central government to concede authority to Scotland regional government as though it were an independent state.

Indian constitution fulfills the basic features of the federal polity as mentioned by Prof. K.C. Wheere Viz. (1) there is a clear division of powers and functions between the Central Government and State Governments and (2) each is independent in its own sphere of activity.

However, it is rightly stated that Indian constitution has several provisions which make central government more powerful than the states. The founding fathers of the Indian Constitution – members of the Constituent Assembly did so advisedly. Independence was accompanied by partition which was a painful blow to the unity of India, so much cherished by leaders of the struggle for independence. They did not want the story to be repeated. They did not want the centrifugal and fissiparous tendencies of which they were fully aware, to threaten the unity of what remained as India after partition when West Punjab, NWFP, Sindh, Baluchistan and East Bengal, Muslim majority areas were made into a muslim state called Pakistan. The unity of Pakistan was broken in 1971 where East Pakistan became Bangladesh.

The makers of Indian nation wanted to preserve unity and integrity of India at any cost. Hence, the provisions to make for a strong central Government Thus, article 355 makes it a duty of the Union 'to protect' every state against external aggression and internal disturbance and to ensure that 'the government of every state is carried out in accordance with provisions of the Constitution Article 356 provides for imposition of Presidents rule (i.e. of Central Government) by issuing proclamation. Under this provision 'functions of the Government of a State' will be assumed by President and the Governor of State will carry on administration under the direction of the Union Government. The President (on the advice of the Central Government) can even declare emergency under article 358 when even basic fundamental rights of the citizens granted under Article 19 like freedom of speech, expression and assembly and free movement could be abrogated. Smt. Indira Gandhi as Prime Minister imposed emergency in 1975 and exercised dictatorial powers bending the constitution at will. Even the Supreme Court succumbed by conceding that even the right to live would stand suspended during emergency

The greater constitutional power of the Centre have been reinforced by greater financial power of the Centre. The constitution gives more liberal and flexible sources of revenue to the centre like Income Tax, Corporate Tax, Excise and Custom. The service tax has been added to enrich the kitty of the centre. No doubt some of the revenues like income tax are shared with the state as per the recommendations of the Finance Commission. But the states are dependent on the financial support of the Centre through the allocation of plan funds by the Planning Commission.

The nature of formation of a federal party in India has been different from that in USA. There the states existed prior to the formation of a federal government. The states came together to form a federal polity. But in India, prior to independence, the strong centre already existed under the Viceroy who was representative of the British sovereign, while provincial Governors, were subordinate to him and carried out administration of provinces under his direction and supervision. Even prior to the British rule, under the Mughal dynasty which ruled over two centuries over large parts of India, the emperor had all powers and provincial *Subhedars* nominated by him were accountable to the emperor.

Under Article 3 of the Indian Constitution, a new state can be formed or its boundaries altered or its name altered by Parliament, making states creatures of the Central Government.

Political Dynamics

Apart from the provisions of the constitution, dynamics of political power determines very much how the Constitution actually functions. Under the first Prime Minister of free India, Jawahar lal Nehru who held the position for a long period of 17 years, the Indian federal polity developed strong unitary tendencies. Nehru was not only the Prime Minister; he was undisputed leader of Parliament, his party and nation. Such was his immense nationwide image that Congress could get power and form governments in all the states. He visualized planning for the country as a whole and set up Planning Commission in 1951, which was not envisaged in the Constitution. He setup National Development Council which was attended by Chief Ministers who while expressing their views, by and large, supported the programmes initiated by the Centre. The officers in the Central Ministries many of which dealt with items in the state held frequent meetings of the state officers so that the entire administrative system would work in unison. The higher officers both at the Centre and the States mostly belonged to the IAS but IAS officers at the Centre were senior to those in the State and could carry the day. These centralizing tendencies were accentuated under Smt. Indira Gandhi who concentrated all political power in her hands. The Chief Ministers of States were her nominees not elected by the representatives of the party in the state legislature. Emergency of 1975 was the culminating point of her authoritarian tendencies. Her son Rajiv, after her tragic assassination in 1984, saw his power weakened by the Bofors episode but even he had a national appeal and could dictate the state leaders. Narsimha Rao who headed Congress minority government from 1990-95 was not an unquestioned national leader or leader of the Congress party and ruled with considerable discretion and with co-operation of the opposition and the States.

After the decline of the Congress as a national party, started the coalition era both at the centre and in the states. The unquestioned rule from the centre has now become a by gone era. Today the Congress party in the UPA Government (a coalition) today inspite of large number of Congress Members of Parliament (207) finds it difficult to have its way. Congress is a dynastic party and writ of its President Sonia Gandhi runs in the party and even in Government. The Prime Minister is her nominee. He is not the unquestioned leader of the party, nor leader of the party in Lok Sabha. He is not elected member of the Lok Sabha but of the Rajya Sabha. He is head of Government but leaves large part of government to Pranab Mukherjee who has emerged as the most influential member of his administration. Congress does not hold power in most of the important States. It was badly defeated in Bihar, UP and Punjab. BJP, the second national party, has power in several large states like Madhya Pradesh and Rajasthan. While the leadership of the Central Government is weak, several Chief Ministers like Jayalalitha, Naveen Patnaik,

Narendra Modi, have emerged as leaders in their own right, popular in the own states with long administrative experience who can standup to the leaders of the Central Government. Clearly the centre of gravity of political power has shifted. It is no wonder that federal aspects of the polity will increasingly be more prominent.

It is high time that Ministers and bureaucrats in union Government fully realize the consequences of the shift of political power and give up their authoritarian tendencies to ride roughshod over the state Chief Ministers, Ministers and civil servants. They have to come to terms will a federal polity in which centre and states are co-equal. That would be the new meaning of the term 'co-operative federalism'.

Chapter - 3

The Issue of States Organisation in India

The December 9, 2009 midnight announcement by Union Home Minister P. Chidambaram that the constitutional process will start for the creation of the new state of Telangana created a veritable hornet's nest in Andhra Pradesh, while it opened up a Pandora's box in rest of the country. While the Telangana Rashtra Samiti leader Chandrashekhar Rao broke his fast leading to the restoration of calm in the Telangana region, it evoked immediate virulent reaction in the Andhra region consisting of Rayalseema and coastal Sarkar regions where mass meetings and processions were held to oppose the carving out Telangana from the Andhra Pradesh to form an independent state with Hyderabad as its capital. Hyderabad, as could to be expected, became a bone of contention. An idea was floated to make Hyderabad the joint capital of the two states – Telangana and Andhra on the Chandigarh model but was rejected outright on the ground that Hyderabad was in the heart of Telangana and had no physical connection to Andhra region. The ideas of making Hyderabad an independent central region was also rejected. A statement by Union Home Secretary that Hyderabad would be the natural capital of Telangana aroused condemnation in Andhra region.

The Chief Minister Rosayya found himself in an unenviable position. He expressed his surprise about Chidambaram's announcement after he had, in earlier consultation with him, opposed the proposal. And yet, as per the Home Minister's announcement, he was expected to get a resolution passed in the State Assembly in favour of formation of the new state of Telangana. Though the legislative assembly session was convened, there was absolutely no possibility of any such resolution being passed. Nearly 150 MLA's from Andhra region including those from the Congress Party and Ministers in his own cabinet tendered their resignation opposing the Telangana proposal. A Congress MP Shri Rajgopal from Vijayawada went on fast against the Telangana proposal as a counter to earlier fast of Chandrashekhar Rao. The non-Congress parties like TDP and PRP, after seeing the Andhra reaction started changing their stand. Earlier supporting Telangana, they now expressed their opposition.

Chidambaram found himself between the devil and the deep sea. To calm down the turmoil in Andhra he made another announcement that the political situation had changed and the proposal for forming Telangana state would be put on hold pending further consultation. This second announcement led to the renewal of agitation in Telangana where the students of Osmania University were at the forefront with their slogan 'Telangana jago, Andhra Bhago'. The State Government tried to stop the mass procession threatened by the students with the use of police force but the students went to High Court which gave the permission to hold the procession so long as it was peaceful.

The opposition parties found an opportunity to severely criticize the Union Government for its flip-flop and for mishandling the situation creating a mess in Andhra Pradesh. The BJP compared and contrasted the incept handling of the issue by the UPA Government with the deft handling by NDA government under the astute leadership of Atal Bihari Vajpayee which brought into existence the new states of Jharkhand, Chattisgarh and Uttarakhand despite opposition particularly of Lalu Prasad Yadav to the partition of Bihar. Chidambaram tried to argue that there was no flip-flop; all that government wanted was that the proposal should have a wider approval and goodwill of all concerned which in the present situation seems to be an impossibility.

There was more than a flip-flop. The Government showed its weakness by succumbing to the blackmail of Chandrashekhar Rao. Earlier, they had betrayed him in 2004 Lok Sabha Election getting his support by promising Telangana but forgot the promise soon after its resounding victory. All that it did was to appoint a committee under Pranab Mukharjee which turned out to be simply an exercise for putting the proposal in cold storage.

Chidambaram invited an eight party meeting under his chairmanship on January 5, in New Delhi. As expected no consensus emerged as the parties stuck to their stated positions. TRS insisted on immediate formation of Telangana. BJP supportred it and asked for a motion to be moved in Parliament to form Telangana State. PRP stood for united Andhra Pradesh. The Congress and TDP were divided – some supporting Telangana state while others asking for the retention of Andhra Pradesh. Chidambaram while conceding differences, emphasized the need for maintaining law and order and creating an atmosphere of peace and harmony so that students could attend schools and colleges and offices could function normally. Meanwhile, consultations should continue. An idea was mooted that a Panel be constituted to enter into detailed discussion on all the pros and cons of the issue and formulate expert recommendations on the subject. The Panel could be headed by a Supreme Court Judge.

Chidambaram warned all parties that the instable situation could provide an opportunity to the extremist Maoist groups to raise their head and overthrow parliamentary democracy itself.

While Chidambaram held discussions on New Delhi and called for restraint, the situation in the field continued to be tense. The Action groups on both sides have stepped up their agitations. Railway time table broke down causing acute inconvenience to travelling passengers. MP from Vijayawada Rajgopal has objected to the Central initiative saying that this is a matter between Telugus of two parts of Andhra Pradesh and there was no scope for a third party intervention on the analogy that third party intervention is not acceptable in Kashmir ! On the other hand Chandrashekhar Rao has been arguing that this is a matter which under the Constitution is entirely within the purview of the Union Government and the resolution by the State Assembly is not required under the Constitutional provisions.

II. Pandora's Box

The Telangana formation led immediately to the demands for other smaller states – particularly Gorkha Land State to be carved out of West Bengal (opposed by both the incumbent Left Government and opposition Trinmool Leader Mamata Banergee) Another demand was for new states to be carved out of the behemoth Uttar Pradesh. Here the Chief Minister herself took the lead demanding trifurcation of Uttar Pradesh. Ajit Singh the Jat leader demanded Harit Pradesh (Western Uttar Pradesh) while Mayawati counter-balanced it by Poorva Pradesh. Then there was the third state of Bundelkhand with capital Jhansi. Vilas Muttemwar, now out of power has started demanding statehood for Vidarbha through his own party (Congress) did not support him. The proposal was earlier made unsuccessfully by Vasant Sathe and N.K.P. Salve- both Congress MPs. Prakash Ambedkar, the grandson of Dr. B.R. Ambedkar, was able to convene a big all party meeting demanding Vidarbha. Even Tamil Nadu could not escape the demand for its partition. Dr. Ramdas rejected by voters in the last election for Lok Sabha, raised the demand for a separate state for North Tamil Nadu region (obviously favouring his Vaniyar caste).

Alarmed by these demands, many Indians have started fearing Balkanization of India which could pose a grave threat to the unity and integrity of the country. Others pointed out that creation of more states does not amount to balkanization' or partitioning of the country but is a legitimate response to the aspirations of the people (or disgruntled politicians?)

All this has created a climate of political instability which does not bode well. Already new investment is fighting shy of Hyderabad which till now was a prized destination of IT and other enterprises. The projected CII

Conference has been shifted to Chennai. The one day cricket match between India and Sri Lanka had to be shifted from Vishakapattanam to Nagpur.

A proposal has been mooted that the best way to get out of this piquant situation is to appoint another States Recognisation Commission on the lines of 1953. Fazal Ali Commission which had recommended both the states of Telangana and Vidarbha through the recommendations was not eventually accepted by Union Government and lay dormant. Now both these proposal lying dormant have resurfaced.

Some have demanded a permanent State Reorganisation Commission on the lines of the Finance Commission to which proposals for the formation of new states can be referred to from time to time for examination in depth.

Both these proposals have not been accepted by Union Government so far. Senior Minister Pranab Mukherjee has rejected the propose out of hand. Government seems to be fearing that resultant political instability would have a damaging effect on the economic growth of the country.

The more basic point is, that they are no well known, well accepted principles regarding the formation of states. Some want that the process of formation of states should have a finality and should stop while others argue that in a large diverse country like India with vast and growing population exceeding 100 crores, there is a scope for forming more states. But how many more and of what size, area wise, population wise or economy wise? There has been no logical thinking on the subject so far. Laying down basic ground rules or guidelines on the subject is necessary.

III. Constitutional Position

What is the Constitutional position? The Constitution in article 3 vests the power to form new States and alteration of areas, boundaries, or names of existing States in Parliament alone which may pass the law on the subject. The Bill for the purpose can be introduced in either House of Parliament on the recommendation of the President which in fact means recommendation of the Union Government as the President acts on the advices of the Union Government.

The Constitution however, is silent on the subject of criteria for forming states doing nothing more than giving the power of formation of States to Parliament. While giving power exclusively to Parliament may be conducive to the integrity and unity of India, it gives no guidance to Parliament or a body created by Parliament as to principles for formation of states.

This brings out the basic deficiencies in the Constitution of our Republic which is often lauded for having stood the test of time but which in fact leaves several important aspects untouched. The constitutional document is basically a framework of the Government of India Act of 1935 of the colonial regime, with the Preamble and Chapters on Fundamental Rights and Directive Principles of the Constitution fastened onto it. The Constituent Assembly consisted of legal stalwarts who were concerned more with procedural and juridical aspects rather than substantive aspects apart from Western concepts of Parliamentary Democracy and rights of a liberal state. There was never an attempt to relate the Constitution to the cultural evolution and values of our country and the genius of our people evolved through centuries. The Constituent Assembly never attempted to discover the 'soul of India' and enshrine it in the constitution. The Constitution makers gave more time and attention to the provisions of constitutional documents of other democracies like US, UK, Ireland, Canada, Australia and some European Countries rather than the cultural history of India making the Constitution a formal document – a lawyer's paradise, but not a reflection of the deep yearnings of the people.

An opportunity to review the working of the Constitution in the light of experience was provided by the Constitutional Review Commission appointed under the Chairmanship of Justice M.N. Venkatachaliah, an Ex-Chief Justice of the Supreme Court. But the opportunity was lost because Venkatachaliah announced at the beginning itself that it would not go into the fundamentals, and take the framework of Parliamentary Democracy and Federal System as given. This settled it and The Committee concentrated only on suggesting procedural and juridical improvements.

IV. Principles of State Formation

We have to go outside the Constitution and Constitutional Review Committee to discover the basic principles for the formation of States.

The only attempt in pre-independence says to provide a logical basis for formation of State was the Motilal Nehru Committee Report of 1928 which recommended the formation of states on a linguistic basis. Major languages, provide the cultural base of the life of the Indian people and should be the appropriate base for state formation.

This principle was accepted by the major party in the forefront of the fight of the Indian people for independence – viz. the Indian National Congress. Even in pre-independence days, the regional Committees of the Congress were formed on the basis of linguistic areas. Thus, the four Kannad speaking districts in Bombay province, went with the Congress Committee for Karnataka covering rest of Kannad region.

The British rulers had no use of the culture of the Indian people and had constituted large provinces purely on administrative criteria. There were the three major 'regulated provinces' of Bombay, Madras and Bengal with the major cities of Bombay, Madras and Calcutta as their Headquarters.

Bombay province stretched from Sindh to Gujarat, Western Maharashtra and Northern Karnataka districts. In 1935 Sindh was separated to become an independent province. Madras province covered Tamil land, Rayalseema and coastal Telugu areas and Karnaraka districts of South Canara. Bengal province once covered the whole of Eastern India. Later Assam, Bihar and in 1935 Orissa became independent provinces. As British rule extended, new provinces were formed. United province covering vast Ganga-Yamuna area stretching from Himalaya regions of Gadhwal and Kumaon to planes of Brijbhoomi, Bundelkhand to Lucknow to Banaras and Allahabad. The Central province consisted of both Marathi (Vidharbha) and Hindi (Mahakoshal) areas with capital Nagpur and also included the largest Baster district and other tribal areas. Punjab in North-west covered the whole of Punjab (Western now in Pakistan and Eastern in India) including hill areas and Hindi speaking Haryana. Each province was headed by the Governor who was the Chief Executive (not ceremonial head as now) who conducted administration with the help of District Collectors and Divisional Commissioners – posts held by the officers of the ICS. Maintenance Law and order and collection of land revenue was the main work of administration.

Indian under the British rule was dotted by 600 states who had rulers who ruled subject to the allegiance to the paramount imperial power headed by the British monarch. After independence the states merged. The biggest state to merge in India was Hyderabad headed by the Nizam. His vast state included Telugu region known as Telangana, Marathi region of Marathwada and the Kanada region of Gulbarga, Raichur and Bidar districts. The Marathwada region eventually become a part of newly formed Maharashtra and Kannad region merged into newly formed Karnataka. Telangana remained for some time as independent State and eventually was joined to Telugu regions of Madras province consisting of Rayalseema and Sarkars.

After the attainment of independence, it was expected that the British time provinces suitable for a colonial regime would no longer continue to exist but would be reorganized on linguistic basis as recommended by the Moti lal Nehru Committee report of 1928.

But this was not to be Prime Minister Nehru himself started having second thoughts. He strongly felt that the maintenance of the unity and integrity of the new fledgling Republic of India should have the first priority. Security and Development were the principal tasks. Concentration on them should not be diverted by the elaborate exercise of state reorganization on linguistic basis.

Even a vastly popular leader like Nehru, however, misjudged the situation. The linguistic identities became more and more assertive and demands grew for state reorganization on linguistic basic. The most prominent amongst linguistic agitations was in Andhra where Potti Sriramalu, a Gandhian went on fast for the formation of Andhra State. His fast lasted for 58 days at the end of which he breathed his last.

There were virulent reactions. Bezwada (now Vijaywada) Railway station was burnt. Nehru realized the gravity of the situation, bowed to public demand and an independent Andhra State was formed into which Telangana region of the Nizam State of Hyderabad, was eventually merged.

Creation of Andhra as a separate state paved the way to a wider process for redrawing India's map. The Fazal Ali Commission was constituted in 1953 to make recommendations for recognisation of states. They toured all over the country, held wide consultations but did not always logically follow the principle of state recognition on linguistic basis. For example, they recommended Telangana and Vidarbha as independent states and not part of a Telugu and Marathi States. They were reluctant to give Bombay, the financial centre and a cosmopolitan city to Maharashtra. Shri. S.K. Patil, a Congress leader known as 'uncrowned King of Bombay' though a Marathi person himself was totally opposed to giving Bombay to Maharashtra. He preferred making it a Central Territory. Ultimately, as a compromise a bilingual state of Gujarat and Maharashtra was created with headquarters at Bombay. The Bilingual Bombay state was not acceptable to the leaders of Marathi people who though belonging to different parties came together and joined hands with popular literary figure and orator Shri. P.K. Atre to form the Sanyukta Maharashtra Parishad for the formation of Maharashtra.

The unpopular leaders like S.K. Patil were no match for them. For a while Morarji Desai another unpopular leader who was the Chief Minister with Nehru's tacit support tried to suppress the popular movement with brutal use of police force. Many became the victims of police bullets when people's procession thronged at Flora Fountain. They became martyrs '*Hutatma*' for the cause of Maharashtra. The spot come to be known as Hutatma Chowk. Nehru saw the writing on the wall and conceded the formation of the new states of Maharashtra and Gujarat on linguistic basis.

Another language which was not given recognition was Punjabi which had been joined to Hindi area of Harayana and hilly region. Soon the linguistic identity got combined with the religious identity of the Sikhs whose leader Sardar Fateh Singh led the agitation for Punjabi suba. The strong Chief Minister Pratap Singh Kairon, with Nehru's support tried to suppress the Sikh agitation but eventually Nehru's daughter Indira Gandhi had to concede the demand and a new state of Punjab (mainly Sikh), Haryana (mainly Hindi) and Himachal Pradesh came into existence.

In the North-East, the insurgencies could be contained only by formation of small states of Mizoram, Nagaland and Meghalaya with its capital Shillong (which earlier was the capital of United Assam in the British days)

After liberation from Portuguese rule, Goa, Daman and Div the Portuguese territories became a Union Territory. Later Div and Daman became part of Gujarat where they geographically and linguistically belonged. It was widely believed that Goa would join Maharashtra. This was the ardent desire of the popular Chief Minister of Goa Shri. Dayanand Bandodkar. But in a referendum, the Goans refused to join Maharashtra and Goa became an independent state. Goa was too tiny to be qualified to become an independent state of the Indian Republic. An idea was mooted to make it a part of Sagar State (a coastal region including portions of Karwar and Konkan region in Maharashtra) or a Konkani State with Konkani speaking peoples of Goa, Karwar, Malwan and Belgaum area. But Goans with a 500 years existence as a separate entity under the Portuguese rule were not interested and Goa remains a tiny state.

This brief historical review of the formation of states in India shows that no single principle or logic was followed invariably and there was much ad hoc action to meet the exigency of the political situation. That is why many issues remain unresolved.

One of them is the question of Border areas. The prime example is Belgaum and surrounding Marathi areas. These were included in Karnataka even though the dream of Marathi speaking people in Belgaum and Nipani area was to be a part of Maharashtra. The Marathi people under the banner of Marathi Ekikaran Samiti have been agitating to join Maharashtra. The Mahajan Commission which was appointed to look into this border dispute did not accept the demand and the area continued to be in Karnataka. The Marathi people at whose instance Mahajan Commission was appointed are not accepting the verdict given by the Commission and the agitation continues with periodic outbursts. Whatever be the decision, guidelines need to be laid down to look after the cultural, literary, educative and administrative aspects of life of linguistic minorities to be followed all over the country so that no feelings are left, of linguistic, cultural, educational and administrative deprivation.

On language one state formula can not obviously be universally accepted. Hindi is the largest linguistic group (albeit with regional variations and dialects) whose population is so large that even now several large states of Hindi speaking population exist like U.P., M.P., Bihar, Rajasthan, Haryana, Uttarakhand and Himachal Pradesh. Yet scope exists for more Hindi states. UP is huge in terms of area and population, it could be subdivided into small manageable units. As C.M. Mayavati pointed out, that people in far off areas of U.P. have to travel 700 Km. to reach the state capital where administration and judicial Headquarters exist. The remoteness creates real problems for the people – the administered and the administrators alike Uttarakhand has already become a separate and smaller states like Bundelkhand, Harit Pradesh and Poorva Pradesh may not be too far.

From the point of view of the Federal Republic of India, acute problems of imbalance amongst constituent states exist. Goa with a small population of one million co-exists as a State as good as a state of UP with 170 million population – to 170 ratio which obviously looks anomalous. Large states are administrationally un-wieldy while very small states are often politically, economically and administrationally sub-standard and non-viable. A state like Goa does not have it's own IAS cadre and has to drawn on Union Territory cadre for its senior administrative and police officials. All states should be within an acceptable band of variation in terms of size, area and population. Very small states tend to have political instability as was seen many times in the case of Goa and Jharkhand. The definition of a small number of MLA's can topple the government. A state to be viable much have a fair number of scientists, educationist, entrepreneurs, political leaders, literary figures etc. as well as a variety of institutions like Banks, Colleges and Universities and economic enterprises and diverse resources to be a viable state. Smaller States develop small mentality, parochial outlook and even undesirable tendencies as is seen in Jharkhand. The late Jaipal Singh, MP an ex-army officer, a champion of Jharkhand on the floor of Parliament who won admiration of even Prime Minister Nehru would have been appalled by the antics and shameless corruption of the likes of Madhu Koda and 'Guruji' Shibu Sorain. Time has come to look comprehensively at the band of variation among states – political, administrative, economic, educational etc. and proper state recognisation taken on hand so as to eliminate the too large a state as well as too small a state. The band of variation can be of the most one to ten.

Obviously a panel of politicians, administrators, industrialist and business people, political scientists, economists , management experts etc. need to be constituted to look at the present scenario and propose changes.

In this exercise shadows of historical past should not be allowed to cloud proposals which should be made on the basis of futuristic thinking. Telangana is a remnant of the past kingdom of Nizam and Goa of the Portuguese empire. How far can the memories of the Nizam and the Portuguese rulers be allowed to continue? Language is undoubtedly the most common acceptable base for state formation. But, as pointed out above, it cannot be an exclusive principle so that we follow one language one state formula. Some modifications and compromises are inevitable. After the formation of states like Maharashtra and Karnataka, the issue of 'emotional integration' of the constituent parts came up. Thus, in Karnataka Gulbarga area was a part of the Nizam Kingdom, Bombay area of the old regime of Bombay Province, South Canara of old Madras Province while the rest Karnataka belonged to the Princely State of Mysore. Similarly in AP., Telangana harks back to Nizam Kingdom with the influence of Urdu and Pharsee while Sarkar and Rayalseema had attachment to old Madras. Similarly in Maharashtra, Vidarbha harked to back to Hindi past, and Marathwada to Nizam past. That no conscious attempts were made to create emotional integration and restore economic balance is a reflection on the political leadership of that state. Vidharbha people continue to have a feeling of deprivation as also 'Bombay' and Hyderabad areas of Karanataka which remain comparatively backward. V.M. Dandekar Committee drew attention to economic deficit of Vidarbha and proposed compensatory measures. It is a pity that political leadership of the states was not able to eliminate 'emotional and economic deficits'. Rigid principles are no substitute to political astuteness and wise leadership.

Chapter - 4

Changing Anatomy of Corruption

When faced with the criticism of widespread corruption in the country, Indira Gandhi said that corruption was a world wide phenomenon. Today, there is a worldwide revulsion against corruption. From a malaise in administration, it has grown into a disastrous debility of the political system. It has pushed all ideological considerations in the political process into a background and has emerged in the mind of the electorate as the single major issue on which Governments should be selected or rejected. What the electorate wants today is clean public life and clean Government – no matter of what political complexion.

In Japan, it was on the corruption. Issue that the monopoly of the liberal party came to an end. The Maverick Hosakaya successfully led the battle against the entrenched liberal party but when he himself was found to have taken in the past a questionable loan from a private business enterprise he had no alternative but to resign yielding power, for the first time in post World War II history of Japan, to a socialist Prime Minister. In Italy, long known for the dominance of the mafia, intrepid judges exposed the involvement of a past socialist Prime Minister Bettino Craxi and many others in the sordidkickback and mafia operations, leading to the electoral victory of a rank outsider, the media tycoon Berlusconi who joined hands with other rightist parties of questionable political ideology, to form Government. In recent Belarus elections, a populist Alexander Lukashenko who vowed to sweep the country of corruption and reverse years of economic decline, was overwhelmingly elected the President of Belarus. Corruption has become hot news in Europe. L.K. Sharma has reported in Times of India July, 12 that business scandals involving top personalities are being reported not only from Italy but also from France, Germany, Spain, Belgium and Britain. Corruption in high places has not remained just a moral issue concerning a individual in public life. The corruption cases have a political context. They arise out of cosy and questionable relationship between business and politics and illicit financing of political parties. There is greater exposure of these secret deals between business and political mafia thanks to a more assertive press, a holder judiciary and a more open co-operate culture. In India, a more assertive civil servant in Bombay Municipal Corporation has recently brought the issue of political corruption into a central focus.

The corruption issue has been there in India since Independence. A.D. Gorwala in his report in 1950-51 referred to corruption as a major malaise of public administration. Over the next two decades, it became a sufficiently important issue for the Central Government to appoint the Santhanam Committee (1966-67) to suggest measures for the prevention of corruption.. These reports analysed the causes of corruption and suggested the remedies. Gorwala attributed corruption to delay in decision-making and suggested streamlining of administrative procedure to eliminate corruption.. Both the Committee recommended the strengthening of vigilance machinery. As a sequel, vigilance commissions were constituted at the level of the State and Central Government. The Central Bureau of Investigation as well as State Anti-corruption bureaus were entrusted with the work of investigation into complaints of corruption in administration. The Administrative Reforms Commission (1966-70) went one step further and recommended the constitution of Lok Pak and Lok Ayukt at the level of Central and State Government to go into complaint of corruption not only against the civil servant (Lok Ayukt) but also the political executives (Lok Pal). The Lok Pal at the Central level is yet to be constituted. Several times the bills introduced for the purpose in Parliament lapsed. The Lok Ayukta have been set up in the State. But apparently they have had little impact on the phenomenon of corruption..

That is because of character of phenomenon has itself undergone a radical change. The phenomenon of corruption traditionally existed in departments like Revenue, Police, and the Public Work Departments. In the first two departments it existed at the lower level like the Patwari, Revenue Inspector or even Tahsildar in the Revenue Department and the police constable or the sub-inspector in the police department. In Public Work Department it reached even higher levels. To these areas of corruption were added cases arising out of rationing of food grains, cement and other essential commodities imposed during the period of World War II and continued thereafter owing to the shortages of commodities. The wartime controls were the beginning of what Rajaji called 'the licence permit Raj' which became well established in the command and control economy attendant to the type of planning we adopted as a concomitant of our concept of the socialist pattern of society.

But as the phenomenon of corruption assumed new dimension, it graduated from the administrative to political level. Politician soon realized that they, not the civil servants, were at the helm of the command and control economy.

The 'rent income' generated by shortages and public contracts belonged to them and not the civil servants. If jobs in public service, transport permits or building sites (which became precious in cities at meteoric rates) were in short supply they were bound to be goldmines of jackpots for the politicians who were justified in tapping them because they needed money for fighting elections. After all by fighting elections they were rendering valuable service to Indian democracy. Another big source to exploit were huge defence, fertilizer and other contracts for which bids and offers came from foreign firms who hired powerful lobbyist to snatch the lucrative contracts through political influence.

The civil servants were in no position to stem this tide of political corruption. With the broadening and deepening of our democracy, as the power of the politicians increased, that of the civil servants declined. They became either collaborators or 'accommodators'. As collaborators they became junior partners in the loot. As accommodators, they did their limited jobs and looked the other way, even when they knew that large scale corruption was indeed taking place. Those few who chose to be 'resistors' took the risk of frequent transfer or getting marginalized by being shunted to inconsequential places. They could do nothing about such treatment being meted out to them because as civil servants they were duty bound to accept whatever position was offered to them. They had to thank their stars if they were not punished for their crime of exposing or resisting corruption.

The power of the politician increased multifold when they joined hands clandestinely or openly with the mafia like the unscrupulous builders or agents of multinational firms suspected of habitually keeping top politicians on their pay roll in India or abroad through the foreign accounts. This was the stage when corruption became the phenomenon of criminalisation of politics.

The old analysis of the cause of corruption. and remedies for dealing with them is no longer valid. Earlier corruption. Was accounted for by low salaries of civil servants with authority to deal with large public spending and weak vigilance machinery. On the basis of this analysis it was proposed that if salaries of civil servants were improved and vigilance machinery strengthened, corruption could be curbed. While these measures are good as far as they go, they have no bearing on dealing with the new phenomenon of political corruption which has gripped many countries of the world including India. The end of 'license permit raj' in the wake of new policy of liberalization may not necessarily eliminate political corruption. Japan and several countries of Europe have no 'licence permit raj'. But it has not saved them from being rocked by scandals of political corruption.

The new phenomenon of corruption is both dangerous and intractable and has disastrous consequences on the national morale. It has destroyed the sanctity of public life. It has called into question not only the credibility of the politicians but to the democratic institutions themselves. If democracy means corruption, then there is no merit in democracy. Democratic institutions and Constitution can as well be done away with!

The phenomenon of corruption has shaken the trust of the common people in authority of any sort. He is prepared to believe in any allegation even against the highest persons in power. When Harshad Mehta made the accusation of bribing the Prime Minister on the eve of Nandyal elections by offering Rs. One crore hidden in a suitcase at his official residence, no less a person than Palkhiwala the great constitutional lawyer of the country publicly stated that such accusation had prima facie credibility. And more recently when Khairnar started hurling accusations of corruption against the Chief Minister of Maharashtra, he publicly stated that while legally Khairnar may be wrong, morally he was right. The public at large also came forward readily to support Khairnar by attending in thousands his meetings in the cities of Maharashtra and Gujarat.

It is a dangerous development when people start believing in accusations of corruption against persons assuming august positions in democracy like the Prime Minister and the Chief Minister without even caring to enquire about convincing evidence. They do so because they have lost trust in the system. They think it is rotten to the core. If we establish a tradition of clean public life, as in days before Independence, nobody would believe in wild allegations.

We have, therefore, to recreate the traditions of pre-independence India of a clean public life the tradition laid down by Mahatma Gandhi that every paisa collected from the public was to be accounted for and properly spent. Dominance of money in public life has itself to be reduced. The dominance of money power in elections is considered to be the course of all corruption in our national life. Mr. Seshan's (he was the Chief Election Commissioner) insistence that limits of election expenditure laid down in the law shall be strictly observed can go a long way in cleaning public life.

The belief of the common man in scrupulousness in public life has to be restored. The response of the people to Khairnar shows that the common man is hankering for cleanliness and decency in public life. He will prefer an honest civil servant to a corrupt elected representative in his quest for clean public life.

Our people in public life specially those who are at the helm of authority in democratic Government should take note of the reaction of the common man lest, sooner or later, such becomes the torrent of his wrath against corruption that it wipes out democracy itself and all that it stands for.

Chapter - 5

The Purpose of Politics

Recent years have seen a rapid disenchantment with politics and the political process in the minds of the Indian people. The behaviour of politicians and political parties has been mainly responsible for such a loss of credibility. People hardly see any connection between politics and the welfare of the people. They have come to believe in the dictum of Dr. Johnson that "politics is the last resort of the scoundrels". People have watched with dismay the nexus between unscrupulous builders and businessmen on one side and the politicians on the other which has given rise to the phenomenon of criminalisation of politics. They have seen persons who have been pennyless with hardly any ostensible means of livelihood entering into the arena of politics and suddenly getting affluent with all the symbols of affluence such as real estate, durable consumer goods, high cost education for their children and ostentatious display during their wedding ceremonies. Indeed, the cynics have started describing politics as the best profession for rapid acquisition of affluence and status in life, needing no qualifications or honest work.

This rapid fall in the image of politics and politicians in the country in post-independence India is particularly striking against the background of politics in India before the attainment of independence. During those days politics stood for the highest standards of idealism laid down by great patriots like Lokmanya Tilak, Mahatma Gandhi, Subhash Chandra Bose, Jawaharlal Nehru and Sardar Patel. They were the best amongst the Indian who could have led an extremely affluent and comfortable life and yet they chose the path of sacrifice in the cause of the people. It, therefore, becomes necessary for all thinking Indians to ponder over the phenomenon of rapid degeneration of Indian politics during a period of less then fifty years from the glorious traditions which free India inherited.

Not that Indians don't realise the change in the political environment after independence. In pre-independence India, the only goal of politics was to fight alien power for the attainment of freedom. After independence, politics was naturally oriented towards success in elections and the formation of Government, whether at the Centre or in the States.

However, this did not necessarily have meant the euthanasia of higher values in life in politics and amongst the politicians. Even though people now join politics and political parties in pursuit of power, and to occupy seats of power in Government, it need not mean the end of decencies and a proprieties let alone higher values in the political life. Politics need not necessarily be dirty. Nor can we do away with politics even though in a moment of disgust we may wish to do so.

It is recognized everywhere in all countries that politics has a role in the satisfactory management of public affairs. Alternative arrangements of public affairs often go in the name of different political ideologies. Political parties are supposed to be built round competing ideologies – liberal versus conservative, rightist versus leftist, socialist versus capitalist or as in recent years, economic development versus preservation of environment. In pursuance of their ideologies, parties formulate their manifestoes on the basis of which they go to the people for votes. On attainment of power, they introduce policies and programmes to give concrete shape to their ideologies. Political parties endeavour to attract people towards their ideologies, aggregate them into their vote banks and draw on their support for ensuring the success of their ideologies, policies and programmes. They do not own the machinery of the government, but use it when in power for the implementation of their programmes. There is nothing abhorrent in this political process, though it involves struggle for attainment of power and the removal of rival parties from power. Such political tussles might create certain amount of tension is a part of life. There is nothing inherently abhorrent about the pursuite of power provided pursuit of power is also in pursuit of the progress of the nation.

Unfortunately, as years passed by after independence, the ideological underpinning of the political parties became weaker and weaker. Ideological coherence was lost and ideological understanding and commitment amongst the ordinary workers and even amongst their leaders progressively diminished and ultimately vanished. After the disintegration of the Soviet Union the ideological issues lost much of their strength or relevance in the world as a whole. In India, it gave a body blow to the last vestiges of the socialist pattern of society initiated as an ideological basis of the Congress party by Jawaharlal Nehru. Long before that, however, ideology for political parties became an external façade, a slogan, a pretense with little relation to the reality of the behaviour of political parties. Radical measures like nationalization of banks were initiated more as part of a battle against political adversaries rather than out of a genuine ideological conviction. Political parties started picking up issues to attract vote banks rather than as a part of coherent ideological approach to the economic and social problems of the country. For purpose of gaining political power, political parties and leaders adopted different postures such as the 'Garibi Hatao' posture adopted by Indira Gandhi, the mandal card played by V.P. Singh to neautralise Devi Lal and the Mandir Rathyatra of Lal Krishna Advani to whip up Hindu sentiments to gather political support.

Worse than the ambiguities in the nature of the ideological commitments of political parties, was the feeling which grew amonst the people that parties did not have a genuine commitment either to any idealogy or even to the progress of the nation as a whole.

If the results of elections are guide, the Indian people hardly seem to appreciate the desperate and radical postures and approaches in dealing with the national problems. The people want that the political power should be used in a responsible manner and in the interest of the nation as a whole. However, politicians and political parties, tend to forget this lesson and political manipulations and gimmicks get the better of the pursuit of national interest.

In digust, people sometime wish to throw away, lock, stock and barrel politics and politicians. But politics and politicians cannot be done away with. They exist in all countries. However, if politics cannot be ended it should be mended. There should be rules of the game which all political parties should follow.

Firstly, all parties should remember that national interest stands above everything else. It is true that the nation does not form a homogenous whole. To be sure, the society does consist of many sections differentiated on economic and social considerations. Different political parties may stand for specific interest of section of society but they have to be subsumed under the unmbrella of national interest as a whole and not inimical to it. Parties cannot forget that society is larger than any particular section of the society, and if the political behaviour of party were to swing in any extreme direction, people are likely to disown it. Above all, the electorate however illiterate and ill informed it may be, has shown that it stands for stability, decency, and fairness. It does not seem to like a party coming into power and behaving in an irresponsible and unscrupulous manner to promote purely sectional interest or to spread mis-information. No party political leader should for example, get away maliging Mahatma Gandhi who sacrificed his whole life and led the country to independence. Nor should it spread hatred, day in day out, against a particular caste – because all the citizens have their place in national life. Persistent propoganda of hatred against a particular caste is behaviour which is out of place in the context of the Indian Constitutional polity.

Secondly, a clear distinction has to be maintained between the Government and the party. A party forming a government cannot use the machinery of the government for aggrandizement of its interest. After years of subjugation of government to the communist political party, the countries of erstwhile USSR and China have come to see the point that it is of paramount importance to keep the two separate and the machinery of government should be independent and serve general interest of the people as a whole.

Thirdly, no party should take up any cause with a view to exciting the emotions of the people and causing a breakdown of law and order. Huge rallies and processions to intimidate the government or state sponsored bandhs, or gheroes have no place in the functioning of an orderly democratic polity. It is strange to see a government in power declaring a bandh. And when the High Court is attacked by the bandh volunteers of the party in power, twenty individuals officers are proceeded against but the government and parties in power are left scot free! It is equally strange to see a Chief Minister inviting people to take law in their own hand and beat public servants on suspicion of corruption or a Minister inviting them to beat tax gathering officials!

Fourthly, the primacy of the public interest will have to be maintained by all those who occupy seats of power in government. Corruption and nepotism in any form should be a total taboo for those who hold reins of government. No public position can ever be used to serve personal and private purposes. Politicians in power may have the ultimate authority to sanction huge defence or fertilizers contracts or sanction huge expenditure on public works. But no part of the money could be siphoned off to political parties or to secret accounts of those who are at the helm of authority. Nor could appointments be made to public positions except on merit, according to prescribed qualifications and procedures and through independent recruitment agencies like Public Service Commissions.

Finally, no party should indulge in naked populism. Unfortunately, parties in India have again and again fallen a prey to the tendency to indulge in populist progammes lime loan melas or writing off loans which have made a permanent damage to the public institutions like nationalized and co-operative banks. All political parties have to uphold the long-term interest of the nation as a whole and haves no business to damage public institutions like bureaucracy, banks or public sector enterprises for short-term gains.

Thus, keeping the nation's fabric intact, maintaining the distinction between government and party, maintaining the law and order, upholding the public interest, and limiting tendencies towards populism at the cost of the state should be essential elements in the code of conduct of all political parties and such a code of conduct must find its place in the constitution itself. The Chief Election Commissioner Shri. T.N. Seshan by enforcing the provisions of the Constitution and Representation of the People's Act has made the electoral code of conduct mandatory for all the political parties but a code of conduct must go beyond the times of election and should characterize politics, political process and governance of the country for all time. It is when such a code of conduct becomes basic feature of the Indian Constitution can the faith of the common man be restored in politics of the country.

Chapter - 6

Separation of Powers in the Indian Polity is Judiciary Undermining the Executive ?

Strictures of the Judiciary against the Executive

On December 14, the Supreme Court fired the Maharashtra Government, while dismissing the appeal of the State Government challenging the Rs. 25000 imposed on it as costs by the Nagpur bench of the Bombay High Court on a petition by Buldhana district farmers – Sarangdhar Singh Chavan and his brother Vijaysingh Chavan – alleging that the police refused to register a criminal case against a Congress legislator Dilip Kumar Sananda's father Gokulchand Sananda, a private money lender The High Court had imposed the fine after funding gross interference from the executive in shielding a money lender belonging to the ruling party. The Chief Minister Vilasrao Deshmukh had stopped the police from filing an FIR. Supreme Court Judge A.K. Ganguly observed that this act was wholly unconstitutional. He further said that in the court and later outside addressing a conference that, 'a politician who was found guilty by the apex court was still in his full glory and thus was shameless' (Indian Express, Feb 5, 2011). Obviously he was chiding the UPA government for 'elevating' in the recent Union Cabinet reshuffle. Minister Vilasrao Deshmukh from the light weight 'Heavy Industries' portfolio's to Rural Development, a portfolio with a huge budget and nationwide reach. Apart from the legal aspects, the act of Deshmukh, Chief Minister, made a mockery of the policy of government to protect the farmers from the extortionate acts of the money lenders. Citizens expected the higher fine of Rs. 10 lakhs imposed by the Supreme Court to be paid personally by the Minister. Instead the fine was imposed on the Maharashtra State Government to be paid out of the public exchequer which it did.

This was not the first or the last occasion when Judges passed strictures on government.

Similar observations were made by the apex court in other cases also such as in the case of the appointment of P.J. Thomas an IAS Officer to the post of CVC. A case was filed in the Supreme Court challenging the appointment on the ground that the officer was involved in the Palmolein corruption case - a huge financial scam while serving the Keral Government and the recent Raja case, when he was serving as Secretary in the Telephone Department The Court asked how Thomas was adjudged by Government as one of the 'impeccable integrity'.

Justice Ganguly asked Government why A. Raja was continued to be Minster in the Union Cabinet when he was under CBI Scrutiny since 2008 in the spectrum allocation case.

Even a subordinate Delhi Court took a swipe at the Congress government saying that the Quotrochi case did not move even an inch in the last 23 years except during the BJP rule when some adverse statements could be recorded. Now the Court would be passing orders on CBI plea to withdraw the case against Otavi Quatrochi in Bofors pay off case. (Indian Express, Feb 11, 2011).

While hearing a PIL petition seeking implementation of traffic rules, the Bombay High Court took note of traffic disruptions during peak hours due to VIP movements including those of the President, Vice President and Prime Minister of India and asked why arrangement cannot be made in such a manner that the common man does not suffer. It may be recalled that during some visits of the Prime Minister, patients died since their relatives could not take them to hospital for treatment on time. (Times of India, Feb 19)

Taking note of the flood of litigation by Government, the Supreme Court observed – 'The government litigation was clogging the wheels of justice'. 'From recruitment to retirement why should', asked the exasperated Court', the Court be deciding everything relating to government officials?'. Questioning the six years delay in diesel scam case in Gujarat, the Supreme Court found CBI plagued by vacancies and asked the Department to follow a time frame to fill them. (Times of India, 17th Feb. 2011).

All these observations were relating to 'Governance deficit' – the failure of the executive to discharge its functions.

Theory of separation of powers

Touched to the quick by the outspoken observations of the Supreme Court, the Prime Minister in his address to the Commonwealth Lawyers Conference invoked the theory of 'separation of powers' and observed that "different limbs of government should stick to their own sphere of activity and not interfere in the activity of another limb (as the judiciary had done he implied). Such acts of the judiciary would undermine the authority of the executive." How far are that Prime Minister's observations valid or justified?

The theory of 'separation of powers' was first enunciated by the French political philosopher Montesquieu. It may be pertinent to recall some of the famous sentences of Montesquieu. He stated, "When the legislative and executive powers are united in the same person or body, there can be no liberty because the apprehension may arise that the senate (i.e. the legislative body) would enact tyrannical laws and enforce them in a tyrannical manner. Were the judge be the legislators or assume executive powers, the judges might behave with all the violence of an oppressors" Endorsing the view, Madison, one of the founding fathers of USA said, "the accumulation of all powers in the same hands is the very definition of tyranny."

Montesquieu had in mind the American constitution and political system where the principle was strictly applied and where the legislature and the judiciary are independent of the executive. The President is the head of the executive but has no place in the House of Representatives or the Senate. To be sure, the President does appoint the judges of the Supreme Court but once appointed, the judges serve for life and are supposed to be independent though they do carry the intellectual baggage of the party of the President who appoints them.

In India, we have followed the West-minister model (i.e. the model of Britain) of parliamentary democracy where the executive is not separated from the Legislature. It is accountable to Parliament and holds power so long as it has the confidence of the Parliament i.e. has majority of members supporting the Government. A Government with huge majority may take the legislative for granted as it happened in the days of Indira Gandhi. But when the government has a slender majority or is a coalition government in which the major party runs government with the support of other parties, the Parliament can be asserative. In India the opposition parties have gone even beyond this and have obstructed the working of Parliament and have not allowed it to function. The Prime Minister is generally a member and indeed the leader of the House though this does not hold good in the current situation in India.

As regards the relationship between the Judiciary and the executive, the independence of the judiciary is the corner-stone of the Indian democracy and is guaranteed in the Constitution which envisages judicial review of the executive decisions. In the early years, the judges of the Supreme Court were appointed by Government. During the emergency, Indira Gandhi made appointments overlooking the seniority of Justice Khanna and Justice Hegde for daring to oppose her arbitrary acts. In a few years the position radically changed. The Supreme Court on its own took over the function of appointment of the judges and the Union Government acquiesced into the decision.

The Supreme Court and the other Courts in India do not suo moto or as a rule deal with administrative matters which are in the domain of the executive. But if the citizens go in appeal in courts against the decision of the executive whether as aggrieved citizens or as a matter of 'Public interest' (litigation which has assumed high proportions), the Courts have to take cognizance of the various aspects of the executive decisions. They have not only to examine the legality or constitutionality of the decision but also whether they are consistent with public interest and whether they are fair and just. To come to a decision, they are bound to call upon Government to provide Government's files and papers along with the affidavit which the government have to submit through their duly appointed attorney. Whether while the proceedings go on, judges should make obiter dicta observations or whether judges should or express their opinions outside, is a debatable matter. But if the executive decisions are objective and in public interest, Government can hold their own and there is no question of the executive authority being undermined.

Judicial Activism

In India, the questionable acts of the executive or executive inaction in important matters have provided Judiciary with the opportunities to take over executive powers as has happened with recent A. Raja case where the CBI was asked to carry on investigation under the supervision of the Supreme Court. Often judges have laid down detailed schemes for compliance by the executive as Jeevan Reddy did in a case about exorbitant fees fixed by non-aided institutions like Manipal. Also government should not be indifferent to important public issues and should take timely action. In India, the questionable acts of the executive have provided opportunities of judiciary to take on.

The refusal of the Union Government to disclose details of 18 Indians holding accounts in the LG Bank, Lichenstein evoked a sharp response from the Bench compressing. Sudershan Reddy and SS. Nijjar. "Make up your mind whether you can make the disclosure." The Court directed that the Government to ensure that Hassan Ali one of the main suspects does not leave the country. Another bench bluntly told the CBI to inform the court who the beneficiaries and conspirators were who befitted from funds in bank parked abroad. In Amar Singh phone tapping case Justice Ganguly noted the four years gap between the filling of the charge sheet in 2006 and the actual trial in 2010. The noted jurist Soli Sorabji observed that the directions of the Supreme Court give the impression that the Supreme Court has been taking over the running of the country !

Seeing that the work of CBI the premier investigating agency was interfered with by government, the Supreme Court Judge J.S. Verma directed that the CBI would work under the supervision of the CVC. Now even the

CVC has become controversial and has recused himself from the most important A. Raja case.

In the absence of Government action, a vacuum is created as in the case against sexual harassment of women at work places. The Supreme Court took upon itself to lay down detailed prescriptions for protection of women at work places from sexual harassment pending enactment of the law on the subject by government which is yet to see the light of the day. In another case taking note of starvation deaths of tribals in Orrisa, the Supreme Court wondered why the food-grains stocks rotting in godowns or in the open could not be used to feed the starving population. When the Food Minister demurred publicly stating that free distribution of food was not a practical proposition, the Supreme Court severely reprimanded the Minister and asked him to take specific action. Thereupon Government was compelled to make some announcement.

Conclusion

Can all this be called 'judicial tyranny' or 'despotism' ? The responsibility lies on government. It has to see that the standards of administration are kept high and the decisions are taken objectively and in public interest and not under the influence of vested interests, that there is no corruption or nepotism and there is complete fair play and transparency. If this had been ensured judicial pronouncements deprecatory to the executive may not have been made nor would the judiciary taken over executive functions.

Chapter - 7

Multiple Executives – A Mistaken Notion

Kapil Sibbal's article ("Can't have multiple executives – CAG policy, prescription have triggered a constitutional crisis." (Times of India, September 15) is full of misttatements calculated to mislead the reader.

Sibbal' thesis is that policy making is the exclusive sphere of the executive and neither the CAG nor the Judiciary has any business to meddle with it. More specifically he asserts that the manner in which public assets are distributed for a particular end must be decided upon by government, not by CAG nor by courts. "We cannot have three executives" he grandly asserts. He invokes the 'theory of separation of powers' to exclude both the courts and CAG from policy making.

Sibbal may be a clever lawyer but he seems to have little understanding of the basic principles of political science and policy making and no concern for the ethics which must govern all acts of government and public administration, including policy making and their implementation.

The theory of separation does not say that there are rigid walls between the three organs of the State viz. the legislative, the executive and the judiciary. In the system of parliamentary democracy such as that in India, executive is not rigidly separated from the legislative. Government is all the time accountable to Parliament. It may take executive decisions on its own without consulting the Parliament. But Parliament has every right – and this includes parties in the opposition as well to call into question every act of the executive including its policies, if they are considered by it as flawed or against public interest. Similarly the Judiciary has every right to strike down executive decisions, if it conscides either suo-moto or on the filing of a case in court including public interest litigation, including those related with public pollcies, if the Court finds them repugnant to the provisions of the constitution. Sibbal should remember that Supreme Court set aside all 122 2G allocations at one stroke as repugnant to public interest. But the government does not seen to have learnt the lesson. Even the Prime Minister probably under the influence of his advisors like Sibbal, has asserted that policy making is the domain of the government and not that of courts.

Sibbal and people like him in government, in the ruling party have deliberating underestimated the role of the CAG as one performing mere 'accountlating functions' Sibbal does not know that long back it was decided that the accounts have to be maintained by Departments concerned and there is separate agency of Accounts both at the Central level and the state level specifically set up for the purpose. After the bifurcation of account from audit, the CAG has been left free to concentrate on his main function of auditing i.e. seeing that, public funds are properly used fulfilling all cannons of financial propriety and there is no loss of public funds, which legitimately should accrue to public exchequer. If a flawed policy leads to such financial losses to the public exchequer, CAG is obliged to draw attention to it in his audit reports. Sibbal states that CAG is not accountable to any constitutional authority. He forgets that CAG himself, in his own right, is a constitutional authority. Sibbal is quite wrong when he asserted that 'PAC examines audit reports and prepares draft reports which are finally adopted by the PAC's with their conclusions and recommendations.' Sibbal does not seem to understand, perhaps deliberately the role of CAG in the hearings of the PAC. CAG is there to assist the PAC. He is not there in the dock. It is the representatives of the Department concerned who appear before the PAC to place their case before the PAC on various observations in the Audit reports. The CAG already had given the opportunity to the departments when the findings of the CAG in a draft form are sent to the departments concerned. It is only after considering their replies on his observations that the CAG prepares his final audit report and sends it to the Parliament. When the Departmental representatives appear before the PAC, they get a second chance. The PAC can come to their own conclusions on the audit finding after hearing the representatives of the department. The representatives of the ruling party are in the majority in the composition of the PAC though a member of the opposition party is the Chairman of the Committee. It is not proper for the members of the ruling party of PAC to pounce on the CAG at its meeting instead of allowing him the role of 'friend, philosophers, guide' to the PAC. Unfortunately in recent meetings of the PAC, the members of the ruling party have started assuming an adversarial role vis avis the CAG. By doing so they are setting up a wrong tradition. The Prime Minister after criticizing the CAG, has now started saying that the CAG report will not 'placed under the carpet' but would be followed up. True to his word he set up inter-departmental working group which started examining the coal allocations and found several of them given to companies without the necessary credentials and experience and recommended either their cancellation or confiscation of gurantee amount. The CBI has also stared investigation and filed several criminal cases against prominent people which included Vijay Darda, businessman who is a Member of Parliament of the ruling party. Another big businessman who is involved is Naveen Jindal an MP of the ruling party. It also came out that several politicians of the ruling party who brought pressure for allocations to particular parties. Among them Shri Subodhkant Sahay who recommended a particular allocation to the Prime Minister who, instead of taking him to task for his unethical conduct, passed on his recommendation for urgent action to the Coal Department! It is unethical to use political position by no less person than a Minister of Cabinet to recommend a case in which his brother was involved. But Sibbal in his assertion of the exclusive right of the executive to make policy decisions has completely ignored these ethical aspects.

Allocation of coal by a screening committee is not a policy decision. A policy decision is a general decision in whose frame work and according to whose guidelines decisions of individual allocations can be made. No such policy decision was taken. This led to questionable allocations causing loss to public exchequer. A policy decision requires precise definition of objectives and to the extent possible quantification of those objectives, input-output or cost-benefit analysis, detailed steps that need to be taken, and proper mechanism for monitoring and evaluation. No such policy decision was laid down leading to arbitrary allocations. The scam in 2G allocations was repeated in coal allocations. Ministers like Sibbal should thank CAG for his audit report instead of pillaring him for doing his duty.

Chapter - 8

Indian Republic in Political Imbroglio

As we approach the next Republic Day on 26.01.2011, the people of India are finding their sixty years old Republic in a state of disarray, with Parliament, our highest representative assembly trapped in a political imbroglio and the governance of the country caught in a creeping paralysis under the impact of successive scams of huge proportions.

Non-functioning parliament

The Parliament has become non-functional over the last more than 20 days – virtually the entire winter session with opposition parties (BJP – Leftist parties including) demanding the constitution of Joint Parliamentary Committee to look into 2G scam while Government remains adamant in rejecting the demand outright. It is not clear to the people why the Government should be so adamant on the issue. Now even the allies parties for their own reasons, are veering round to the view that the Government should agree to the opposition demand. The head of the biggest ally. Mamata Banerjee fears that her opposition to the proposal will be used by the incumbent leftist parties in power to her disadvantage in the on coming elections to the State Assembly. The DMK would be looking for its pound of flesh now that it was required to agree to dislodge. A. Raja from the Union Cabinet. The Congress, the biggest party in power, seems adamant on the issue because of many reasons – first because it would be in minority in the JPC; second it fears that the JPC could drag on for two or three years casting a shadow on 2014 elections as well assembly elections in different states; thirdly they fear that the JPC would involve the Prime Minister and his office in the course of the JPC probe. It is yet another example of purely political considerations, getting the better of the paramount need to ensure smooth running of the Parliament.

Corruption Scams – The Raja Case

Scams after scams of corruption have tarnished the image of not only the government and the political system but of the country as a whole. Already the doyen among Indian Industrialist Ratan Tata has openly talked, in course of a Television interview, of Banana Republic type situation developing in the country. The worst of the scams in many ways was the 2G Spectrum sale scam. The sale in 2008 of the spectrum at 2002 rates led to a loss to Government of, as clearly stated in the recent CAG report, Rs. 17,6000 cr. A draft of the report before its finalization was sent to the Telecom Department. Instead of responding to the observations in the draft report of the high constitutional authority, the Union Minister A. Raja brazenly brushed it aside claiming that it was 'a policy decision' of Government and the CAG had no business to comment on it. The Minister apparently neither knew what 'a policy decision was nor the weight that needs to be given to the observations of the CAG. When there was parliamentary demand for sacking the minister, DMK Chief and Chief Minister of Tamil Nadu specially found time to call upon the Prime Minister and tell him that Raja should not be victimized just because he was a SC Minister ! The weight of the Chief Minister and head of DMK a staunch ally of UPA Government had obviously the needed effect and the Prime Minister chose not to sack Raja for two long years despite a nationwide demand to do so. The nation wondered how and why under a Prime Minister, known for his personal integrity, a Minister like Raja could be allowed to function. In a press interview the Prime Minister was content to say that law would take its own course, which was hardly convincing. Now it has come out that despite Prime Minister's letter warning the Minister in the matter, the Minister not only arrogantly brushed aside the Law Ministry's opinion but also used disrespectable word in his reply to Prime Minister which was hardly becoming of a minister in Cabinet. Just because it is a coalition government depending, among others, on DMK support, could not justify such a Ministerial behaviour. The Minister stuck to his job; finally he was sacked. Even after that he continued to open his big mouth justifying his action. Now it has come out that the Minister has been a 'habitual offender'. He threatened a Judge of Madras High Court in a criminal case pending before him. The judge, instead of immediately giving the Minister a 'contempt of court' notice, chose to write to Chief Justice of Supreme Court Shri. Balakrishnan. The latter summoned him to Delhi but even after the meeting, the Chief Justice, now retired, chose to speak in a vague manner without mentioning the name of the Minister. Nothing happened and the Minister was left scot free. The Minister setup a bad example of conduct of a Minister in Union Cabinet but still the Tamil Nadu Chief Minister continue to stand behind Raja and people in his constituency gave him a big reception after he resigned. So much for the democratic conscience of the people in the world's largest democracy !

In a case in Supreme court filed by Shri Subramaniam Swamy, head of Janata Party in regard to Raja's involvement in 2G scam, Supreme Court asked as is to why no action was taken against Raja for two years. It was explained on behalf of Prime Minister that action against Raja was delayed because the Law Department's advice was pending. Shri Subramaniam Swamy who had filed the case has exonerated the Prime Minister and put the blame on 'bureaucracy'. How much value can be attached to the certificate given by Swamy to Prime Minister is another question ! The national outrage against Raja compelled the CBI to take same concrete action against Raja after dilly dallying for 400 days after the case came on the file of CBI. They carried simultaneous raids on his residences and those of his associates and seized, documents and other incriminating material.

The ramifications of the Raja case were not confirmed to politics. They extended to the corporate world as well. It was long known that the Corporates exercises a powerful influence on Government to bend its machinery to subserve its interests. The supreme example of the working of capitalism is USA which is based on the premise of ''less government in business and more business government'. The Raja case provided a striking example of this corporate influence in India which has become more and more apparent after the new economic polity was introduced in 1991 characterised by marketisation, privatization, liberalization and globalisation. Shri Rajiv Chandrashekhar an MP of Rajya Sabha alleged that the Tatas were the main beneficiaries of 2G scam. The Neera Radia tapes had clearly exposed the conversation between Ratan Tata and Neera Radia. Tata rushed to Supreme Court to stop the publicizing of 'private conversation' between him and Neera Radia. But is was not really that personal but related to business. It further came out that public relation work relating 90 units of the vast Tata empire was handed over to Neera Radia, who in a short period miraculously developed cordial relations with people in Central Government including the influential politicians and the burocrates. The lady had arrived only 15 years ago from London after her divorce with only one lakh rupees and has through her 'public relations work amassed' a fortune of Rs. 400 cr ! Thorstein Veblen the maverick American Economist of Norwegian origin a century ago had drawn attention to ostentatious consumption waste and misleading advertisements as some of the evils of capitalism. To those should be added 'lobbying and public relations' industry which has started exercising in a big way its evil influence on Government at the cost of public interest.

The case of P. J. Thomas

Another case closely connected with Raja scandal was that P.J. Thomas who was Telecom Secretary under Raja. Earlier in his career he was Civil Supplies Secretary in 1991-92 when the controversial import of 15000 tons of palmolein from Malaysia took place, allegedly costing the State Exchequer a loss of Rs. 200 cr. as found out in a latter CAG report. Inspite of this the Union Government appointed him to the high post of Chief Vigilance Commissioner despite the written objections received from the leader of the opposition Smt. Sushama Swaraj, who was a member of the three member committee constituted as per the guideline of the Supreme Court. Smt. Sushama Swaraj in her objections pointed out to the Palmolein scam and a 2G Scam in which Thomas was involved. A panel of three officers was before the Committee for its consideration. Swaraj asked the two other members, the Prime Minister and the Home Minister, to consider two other names in the panel, but the Prime Minister was adamant and insisted on the selection of Thomas for the post. It was difficult to understand why the Prime Minister was so insistent on Thomas. His appointment as CVC caused national outrage. On TV channels the appointment was severaly condemned. But Thomas chose not to be embarrassed and stuck to his post ! Nor did the Government ask for his resignation ! All that he did, was to say that he would recuse from the CBI enquiry into 2G scandal ! The CVC recusing himself from the most important enquiry viz. 2G Spectrum scam in which an ex. Union Minister has been involved was strange. He forgot to tell that the person who would be responsible to investigate into the scam was appointed only recently by him creating doubt whether he would be able to be objective regarding the role of Thomas as Telecommunication Secretary !

Now the case has taken a new turn. Two separate petitions have been filed in the Supreme Court one by NGO CPL and the other by a group of civil servants led by Former Election Commissioner J.M. Lyngdo challenging the appointment of Thomas a CVC and asking for his removal from the post, citing his role in the Palmolein import and 2G spectrum cases. The Supreme Court bench headed by the Chief Justice of India S.H. Kapadia has issued a notice to Thomas to appear in person. The Supreme Court has raised two basic issues. One, how will Thomas perform his duties with a charge sheet pending against him? And two and more importantly, whether he 'fulfilled the criterion of 'unimpeachable integrity' required for appointment as CVC. Thomas will have to answer some tough posers in the Supreme Court. The Court has noted that in the conditions in which he finds himself, he will feel embarrassed and will not be able to function effectively. Apparantly Thomas does not feel so ! The Government in turn will have to explain why they chose Thomas despite the dissent of the leader of opposition. Since Prime Minister himself was adamant in appointing Thomas, he will be directly involved.

The credibility of CBI was already at a low ebb due to its non-performance in a number of cases including the Commonwealth Games Organisation Committee case when it has omitted the name of Shri. Kalamadi the Chairman of the Committee from the FIR. Now the Thomas case has called into question the credibility of CVC itself which is supposed to supervise CBI.

Vulnerabilities of Prime Minister and the Congress

These two cases have certainly added to the vulnerability of Dr. Manmohan Singh as Prime Minister. He is head of Government but not the leader of the Congress Party in power nor of the UPA. The political ascendancy of Sonia Gandhi over him has been acknowledged by him. The Prime Minister is normally expected to be not only the head of Government but also the supremo leader of the party and of the nation – as Jawaharlal Nehru was. And yet Dr. Singh claimed that his government was more cohesive than that of Jawaharlal Nehru which hardly seemed plausible !

In fact, the situation seems to be quite the opposite. Despite the resounding success of the Congress party in 2009 General Elections and the severe defeat suffered by BJP which expected to come back to power. It was reduced to 116, also of the leftist parties which was reduced from 60 to 30. The Congress did much better than expected crossing 200 mark and reaching 206. The leftist parties were apparently punished by the electorate for withdrawing 'outside support' to UPA Government. They had withdrawn support when Prime Minister Manmohan insisted on the Nuclear Deal with USA to which the leftists were opposed tooth and nail. Even after the left withdrew support UPA, It survived the vote of confidence with the unexpected support of the Samajwadi Party and the Congress Party's manipulation which successfully ensured several opposition MP's deserting their parties and crossing over to UPA. They included BJP and Shiv Sena MPs as well. The UPA-I survived. The Prime Minister described the withdrawal of the support of the leftist parties as good riddance since they opposed several of his so called 'reforms measures'. It was a great relief, the Prime Minister said, that "he had no longer to be a slave of the leftist".

The UPA Government again formed under the leadership of Dr. Manmohan Singh after the General elections was expected to be much stronger. Though the Congress won 206 seats it was short of 272 mark and had to have the support of other smaller parties to have a majority in Parliament. That it easily got with the support of Trinmool Congress of Mamata Banerjee dominant in West Bengal, DMK in power in Tamil Nadu and NCP with whom congress had formed Government in Maharashtra. Soon the Congress realized that while the leftist support to UPA was based on principles, the coalition parties of UPA-II were opportunist. Mamata all the time had her eye on West Bengal Assembly elections where she wanted to demolish Marxist led government. She went on pressing premature dismissal of the leftist government which Congress refused to agree to. She went to the extent of supporting the Maoist while Chidambaram, the Union Home Minister supported the State Government in the fight against the Maoists. Mamata was more in Calcutta than in Delhi. DMK was all the time interested in loaves and fishes of office. Pawer of NCP always sought to get more political mileage than his numbers warranted and succeeded in that. He personally held several portfolios including Agriculture, Food and Civil Supplies but had more interest in Cricket politics than in his several Ministerial assignments which he mishandled. His import of rotten wheat from Australia created national outrage. And now there is a big food scandal in UP in which large quantities of food grains meant for distribution amongst the poor are directed to export and the blame was laid not just at the doors of State Administration but also at the Union Minister. The scandal has yet to blow out in all its proportions. With a much smaller number of MLA's in Maharashtra, Pawar's party has all the significant portfolios including Finance and Home.

The Congress has dubious coalition at the centre with unreliable partners. Additionally it is conspicuously weak in the States. It snatched Rajasthan from BJP but is without power in several states, with BJP in power in states like Madhya Pradesh, Gujarat and Himachal Pradesh. The Lefts are in power in West Bengal and Kerala. The Shiromani Akali Dal with the BJP in Punjab. The Congress suffered a severe defeat in Bihar Assembly elections with Nitish Kumar's JDU in alliance with BJP capturing 85% of assembly seats. The Congress went down from 9 to 4 and Lalu Paswan alliance was reduced to 25. It was Rahul Gandhi who had decided that Congress would fight alone. Now everybody blamed him for miserable performance of the Congress. Actually it was the weakness of the Congress Party at the field level which was the cause of the miserable performance. The grass root organisation can be built only over a period of time.

The Congress got into trouble in Maharashtra and in Andhra Pradesh where it had a re-sounding victory under YSR Reddy's leadership. The Congress came to trouble in Maharashtra when Adarsha Housing Society scam reached such proportions that it caused a national outrage. The multi storied apartment building in a Mumbai was originally meant for the families of the Kargil victims. But the flats were grabbed by senior army officers, bureaucrats and above all powerful politicians. Among the beneficiaries were the mother in law of Chief Minister Ashok Chavan and several of his relatives through his wife. Chavan pleaded innocence. And still does so but had to be removed and replaced by Prithviraj Chavan a Minister of State in Prime Minister Office incharge of several departments who has a comparatively clean record.

In Andhra Pradesh the situation is very difficult for the Congress party. After the sudden demise of YSR in a helicopter accident, the Congress put his finance minister and a senior member of Cabinet, Rosayya in the seat of Chief Minister. But YSRs' son Jugan Mohan Reddy had the ambition to succeed his father. He was supported by his mother, but Congress President Sonia Gandhi cold shouldered him and ultimately he left the Congress and has decided to form his own party. The Congress removed the ineffective Rosayya and replaced him by Kiran Kumar Reddy. Once what happened under Rajiv Gandhi is being repeated within Congress leadership showing that the local politicians do not count and the privilege of appointing the Chief Minister is that of High command. This led once to the downfall of Congress. The story may be repeated in Andhra Pradesh. Already situation became grim with the Telangana agitation taking serious turn. With the appointment of Shri. Krishna Committee the situation in Telangana has no doubt calmed down but may explode again.

Grim Security Scenario

The Congress is accused of being soft on terrorists. Major security challenge are faced by several states and the terrorist challenge is a constant threat. The 26/11 criminals are not yet brought to book and the judicial process is working at a ponderously slow speed. Chidambaram boasts this as the vindication of the Indian democracy but people have lost patience. The recent attack on Varanasi has come as a severe blow. The terrorist threat is ever alive in several big cities and sensitive places like temples. The situation in Kashmir had gone out of control and that the Chief Minister is ineffective in dealing with the situation is apparent. The Maoist challenge is faced in several states.

The depredations of Free Market Economy

The economic policy of free market economy has created apoplexy at the centre (certain part of metropolitan cities) and anaemia at the periphery (rural areas and poor people). The luxury sector, has prospered while the poor in slums suffer. The infrastructure is woefully inadequate Prime Ministers talk of turning Mumbai into Shanghai looks like an empty boast. Despite Jagdish Bhagvati's claims in the Hiren Mukerjee lecture that the poor have benefitted from the policy of liberlisation, the ground reality is that a few have prospered while the poor have suffered. There is unholy alliance between builders, businessmen, politicians and few bureaucrates which at present has led to the ugly urban scenario. The inequalities are glaring and cannot be accepted by people all the time. They are bound to revolt. The social situation is also precarious. Instead of national unity, there are fissures on caste and communal basis.

Inflation in prices of essential commodities like food grains, pulses, milk and vegetables have put them beyond the reach of the common people. But the Minister directly concerned Shri. Pawar looks the other way and expects the Finance Minister to take the blame. The Finance Minister accepts that inflation is rampant but attributes it to 9% growth ! This argument is fallacious. If there is growth in the productive sectors, the supply of essential commodities will grow and would absorb the inflationary pressure caused by developmental expenditure. The Prime Minister and Deputy Chairman Planning Commission both economic experts go on saying and predicting that inflation would get moderated by December (or even earlier) but inflation does not seem to respect their economic expertise.

Glimmer of Hope

But recent Bihar elections have shown that there is a glimmer of hope. Bihar has shown that people even in rural Bihar are alive and awake. They want security and good government. The Chief Minister Nitish Kumar gave them after the Jungle Raj of Lalu Prasad for 15 years. It is wrong to attribute victory to his 'social engineering'. The sophisticated analysts who do so are more castiest and communal than the common people. The people of India despite existence of caste, creed and community have a basic sense of unity and all that they want is honest good government.

This lesson of Bihar elections is a glimmer of hope for the Indian Republic which can yet overcome the multi-dimensional crisis in which it is entangled at present. People can and should throw away power drunk politicians who misuse political power, and the political parties who have no principles, no ideology, no coherent programme to benefit the people and who do not put national interest above partison interest whether of caste or family. That is the lesson of the recent Bihar election which has a national significance.

Chapter - 9

Coalition Culture

An economic textbook talks of the phenomenon of the 'importance of the unimportant'. The phenomenon is visible in coalition politics as well when small parties claimed and receive importance disproportionate to their numbers in the elected bodies.

Britain traditionally has been a two party democracy in which in the election outcome, one party gains absolute majority and forms government. There is no ambiguity or uncertainty. But the May 6 election results brought out a different outcome. For sometime now, Liberal Democratic Party has been emerging as a third national party which could provide an alternative to the existing two national parties viz. Labour in power and Conservative in the opposition. In the presidential style of discussion on TV, Nick Clegg got the better of Prime Minister Gordon Brown of the ruling party and David Cameron, the leader of the main opposition who was widely believed to be a serious candidate for the top post. The results were however disappointing for the Liberal Democratic party which emerged as poor third with meagre 57 seats way behind Labour (258) and Conservative (306). And yet in a situation in which no party gained a clear majority, Liberal Democrats had the opportunity to be the kingmaker. Both the major parties had to solicit the support of Liberal Democrats in order to gain majority and form government – which the leaders of two major parties set out to do. Stating that the Conservatives with the largest number of seats should have the first chance to form government, Clegg setup a team for discussion with the team of conservative party led by William Hague, the right hand man of David Cameron. When the discussions were going on, Clegg had no compunction in having long telephonic talk with Gordon Brown. He felt that Labour party was ideologically much nearer to his Democratic and coalition between the two would be more natural and tenable. There were days of anxiety and uncertainty for the Conservatives. Eventually the conservatives-liberal alliance was formed and Brown gave up his claim. He met the sovereign to tender resignation. The Queen lost no time in inviting Cameron to form government. Brown vacated 10 Downing Street and Cameron made his appearance.

The alliance could not have been easy. Liberal Democratic party have been keen on many points which would not be accepted to the Conservatives. Above all Liberal Democrats want electoral reforms – introduction of proportional representation as in European Countries, since 'the first past the post system' does not reflect the electoral support. Thus, in recent elections 23% of voters voted for the Liberals, but their number of seats was less than 10%. For Conservatives to accept the reforms was to commit itself perpetually to a coalition system abandoning the ambition to form government on its own in the succeeding elections. Cameron did not immediately accept the proposal for introducing the system of proportional representation but agreed to set up a committee to examine the issue in depth. A second important difference is the relationship with the European Union. The Liberal want a much closer integration with possible acceptance of Euro as currency, the Conservatives, as always, want to keep distance and retain British identity. The proposals of the two parties to tackle the economic crisis are some what different. Both agreed that the recession is not yet over and recovery is weak. But the Liberals are more keen on maintaining employment while Conservatives are keen on ending huge budgetary deficit. Cameron wants fiscal toughness to be the hallmark of his government.

Despite these major differences in approach to political and economic issues, the lure of power was too much to resists. For the first time after many years, the Liberals had a chance of being in Government. And that is what happened. Clegg became the Deputy Prime Minister and five of his colleagues became Ministers. Cameron however, retained all the major portfolios for his colleagues - William Hague, became the Foreign Secretary, thirty eight years young George Osbourne became Chancellor of the Exchequer, Lian Fox became Defence Secretary, Taresa May became Home Secretary and Ken Clarke the Justice Minister.

Despite major differences on policy issues both Cameron and Clegg assured the British people that the Government will last for five years. They expressed their intention to introduce law for setting the next date of election after May 2015, replacing the current system in which the Prime Minister could call election any time. Both assured a government with a 'strong and secure majority in the House of Commons". What helped Conservative-liberal alliance was the fact that Cameron was no Thatcher with her hide-bound conservatism. He stands for 'compassionate conservatism. He also denounces unbridled greed and selfishness as the basis of capitalism and free market economy. He wants a more responsible society" in which "we just don't ask "what are my entitlements but what are my responsibilities – we don't ask just what I am owned but what can I give" Cameron is a defender of national health service influenced by his experience of his eldest child who suffered from cerebral palsy and epilepsy and died at the age of six.

Despite Browns desire to hang on to power, he ultimately had to bow down to openly expressed views that "we have got to respect the results of the general elections. We cannot get away from the fact that Labour did not win. Barganining to stay in power at all cost is unacceptable. A Labour-Liberal pact would lack Legitimacy and anger the public".

The formation of coalition government in Britain after May 6 election has been neatly accomplished without ugly bargaining or massy compromises. Appointment of Nick Clegg as Deputy Prime Minister and bonohmie exhibited by both the Prime Minister and Deputy Prime Minister (taking in good humour the jibe of Cameron in Course of election propaganda that the biggest joke was Nick Clegg) at the time of their first press conference was a good augury for a smooth two party government. Only the performance of the coalition government over the next five years would show how far the first coalition after the wartime coalition between conservatives led by Winston Churchil and Labour led by Clement Attley , would show how for the coalition experience has been successful. It might well be the beginning of a new coalition era in Britain.

II. The Indian experience

We in India, of course, have been a witness to coalition governments for many years in the states and even at the center after the end of single party domination of the Congress for over two decades after the attainment of independence. The scenario of multi-party coalition governments in India is far more complex than the two party coalition in Britain. Many of the parties are of regional nature which after forming government in the State have made their presence felt at the Centre. Congress which was reluctant to form coalition governments was forced to swallow pride and accept the inevitability of coalition after being out of power from 1996 till 2004. The prelude to Congress coalition experience was the minority government of Narasimharao which stayed in power for a full term of five years, but at the cost of its image of moral rectitude being badly tarnished. It survived with the support of the MPs of Jharkhand Mukti Morcha led by Shibu Sorain who wanted bribe as a price for their support. This created a national scandal. A PIL was filed in the Supreme Court but it held that the phenomenon of acceptance of bribe took place on the floor of Parliament and hence was outside the purview of the judiciary. The judgement outraged all those who stood for moral standards in politics but the judgement stands till today.

The Congress led UPA coalition government completed full term from 2004 to 2009 but not without making serious compromises with its policy preferences and decent standard of political morality. India's original contribution to coalition politics is the existence of a coalition government based on 'outside support' of a party which refuses to join the Government. The Leftists won more than sixty seats and their support was crucial for the government to have the confidence of the House. They agreed to give outside support on the basis of 'common minimum programme'. The leftist kept a close watch on the policy initiative of UPA Government and did not allow the government to undertake 'disinvestments' of public enterprises nor the entry of foreign investments in banking and insurance nor the investment of provident fund in the stock market. They also opposed the Nuclear Energy and strategic fact with US government which was agreed upon between Prime Minister Manmohan Singh and President George Bush. The Prime Minister put up with the leftists resistance for a long time trying various ways to win over the leftist and get their support but when the time ran out he took the plunge and the leftist withdrew support putting the government in minority. But when the crunch came, the government was able to win the confidence vote by winning over the Samajwadi Party which hitherto had kept company with the leftists and wining over some opposition MPs including those belonging to BJP with it was believed with bribes and blandishments. The ugly phenomenon of bundles of notes given by way of bribe on the speakers table in an open house created outrage and a parliamentary enquiry committee was appointed with hardly any consequences. What was material was the government survived with a handsome majority. Government took it as a stamp of approval to the nuclear agreement.

The UPA government not only completed its full term but came back with better results, specially for the Congress which crossed 200 mark. (206 to be precise) to the utter discomfiture of the BJP which had hoped to gain majority but got just 116, 90 less than Congress. The leftist fared even worst and being reduced to half. Congress again formed a coalition with the participation of DMK, NCP and Trinmool Congress under the leadership of fiery Mamta Banergee who after a long struggle was able to humble the long entrenched Marxists and their associates in West Bengal. The two main opposition parties were in utter disarray. The regional parties BSP and SP, for their own reasons, gave outside support to Government further weakening the opposition.

Apparently the UPA-II was in a far more comfortable position than UPA-I. However, it soon found itself in knots. The relentless rise in the prices of essential commodities caused hardships to the common people. The government took a number of measures like resort to imports, restrictions on exports, subsidized supplies through public distribution system and tightening money supply but they all proved ineffective. On the contrary additional tax levies on petrol and diesel raised their prices and had all inevitable cascading effect on prices. Government was of its wits end in dealing with the price spiral. The Minister in charge of several relevant departments like agriculture, food, public distribution and consumer welfare refused to take responsibility and passed it on the Prime Minister and Cabinet. Government in turn, attributed it to the drought situation, global rise in prices and higher price given to farmers for their products. The opposition refused to accept these as valid reasons and drew attention to bungling in international trade such as import of rotten wheat at high price, export of sugar at subsidized rates and import of sugar at high prices, and future trading in agricultural commodities. They tried to whip up agitations including a huge rally in scorching heat in the nation's capital. They moved cut motion on the Budget in which both BJP and the leftists joined. They were confident of success which would have put the government in jeopardy. But the floor manages of UPA were able to turn the tables by manipulating the regional parties. BSP with which the Congress party is at logger heads for gaining power in UP surprisingly declared support to government. Their 23 votes came in very handy. At about the same time the CBI had withdrawn cases against Mayavati which action was seen as quid-pro-quo for gaining BSP support on the cut motion. What was more surprising was that the SP and RJD which were with the leftists in decrying government for inflation of food prices chose to walk out instead of supporting the cut motion. Even the Chief Minister of Jharkhand who was still an MP and who was Chief Minister of Jharkhand with BJP as coalition partner and in opposition to Congress, chose to cast his vote in favour of UPA to the utter discomfiture of BJP. The motion consequently was lost decisively with substantial margin in favour of UPA. The government interpreted the vote as a mandate in its favour, though it was quite clear that but for the support of BSP and the walkout of SP and RJD, the government would have been in a minority. UPA was clearly buying support through political bargaining. The leftist accused Mulayam Singh of perfidy. As for SP and RJD who had joined the leftist parties in demonstrations against price rise, the last minute decision not to vote in favour of the cut motion shocked the leftist parties particularly because only a few days in the teeth of opposition of SP and RJD, Congress had got passed the Women's Reservation Bill in Rajya Sabha. It appeared later that in return for the favour of 'not voting', Congress quietly dropped the proposal to place the Bill before Lok Sabha. Such is the power of the small parties to make the much bigger parties to act according to their wishes. The decision not to include 'caste' in the census which had already commenced was also the concession to SP and RJD. Nor do the regional parties trust the Congress, just when it seemed that the SP was moving towards evolving a working relationship with the Congress the Government decision to refer the civic liability Nuclear Damage Bill to the standing committee of Parliament on science and technology and not the one on energy headed by Mulayam Singh

Yadav, had led to fresh heart burn between the two parties. Congress knows the unreliability of the regional parties who cannot always be depended upon.

BJP betrayed by Shibu Sorain withdrewed support to his government in Jharkhand had a second thought when Shibu's son Hemant came forward with a compromise solution of BJP chief Minister supported by Jharkhand Mukti Morcha. The wily Guruju (Shibu Sorain) once again showed his political skill by throwing in the idea of rotational CM. After some pre-verification BJP succumbed to this idea. Such is the lure of power !

Another serious case showed how a regional party could hold Congress to ransom by insisting on its pound of flesh. The DMK joined UPA government as its constituent by asking for and getting crucial and lucrative portfolios and nominating its own candidates to those Ministerial positions. One of them was Tele Communication Department held by A. Raja who was involved in a huge scandal relating to sale of G2 spectrum in 2008 which was sold at 2002 prices landing government in huge losses calculated any where between 60,000 Cr to 100,000 Cr. There was wide spread exposure in press and electronic media creating national outrage and demand for Rajas's ouster from the Cabinet. But Prime Minister known for his own personal integrity was unable to take any action against Raja especially after the 85 years old Chief Minister of Tamil Nadu and DMK patron made a personal visit to Delhi and met Prime Minister to support Raja and his continued position as Cabinet Minister in charge of Telecommunication. He dismissed all charges against Raja as false and made just because he was a Dalit forgetting that the CAG and many other independent bodies had clearly established the huge scandal. Even the CBI had 'raided' his office and yet he continues to be a Union Cabinet Minister, seriously compromising high stand of political integrity and morality.

Opportunistic political bargaining and massy compromises and condonation of serious scandals have been undermining the very foundations of confidence in our democracy. We have to establish tradition and culture of coalition working on the basis of principles rather than mere expediencies, going from one political crisis to another.

Chapter - 10

Whither Parliamentary Democracy in India

Fasts of Anna Hazare regarding passing of the Lok Pal Bill and Baba Ramdev against corruption and events that followed have raised fundamental questions regarding the functioning of Parliamentary Democracy in India.

The 97 hours fast by Anna Hazare at Jantarmantar which evoked huge response of people in Delhi and all over the country, compelled Govt to concede to his demand to constitute a joint committee of 'Ministers and members of 'Civil Society' to formulate a draft by the end of June 30 on the basis of the drafts formulated by Government and the one by the 'Civil Society'. After some initial smooth sailing, serious differences have arisen, as could only be expected, regarding different issues such as the inclusion of the Prime Minister and judiciary within the ambit of Lokpal.

While this was going on, Baba Ramdev began his fast at Ramlila Ground (after permission was denied to hold it at Jantar Mantar) regarding the wider issue of elimination of corruption and black money. To dissuade Baba from embarking on fast, four Ministers of Union Government headed by no less than Pranab Mukherji went to the airport to meet him but Baba was adamant on his fast. Thousands of his followers, young and old, women and children assembled in the huge pandal specially erected for the purpose at Ramlila Ground to fast in sympathy. The exchanges between the two parties nevertheless continued. When Kapil Sibbal, the Minister negotiating with Baba, publicly announced that Baba had agreed to give up 'Tapa' after three days, Baba felt he was compromised and exposed, while his followers were still coming all over the country to join the fast. Baba immediately hardened his stand and announced that he would continue his fast till government issued an ordinance to declare as 'public assets' black money stashed abroad in overseas banks.

Government accused Baba of betrayal. Past night on 4th June 5000 police of rapid action force of the State Government armed with tear gas and lathi swooped on the sleeping congregation while trying to arrest Baba. A drama followed, Baba escaped from the Pandal but to the relief of Government was apprehend by Delhi Police while running away surrounded by his female followers himself disguised in female dress. More important sleeping men were rudely woken up by police who burst tear gas shells and resorted to lathi charge even on women and children. 70 injured persons were admitted to hospital and some to intensive care units. A particularly bad case was Rajbala who was paralysed.

The nocturnal crackdown was condemned not only by Baba's followers but people all over the country. L.K. Advani, leader of BJP, said that the crackdown reminded of Jaliyawala Bagh massacre by Gen. Dyer during the colonial days. Anna Hazare and 'Civil Society' activists condemned the crackdown as 'Kalank', a blot on humanity and democracy. Shanti Bhushan the senior lawyer demanded that the Union government should resign.

Government representatives tried to defend the action. First Sibbal claimed that none was injured. But when seventy injured persons were admitted in the hospital his claim was found to be not correct. After waiting for a day after the crackdown, the Prime Minister said that the incident was 'unfortunate' but in the situation as is developed, was 'unavoidable'. The Home Minister Chidambaram took a press conference even to declare that the crackdown was necessary for maintenance of 'Law and Order'. None was convinced. When the crackdown was described as a panicky action of a weak vacillating Government, it was asserted that the plan for removing Baba if necessary by force was already decided upon. This was proof enough that the crackdown was not a reaction to a situation but a pre-meditated coldblooded assault on defenceless people. Then there was an attempt to malign the Baba's fast as instigated by the RSS which Rahul Gandhi, in a controversial statement, had equated with SIMI! Chidambaram cited an intelligence report to support the allegation. The presence of the 'notorious' Sadhvi Ritambara on the dias with Ramdev Baba was a further proof of the 'communal' nature of Baba's fast. Government was not prepared to accept that fight against corruption and blackmarket cannot be curbed by such allegations. Actual, only a few days earlier Chidambaram along with other Ministers had gone to the airport to receive Baba despite his knowledge of the intelligence report. The Congress party spokesman first tried to distance itself from Government and objected to the senior ministers going to the airport to receive the Baba giving the impression that the party and Government were working at cross-purposes.

Why were the government ministers trying to placate Baba? They had found Anna a hard nut to crack. They felt that the egoist Baba would be more manageable and vulnerable. When this did not happen within the time limit contemplated by Government they suddenly reversed the gears and took aggressive action in the form of the nocturnal crackdown.

Ramdev Baba continued his fast even after he was shifted by govt from Ramlila Ground to Patanjali Ashram in Haridwar. After days of fasting his health seriously deteriorated and he had to be shifted by the BJP state govt to Dehradun Hospital (the union govt had washed off his hands once he was shifted to Patanjali Ashram). Even in hospital, Baba continued his fast. It was left to Shri Shri Ravi Shankar to persuade him to give up his fast after 9 days. It was stated on behalf of Baba, that his fight against blackmoney would continue. In the meanwhile Shri. Digvijay Singh, General Secretary of the Congress Party publicly accused Baba of money laundering and demanded that the vast accumulation of wealth exceeding Rs. 1000/- Cr. should be investigated. Even while he was fasting, Baba publicly announced details of his wealth.

Anna was also subjected to maligning by Digvijay who alleged his association with RSS in view of the picture of Hindmata displayed in course of his fast was similar to that of RSS. Touched to the quick Anna angrily stated that Digvijay should be sent to a lunatic asylum. He wrote to Sonia Gandhi complaining about smear campaign agaisnt him and demanded evidence to prove his association with RSS. The public discourse is obviously getting shriller and shriller.

After surrendering to Anna's demand of a joint committee and placeting Baba by four minutes going to airport, Congress leaders and UPA Government have taken a hardline. In an interview at Kolkatta, Pranab Mukherjee stated that the Civil Society movement is undermining democracy and elected government at the centre. Parliament is supreme to pass law and a handful 'civil society' activists cannot dictate terms to a government which has confidence of the Parliament (Times of India, June 13, 2011).

The emerging political scenario is worrisome. When the country is facing major challenges like terrorism, violent Maoist movement, resistance to land acquisition by people, deteriorating law and order situation in the country, hostile Chinese action on Northern Himalayan border and major corruption scandals, leading to loss of confidence of foreign investors, instead of taking a united national stand in firmly dealing with these problems, the nation is engulfed in intensive conflicts. The future of the joint committee on Lokpal scams to be dismal. No consensus is likely to emerge. The government may even decide to windup the work of the committee. And even if a 'final' draft would be ready by June and introduced in Parliament, passing of the Bill is likely to be no smooth sailing and may not be passed by August 15, the date by which Anna insists it should be passed on else he would again go on fast. The Government would not allow the kind of response Anna's fast had at Jantar-Mantar.

Government attempt to communalise Baba's movement against corruption was an attempt to drive a wedge between the communal Baba and the

'Gandhian' Anna. The civil society activists were earlier not enthusiastic about Baba but once the nocturnal crackdown on the defenceless man, women and children took place, the two sides forgot the differences and came closer to each other. The civil society activist used strongest words to condemn the crackdown.

The BJP declared that the Government was bringing back the emergency days and the party would organise nationwide protest against corruption, blackmarketing and supression of fundamental rights of the citizens to express opinion through peaceful demonstration'. The Congress party in reply decided to organise national movement against fundamentalism and communalism embodied in BJP, the RSS and allied organisations.

But for government more serious than the challenges of BJP, the Leftist parties and regional parties like SP which spoke against the noctural crackdown on peaceful assembly of people, was the 15 days notice issued by the vacation bench of the Supreme Court to the Union Home Secretary, Delhi State Government and the Delhi Commissioner of Police to explain the crackdown. Chidambaram has blithely stated that the Delhi Police will file the affidavit forgetting that the Supreme Court is not likely to be satisfied with the explanation of the State Government and will hold the Union Home Ministry as well accountable, if not the Union Home Minister and the Prime Minister themselves.

Law and Order

Politicians in power are often inclined to pass on the buck on 'law and order' matters, to the police forgetting that the issues behind any serious law and order situation have to be handled well on time by the politicians in power and the civil servants who work under them. In the present case the issues of corruption and black economy and the passing of Lokpal Bill have been long neglected and not tackled with any sense of urgency and sincerity. The most glaring instance of this was the fact that Lokpal Bill has been pending since 1968 i.e. over the last forty two years. The mega scams relating to 2G Spectrum, Commonwealth Game and Adarsh Society apartment in Mumbai, were attributed to politicians in power like union ministers and chief ministers. Even after the Spectrum Scam was exposed by CAG, Kapil Sibbal additional in charge of the Telecommunication Ministry brazenly stated that there was no loss to public exchequer and attacked the CAG for giving a wrong report alleging presumptive loss of 176000 crores of rupees to the public exchequer. Prime Minister defended minister Raja responsible for 2G scam for a period of over two years. Suresh Kalmadi was allowed to run the show of Commonwealth Games despite the fact he was accused in corrupt deals six months before the commonwealth games. The media gave wide publicity to these scams and the nation was outraged at the studied inability to prevent and control corruption. The Finance Minister doggedly refused to disclose names of those whose funds were stacked abroad citing the secrecy clause of the taxation evasion agreements with foreign governments. People started losing confidence in Government and their pent up anger was articulated by Anna Hazare and Baba Ramdev through their fasts which evoked nationwide response. Even after the fast started and people gathered, politicians of the ruling party did not care to meet the people and convince them about sincerity of Government Government must actively communicate with people to prevent popular agitation going out of hand instead of letting loose police. If serious consequences follow in the shape of injury and loss of lives, police are exposed to judicial enquiries. The politicians and administrators mostly remain aloof, when they should squarely be blamed for allowing the law and order situation to drift and assume serious proportions. When we became independent we declared that the 'Police state' of the British Raj will be replaced by 'welfare state' of people's government But in free India police raj seems to have come back with a vengeance.

Legitimacy of Elected Government

After some initial hesitation, the Congress has decided to go on the offensive. They are asserting that the Congress and its allies have been voted to power by the people and the opposition parties and 'civil society' activists have no business to destabilize them through their agitations and by people like Hazare and Ramdev Baba going on fast to coerce government How far is the argument valid?

It is true that the government has every right to decide on legislation, policies and programmes. At the same it is also the duty of the opposition to oppose actions by Government through constitutional means. The government should recognise the legitimacy of the opposition to oppose as much the opposition should concde the right of the government to govern. But if the government treats the opposition with contempt and gives short shrift to the reasonable demands of the opposition, the opposition gets frustrated and resorts to action which immobilizes the functioning of the Parliament. This was what happened to Parliament in the last winter session. The whole session was washed out. Eventually the demand of the opposition was conceded before the Budget session could go on smoothly. If this had been done at the beginning of the winter session, the nation would not have had to suffer a non-functioning Parliament. The government and the opposition are equally responsible.

What about the people? Should they helplessly suffer an inept or corrupt government? Have they not the right to call the government to question in between the elections? Do the duties of the citizens end, once they have voted? Surely that is not so. Even in between elections, the government is accountable to the people and people should be able to express their dissatisfaction through all means allowed by the Constitution. The active groups of citizens can take the lead in mobilizing public opinion through all means allowed by the Constitution. This does not amount to 'blackmailing' of an elected government as alleged by some Congress spokesman like Digvijay Singh? Hazare reply was that if fast and dharana amount to blackmail then he will 'blackmail' the government.

In the context it is necessary to recall what Dr. Ambedkar, the principal architect of the Constitution said in his address to the Constituted Assembly – "We must hold fast to the constitutional methods of achieving our social and economic goals. It means we must abandon the bloody methods of revolution. It also means we must abandon the method of civil disobedience, non-co-operation and Satyagrah. When constitutional methods are open, there can be no justification for unconstitutional methods. Sooner these methods are abandoned the better for us." Dr. Ambedkar's warning was prophetic. He feared that the Gandhian legacy will be continued even after the government starts functioning as per the Constitution of the Indian Republic. But government also hold the responsibility of running the govt in a transparent, open, manner without making an ugly display of arrogance of power. As Hazare reminded, the government Ministers and legislators are servants of the people; people are not their servants. Unfortunately our politicians have became so arrogant and self-serving that they have forgotten the basic premise of democracy that it is the bounden duty of politicians in power to serve the people with sincerity, honesty and dedication. If the current agitation teaches this lesson to government and politicians, its purpose would be served. But if Govt resorts to repression and intolerance of any opposition, makes all kinds of defamatory statement against those who oppose them, if public opinion is stifled and evils like rampant corruption are allowed free play, the future of Indian Parliamentary democracy may be very dismal.

Chapter - 11

Power to the People

When India attained freedom on 15th August, 1947, the political power was transferred from the British rulers to the Indian people. The Indian Constitution provided for a federal poloikty in which the legislature and executive power was divided between the Central Government and the State Government. It also provided for a parliamentary system of Government under which the power was exercised by the elected representatives on behalf of the people. Under this system the leader of the party which commands majority in the legislature becomes the Prime Minister at the Centre and Chief Minister at the State. The Prime Minister and Chief Minister constitute the cabinet or the Council of Ministers consisting of members of his or her party in the legislature whom he or she selects to join his cabinet. The cabinet constitutes the political executive and exercises/ political power on behalf of the people.

The political executive is expected to exercise the power to translate the hopes and aspirations of the people into a concrete reality. It is also expected to devise policies and frame plans and programmes so as to satisfy the aspirations of the people.

The political executive has to rely on the members of the civil service in its task. The civil servants help the political executive in the formulation of plans, policies and programmes. They also implement them at various operational levels both in the State and Central Government.

The State in independent India is a expected to work as a welfare State. The welfare State is expected to undertake a whole spectrum of developmental activities for the welfare of the people. These include a wide range programmes for rural and agricultural development, promotion of industry and infrastructural development including irrigation, electrification, transport, communication, education, health etc.

In 1951, the nation embarked on a planned process of economic development. A nation wide community development programme was ushered in through the medium of community development blocks. Each block had a machinery consisting of Block Development Officer and team of Extension Officers for subjects like agriculture, animal husbandry, rural industries, rural engineering, social education, co-operation, etc.

After few years of working of the Community Development Programme in the country, it was evaluated by the Balwantrai Mehta Study Team. On the basis of an indepth analysis, the Balwantrai Mehta Study Team came to the conclusion that the success of the Community development programe depends on the participation of the people and such participation would not be forthcoming, unless the block development administration is placed under the elected representatives of the people at the local level. They, therefore, recommended a three tier system of Panchayati Raj Institutions with Panchayat at the villasge level, Panchayat Samiti at the block level, and the Zilla Parishad at the district level.

Soon the recommendations of the Study Team were accepted by the State and Central Government and Panchayati Raj Institutions were set up in different states in India, beginning with Rajasthan and Andhra Pradesh. There were many local variations in the pattern suggested by Balwantrai Mehta Study Team. There was initially a great enthusiasm for the Panchayati Raj set up. It was hailed as a 'transfer of power' to the people – as a change from people's participation in Government's programme to of Government's participation in people's programme.

However, after few years it was realized that for a variety of reasons the Panchayati Raj institutions did not make a success in many states. Firstly, the elections to the panchayati raj institutions were not held regularly. After their terms were over, the administration of these institutions was entrusted to the administrators consisting of the civil servants. Secondly, where they continued to function, their scope of activities was progressively curtailed. Thirdly, in many Panchayati Raj institutions, there was excessive politicization leading to rivalries between factions which hampered the work of the pancyayati Raj institutions. The positions of the Panchayati Raj Institutions were used more for acquisition of power than for the service to the people, thus defeating the very objective of establishing Panchayati Raj institutions. The whole system went into dolldrums.

It is in this context, that it was felt that it would not be allright to leave the Panchayati Raj Institutions as only creatures of the State Government. The State Government cannot be left free to meddle with the Panchayati Raj institutions or supercede them at will. In a large country like India, the development programmes and indeed governmental power cannot be concentrated at the Central and State level. There has to be decentralization of power and demolition of functions which should be transferred to the local levels viz. district, block and the village.

For such decentralization to be effective, it was felt that the institutions at the District, Block and village levels should be recognized as constitutional entities i.e. the local self government institutions should have the same constitutional sanction as the government at the State and Central levels. This led to the revolutionary concept that Panchayati Raj institutions should find a place in the constitution itself. In other words, the constitutional authority should be divided between central, state and local government as co-ordinate entities.

This concept was given expression by the 73rd Amendment to the Indian Constitution which has been passed by both the Central and the State legislature. Now, the Panchayati Raj institutions have become the organs of the constitutional scheme of the country.

Let us understand the implications of this change – Firstly, the 73rd amendment envisages a 'local sector'. Hither to there were only three lists of constitutional powers and functions viz. The central list, the state list and the concurrent list. Now there is the fourth list, the list of local government powers and functions. Secondly, to ensoure timely an orderly elections to the Panchayati Raj institutions the amendment envisages a separate Election Commission for the Panchayati Raj institutions just like the Election Commission for the Parliamentary and State legislative elections. Thirdly, to ensure proper allocation of finance to the local bodies, the local finances commission has also been envisaged.

With the secure basis provided by the Indian constitution, the Panchayati Raj institutions can emerge as effective local self government institutions. However, it has to be realized that a constitutional mechanism by itself cannot achieve the objectives envisaged. A constitution will deliver of goods only if the institutions created under it function in a manner they are expected to function. In other words, the Panchayati Raj institutions even though regularly elected and clothes with necessary power and supported by finances of their own, cannot succeed unless those who are elected to the Panchayati Raj institutions are aware that the power given to them has to be used for the benefit of the people and not for personal or partisan interests. The Panchayati Raj institutions have also to be efficient and effective bodies. If they become hot beds of local politics, and dens of Corruption, then the very objective of 'power to the people' will be defeated.

It is rightly said that eternal vigilance is the price of liberty. It is for the people to be awake and see that the Panchayati Raj institutions work with dedication, objectively and sense of commitment for the welfare of the people.

It could be expected that the Panchayati Raj institution being nearer to the people, would be more answerable to them. It is only an enlightened body of citizens who can ensure the answerability of the local governments to them.

One can hope that 73rd amendment will usher in a new era of Panchayati Raj in the country and ensure fulfillment the concept of 'power to the people' through decentralized democracy.

SOCIAL - II

Chapter - 1

Role of Social Activism in National Life

Activism has gained currency in our social lexicography. The term 'activism' does not appear in the dictionary though the terms 'act', 'action', and 'activity' do. Activism may be defined as a intensive concern with activities.

Activities may be divided into three categories. Firstly, activities of those engaged in public agencies like ministers, bureaucrate or judges for the fulfillment of the public purpose. Secondly, of those in private agencies for the fulfillment of the private purpose such promotion of self interest or accumulation of profit; and thirdly, of those in private agencies for the fulfillment of the public purpose. It is the last which is generally in view when we talk of social activism.

Though the term social activism has come into vogue recently, we have a long tradition of social activism. Thus, the father of modern Indian renaissance, Raja Ram Mohan Roy was an activist in the cause of economic and social reform and abolition of sati. Mahatma Jyotiba Phule and later on Dr. B.R. Ambedkar were activist in the cause of the backward and the depressed classes. Maharshi Dhondo Keshav Karve took up the cause of women education and widow remarriage. His son Bhaskar Karve and later Shakuntala Paranjapye devoted themselves to spreading the awareness of the need for birth control. Karmaveer Bhaurao Patil established educational institutions throughout the length and breadth of rural Maharashtra for dissemination of education amongst the rural people. Gopal Ganesh Agarkar was a great social reformer and together with Lokmanya Tilak, the fiery patriot, founded institutions of higher education. Mahatma Gandhi was social activist par excellence who while leading several political movements for freeing the country from the yoke of foreign rule, nevertheless combined it with his constructive programme which promoted social activism in many fields – abolition of untouchability, emancipation of women, village industry and swadeshi, basic education, and abolition of the scourge of drinking. These are only a few leading examples of social activism in the pre-independence period.

After the attainment of freedom, the State became a Welfare State. Nehru thought that through the administrative machinery of the Welfare State, a broad based programme of economic development and social change could be introduced. This led to the widening of the ambit of State activity. The State would look after the citizen from cradle to grave. There was a proliferation of the voluntary and peoples' agencies like Bharat Sevak Samaj and Mahila Mandals but they became a part of the State activity. The voluntary bodies started springing up not because there was the spirit of social work and the force of social activism behind them but because State financial assistance was available. No wonder, this gave a setback to the very movement of voluntary social work and social activism itself. Genuine social workers were hard to find.

It was only after about three decades of State activism, that the realization dawned that the State apparatus may not be the exclusive or the best instrument of development and social change. There are several limitations on what the State can achieve through its administrative machinery. Development of even a single village community may require devoted work of several years and cannot be done in a few years through nation wide streaotype schemes like IRDP and SFDA and MFAL. Social activism in the fields of sustainable development, environmental preservation and poverty alleviation showed that voluntary effort can provide a better and an innovative alternative. Shri. Anna Hazare was able to transform his native village Ralegansiddhi through years of effort beginning with the abolition of the evil of drinking. Vilasrao Salunke through his programme of Pani Panchayats in Purandar Taluka could deal with the problem of drought through a programme of watershed management in a manner in which the nationwide DPAP could not. Both of them belonged to the rural community and evolved techniques of work which were foreign to the governmental methods of functioning. The Chipko movement was spontaneous initiative of the hill people under the leadership of Sundarlal Bahuguna and Chandiprasad Bhat for the preservation of forests from the ravages of the forest contractors. Madhukarrao Deval showed at Mhaisal, Maharashtra how the harijans can run successfully a co-operative farming society. Baba Amte organised leprosy patients to grow vegetables at Anandvan and showed how far from the curse of social ostracism, what these unfortunable people require is sympathy and help to become self reliant and be an asset rather than a drag on the society. Pathak introduced 'Sulabh Souchalaya' and thereby initiated a programme for rural sanitation. Movements like a Grahak Panchayats sprang up for the protection of the consumer from exploitation through indiscriminate price rise and passing on shoddy goods. Rural women came forward to Andhra Pradesh and Kerala to close toddy shops to prevent their menfolk from the evil of drinking. Women raised their voice against atrocities on women in the shape of dowry, bride burning, rape, desertion and denial of the right of maintenance. In each of these areas of action, the State was found to be ineffective.

Social activism also took the form of exposing and resisting the socially and ecologically destroying consequence of State projects. Medha Patkar led the campaign against the Narmada irrigation project – the Sardar Sarovar becaue it led to the uprooting of life of the tribals and submersion of forest areas. The silent valley in Kerala was saved by the alertness of the social activists. Bharatiya Gyan Peeth award winner Shivram Karanth gave his support to campaign against Kaiga atomic power plant in North Kanara district.

The new policy of liberalization may trigger off private initiative for the promotion of self interest and accumulation of profit. But it cannot generate voluntary action for the promotion of social good and prevention of social evils. That can only come from the springs of deep compassion, and spirit of self-reliance and social service. These qualities are always deep down in every society but it requires some social worker to bring them out and galvanise them into social action.

Social activism may be negative or positive as the examples cited above show. Negative social activism takes the form of social protests. Even this has its own value. But more valuable is positive social activism which goes beyond protest and advocacy and shows through constructive action and projects how social evils can be eliminated and social causes promoted. While negative social action can peter out after the initial burst of protest, positive social action can be abiding. That is why Gandhiji always combined his constructive programme with his fight for independence from the British rule.

Chapter - 2

Our National Identity

Competitive claims on share in political power and material wealth have sharpened over the years in our country and with them the conflict and strife in our social life. Caste and community identities and divisions have become the focus of an aggressive politics. Different segments of the society seem to forget that only fifty years ago we fought together as one nation for the emancipation of the country and did not stop to consider as too great any sacrifice of life, liberty and property as a price for national freedom.

As sectional loyalties have got the better of the nation and as forces of regionalism and sectoralism have got an upper hand, some of our academicians, drawing inspiration from dubious intellectual conceptualization and formulation of 'think tanks' abroad ever interested in the fissures developing in the Indian society and thereby weakening Indian State, have started spinning out theories couched in academic jargons, to rationalize and thereby legitimize the rise of those disruptive, separatist, centrifugal and disintegrating tendencies against which all our national leaders like Tilak, Mahatma Gandhi and Subhash Bose fought in the past – Fiery patriot like Bhagat Singh, Chandrashekhar Azad and Khudiram Bose went to the gallows for national freedom. Apparently their lives and deeds wiped out these tendencies from our psyche. These tendencies are raising their ugly heads again and the rationalization of these tendencies by doubtful theoretical formulations of sociologists and political scientists has let loose an insidious process of subvertion of the very basis of our nation State viz. the overwhelming consciousness of belonging to one nation.

Nation in the making?

One of these theories describes India as not a nation, but as 'a nation in the making' forgetting that India that is Bharat has been a nation in the making for the last 5000 years! History and geography, culture and civilization, nature and nurture, language, literature and legend, philosophical thoughts and ways of living, all had created a national consciousness throughout the length and breadth of our country despite the problem of transport and communication in the past. The feeling of one nation which had been deeply implanted in the psyche of our people was greatly consolidated during the fight for freedom. It is astonishing that the pulsation of that feeling is not felt by those Rip Van winkles who think of India as a ;nation in the making'. Anyone who like Swami Vivekananda has been a parivrajak i.e. a wandering mendicant visiting the different parts of India and lived and moved with the ordinary people of India will get the sensation of India as one nation, but those academicians and intellectuals who live in their ivory towers and nourish themselves on the diet of borrowed learning would have no feelings for the oneness of the Indian people. However, sophisticated their theories and whatever be the sophistry of their phrase and diction, they would never be able to comprehend the reality of India.

Federal India

Less offensive than the theory which describe India as a 'nation in the making' is another that describes India as a 'federal nation'. Federalism is an attribute of the political organization of a State and not a category of nation. Those who describe India as a 'federal nation' have in mind the vast and diverse nature of our population and the variety of our languages, culture and regional traditions. While these features may be on a much larger scale in India than in any other State in the world, the fact remains that even small nations like Belgium and Switzerland have linguistic and cultural diversity but these are not called 'federal nations'. The single our India for the use of the special epithet and, therefore, to suggest that India is somewhat different than a single nation is to do injustice to the pervasive sense of oneness of the India people. The treatises on political science mention a number of attributes of a society which constitutes a nation such as a single language a homogenous culture, a common historical past, and common future, a defined territory, and a sense of belongingness amongst the people. At the same time they recognize that all these elements may contribute to the national consciousness, despite being divided amongst many kingdoms and principlalities. So India does not need a special attribute to be allowed to be described as a nation.

Nation of many nationalities

Another variance of such a theory is one which describes India as a State consisting of nationalities. This description of India was on the erstwhile Soviet model whose constitution described it as a federation of many nationalities. The camp followers of the erstwhile Soviet Union who blindly propagated their theory never understood the difference between the making of the erstwhile Soviet Union and India. The so called other nationalities in the Soviet union were actually those people who were forced in the Russian polity first by the imperial cars and later on by their communist successors. On the other hand, the emergence of the common consciousness of the Indian nation has been a gradual process evolving over centuries, sanctified by religious and cultural traditions, legends literature and folklore.

Composite culture

Those who describe India as a 'federal nation' link it up with the so called 'composite culture' of India. What they have in mind is that people professing several religions (specifically Muslim not just Hindus) have contributed to the kaleidoscopic culture of India. Sayed Naqvi through several short films on places of worship in India exhibited on Telvision has shown how even Hindu shrines are looked after by Muslim 'pujaries' and at Hindu and Muslim shrines both Hindu and Muslim devotees congregate. This of course is true of other religious communities as well. For example, half the devotees of the Kamakshi temple at Shiroda in Goa, I am told, are Catholics. All this is a part of the Indian ethos, its tradition of tolerance and the basic principle of 'live and let live' round which India social life is organised. Indian culture is like a river with many tributaries. But just as a river which is enriched by many streams joining it over its meandering course is not described as a 'composite' river, so also it is not necessary to describe Indian culture as a composite culture. For that matter the culture of every society is in someways 'composite'. It is not necessary to single out India culture as a composite culture.

Plural Society

A term which has recently gained currency and legitimacy is the description of India as a 'plural society'. Before independence, this term was not in usage. Jawaharlal Nehru described the India as characterized by 'unity in the midst of diversity'. This is not the same as plurality. Plurality implies co-existence or co-habitation of different groups without anything in common. This is not a correct description of India. Indeed it does grave injustice to it. India is like a bouquet of many flowers or a flower with many petals. In both these cases diversity is subsumed under a unity. To describe India as a plurality is to overlook the basic unity of India. Without unity, diversity would lead to disintegration. To insist on the description of India as a plural society is to provide a rationale for the disintegration of India.

The term 'plural society' is further amplified by its users in terms of a 'multi-ethnic, muti-cultural society. The term 'multi-ethnic was seldom used in the past in the Indian continent. It is a word appropriate for the USA which is the 'melting pot' of many races – Red Indians (who were exterminated and confined to reserves), whites from many European countries, and now Indians, Chinese, Vietnamies etc. Though the Indian society has assimilated people of different origin in its historical past, it is not characterized at present by racial divides except in some peripheral parts of India or in isolated pockets. Nor is it a multi-cultural society in the sense that people of India do not share a common culture. The cultures of different regional or religious groups of India are variations of a common theme – in terms of food, dress, festivals, folklores, etc.

Perceptions differ

Ultimately concepts and theories are a matter of perception. Those who look at the woods will emphasise the unity of the overall design while those who look at the individual trees would miss the overall design. In the ultimate analysis, Indians do not need to be guided by the perceptions, paradigms and prescriptions of the others, if they have the self-confidence and the sense of self-assurance to be guided by their own perceptions and experience.

Unfortunately colonialism seems to be assuming a new form. Political colonialism has gone but intellectual colonialism seems not only to have survived but seems to have returned with greater force and potency under whose impact we seem to be blinded and losing our own perceptions. If this process goes on, the future of the Indian nationhood may well be endangered. Since the very basis of that nationhood viz. common consciousness in the Indian mind will get weakened and ultimately destroyed. If this happens, disintegration and destruction of India will not be very far.

India is not one State with many nations but one nation divided into many states. Many articles have appeared from time to time in newspapers that Indians visiting Pakistan and Bangladesh are often treated with warmth, usually reserved for longlast kith and kin – despite the persistent political animosities between the three States of the sub-continent. The secret of this lies in the essential oneness of these people. Instead of splintering of India in many bits, what should happen as a natural process is for people of these estranged 'nations' – India Pakistan and Bangladesh to realise this essential oneness and develop institutions, programmes and procedures which will bring them together in a spirit of tolerance and 'live and let live' which is our hall mark and our historical heritage.

Chapter - 3

Taslima Nasrin's 'Lajja' – A True Assessment – Growth of Intolerance

'Lajja', a book which has attracted world wide attention and which has been translated from original Bengali into English (by Tutul Gupta) and several other Indian and world languages has been described by several readers and reviewers as a 'boring novel'. This shows lack of understanding of the nature of the book. It is not just a novel; it is also a political history of Bangladesh after 'liberation' (and to some extent before it and of the Indian sub-continent as a whole since partition) and a documentation of certain events related to the central theme of that history. The 'novel' part is developed against the backdrop of that history and chronicle of events. The history is notable for its insight; and documentation for its accuracy, and the novel for the dramatic depiction of a human tragedy. Not to take note of each of these aspects, it to do less than justice to the book and the author.

1971 was a watershed in Bangladesh history. That was the year of her liberation from the oppressive tyranny of Pakistan rulers ever since the creation of the geographically, linguistically, and culturally anomalous state of Pakistan. The Muslims and Hindus of Bangladesh brought together by their Bengali identity, fought shoulder to shoulder for their liberation. The military strength and strategy of India hastened the process of liberation. India was generous in her hour of victory. All that India expected in return was genuine friendship of Bangladesh.

But alas that was not to be. Things began all right. The State of Bangladesh was founded on the basis of the principles of the Freedom Movement of 1971 viz nationalism, secularism, democracy and socialism. But soon religious fanaticism of the Muslim majority got the better of Bengali identity. Even Mujibar Rahman who owed his life and power to India passed the law to declare the property of Hindu migrants to India as enemy property. After he and his family were killed in a bloody coup. Things went from bad to worse. India was disappointed but Indians never knew the reality in neighbouring Bangladesh. Reading of Bangladesh history in Lajja would surely open the eyes of the complacent Indians to the realities in Bangladesh.

Zia Ur Rahman who seized power after the assassination of Mujub started tinkering with the constitution introduing at the beginning of the Constitution the Arabic words – 'Bismillah ir Rehman ir Rehim'. The articles declaring Bangladesh as a secular state were deleted. The citizens of Bangladesh were not to be called 'Bengalis' but 'Bangladeshis'. Gen Ershad who succeeded Zia Ur Rehman went a step further and inserted a clause in the constitution declaring Islam as the state religion. This was the signal for the fanatics to force the dictates of Islam on Hindus and other minorities. All T.V. and Radio programmes started with Quran as the holy text. The secular forces were progressively weakened and became unable to resist the onslaught of communal forces led by the fanatical Moulavis and Jamati Islami Party. Even the daughter of Mujib, Hasina Wajed had to come to terms with these fanatic elements to maintain her position in the politics of Bangladesh. Even the Communists became communalists. And people who called themselves friends of Hindus became indifferent if not actually inimical. The Hindus were discriminated against in every walk of life – in army, services, business, academic institutions. Hindus became worse than second class citizens. Hindu names of roads were Islamised. An Islamic Foundation was created and was awardes sizeable budget to help Muslim religious institutions and for renovation of Masjids.

The charge in the character of the state and polities of Bangladesh soon started taking many inhuman form in day-to-day life. Hindus could not celebrate their festivals. Hindu women could not sing in public Rabindra Sangeet. If they did, they were called shameless. The Hindu men could not wear dhoti and Hindu women could not display sindhur, kumkum and sankh, their sacred symbols. They had even to change their Bengali vocabulary. They could not ask for 'jol' but for 'pani', lest their identity be revealed. Hindu students were perforce required to recite passage from Sura in the schools. Hindus were forced to part with their properties – their ancestral homes and gardens in favour of their Muslim neighbours who used all tricks to pressurize them and ease them out of their rights. Hindus became the targets of Muslim hoolingans and were beaten up in towns and villages. If they went to the police station for help, they were further beaten up. While Muslims minority could retaliate in India, the Hindu minority could not do so in Bangladesh – this was the extent of their demoralisation! Ancient sacred temples were torched and Maths of the Hindus were pillaged. Children played on the top of their ruins and pissed on them. 'Leave the country if you want to live' – Hindus were told. Hindus had to live in state of fear, uncertainity and insecurity. The Hindu men and women had come out with Muslim names in case they fell in the hands of Muslim fanatics. Young Hindu girls were abducted and raped and forced to marry their Muslim abductors.

Taslima has given long litany of destruction – list of depredations at various stages of the book – lists which readers only on the look out for entertaining fiction may find boring. But they should realize that more often than not facts are stranger than fiction. And if not given as facts could be dismissed as fiction! If they have the patience to go through the lists of these depredations they would soon realise that more often than not facts are strange than fiction! If they have the patience to go through the list of these depredations they would soon realise that what happened over years in Bangladesh was nothing less than the slow strangulation and destruction of a beautiful culture and civilization built over thousands of years.

No wonder there was continuous haemorhage of Bengali Hindu population from Bangladesh. In trickless and torrents Bengali Hindus were forced to migrate to India leaving their dear lands and homes behind. And yet apparently India never found it necessary to take up the issue of denial of human rights to Hindus in Bangladesh. Deprived of any support, the proportion of Hindu population in Bangladesh rapidly slumped meeting them progressively weaker. In a way, the tragedy of the Hindus in Bangladesh was worse than that of Hindus in Pakistan. They were pushed out in one bloody carnage in 1947 from West Pakistan but Bangladesh became for Hindus slow death.

It is against this background that Taslima has given the story of the fate of Bengali Hindu family – Dutts, as an aftermath of the destruction of Babri mosque in Ayodhya on 6th December 1992. The Dutts were proud of their motherland – the only motherland they knew was their dear Sonar Bangla immortalized by Rabindranath Tagore in his poems. It was a family based in Mymensigh. They had to paret with their ancestral home to a Muslim neighbour for a paultry sum and seek shelter in a small flat in Dhaka. Yet they put up with this deprivation and never thought of leaving Bangladesh even though many of their relatives and neighbours had already done so. The head of the family, Sudhamay Dutt was a doctor in Government service but he was denied promotion due to him in service. Only Muslim could hold high positions in Bangladesh administration irrespective of merit. No Hindu Generals, Secretaries or Heads of departments – no matter what their seniority or competence. And yet Dutt struggled on with his meager earnings from a private practice. His wife Kironmoyee was a good singer but she had to stop giving public performances since Muslim fanaties considered singing in public by women as a shameless behaviour! Their son Suranjan was at the forefront of progressive movements of Bangladesh including students agitation and had many Muslim friends dear to him but he got nothing in return and no position in Bangladesh polities. Despite this, none of the three could even think of leaving their motherland except daughter Maya who feebly suggested it from time to time. But her poignant cry 'let us live, let us get away' fell on deaf ears. She was in love with a Muslim boy Jahangir who ditched her and went abroad just as Surganjen was disappointed with Parveen, sister of his friend Hyder whom he loved. Both wanted to marry each other but her family denied and she insisted that Suranjan should convert himself into a Muslim and Suranjan would not have it. The proposed marriage could not take place and Parveen married to a Muslim only to be soon divorced.

But the worst blow fell on the Dutt family on the day following demolition of the Babri Masjid. Hatred of Hindus reached great heights. In the atmosphere of that hatred, Muslim hoolingens entered into Dutt household, destroyed household belongings, beat ailing Dudhamay and gentle Kiranmoyee and before their eyes forcibly abducted Maya when Suranjan was roaming in the town oblivions of his family responsibility. When he returned, he saw his house is shambles and family in a state of desolation. He rushed out with his friend Hyder to locate Maya but neightlong chase led to nothing! Days and nights became insufferable agonies for Dutt family. In an impotent rage all that Suranjan could do was to get a Muslim whore and rape her in his own house!

The story ends by the decision of the three members of the Dutt family so much attached to their homeland deciding at longlast to migrate to India. Their sense of alienation was complete; they had come to the end of the road; their passionate attachment to their land had finally ended! It was obvious to them that it was pointless for Hindus to try and survive in Bangladesh.

The Muslims in Bangladesh justified the carnage by (a) holding the Bangladesh Hindus responsible for the destruction of the Babri mosque and (b) the depredations on Muslims in India. They should realise that India had Muslim Presidents of the Republic and Muslims holding high ranks in all walks of life including polities, administration, army and education. Yet to justify the inhumanity, all kinds of wrong facts seem to be propagated in Bangladesh to justify their outrages.

What is the 'Lajja' in all this story? Not of Maya who was abducted and raped; nor of Sudhamay Dutt who had to sell his ancestral house in Mymensingh, nor of Suranjan who at long last decided that Bangladesh was no longer his mother but is of those who abducted helpless Maya and robbed helpless Hindus of their hearths and homes. The Lajja is of 'indecency' and perversion of humanity Taslima is a proud Bengali – proud of her beautiful Bengali cultural heritage and for her the indecency is a blot on Bengali heritage.

Indeed it is a blot on the civilization of the entire Indian sub-continent and its uninterrupted history of 5000 years of civilization and culture based on broadmindedness, tolerance and compassion. The very formation of Pakistan is 1947 – what happened before and after in all the three countries has been a Lajja.

But would people of these three countries understand the message of this true daughter of the Indian heritage as we have known through centuries? The purpose of the book would have been served if this lessens dawns on the people of the three countries, if they feel the shame of what happened and go back to the traditions of broadmindedness and tolerance. People of Pakistan and Bangladesh should make the start and totally get out of the grip of religions fanaticism. The predominantly tolerant Hindus would undoubtedly extend their hand of friendship.

The Muslim in India should go through the book and realise the vast difference between the treatment meted out to Muslims in India as compared to Hindus in Bangladesh (let alone Pakistan) and consider themselves as loyal citizens of the country as citizens of other religions denominations do without demanding any provisions by way of special programmes for the protection of minorities. The Hindu on their part should stick to their traditional tolerance and broadmindedness, never think of retaliation and consider the deed of destruction of the Babri Mosque as their own lajja which should never be repeated.

Unfortunately Hindus have also become intolerant, as shown by recent slaughter of Muslim individuals for no faulty of theirs in the name of 'Gomata' and ban on eating beaf.

Chapter - 4

Quiet Violence in Bangladesh

There are two ways of understanding and describing the social reality – the macro and the micro. The macro way provides statistics – global or national – regarding the GNP and its distribution, employment and unemployment, and pattern of occupational distribution of population. It provides the larger framework in which the reality in a small villages community and its problems could be understood. The micro approach goes deeper into the reality of life in the village community and provides an intimate picture and sensitive understanding of individual familities and thereby lends meaning and feeling to dry statistics. The first approach is followed usually by the economists and the second by the sociologists. The book under review belongs to the latter category.

Both approaches point out to the same reality – the reality conveyed by the term 'quiet violence', which constitutes the title of the book. The violence of needless hunger quietly takes the tool of life of hungry millions in Bangladesh countryside. The hunger is needless because it is avoidable. Bangladesh like India of which it was a part, is a 'rich country inhabited by poor people.' The land is fertile, lush green and golden at the harvest time, which can sustain even a large population. But what comes in the way is the concentration of land in a few hands while the large majority is of the landless, the sharecroppers and the marginal holders. And this inequality gets worse every day owing to the vicious circle of poverty which makes the rich richer and the poor poorer. It drains the surplus of wealth generated by the labour of the poor who are unable to get bare where-withals of living – the morsel of rice for them and their famished families. Forces to borrow, the poor are forced to part their meagre land holding to the rich and join the army of the landless.

Functioning of the institutions and administration of the programmes aided by the World Bank, USA, and other donor agencies is such that ostensibly brought into existence to help the poor, they only accentuate the tendency of the vicious circle to make the rich richer and the poor poorer since they are palpably distorted by the influence of the rich, the powerful and the influencial. Thus, food for the poor goes to the rich who have access to the ration card and ration shops. Work for the poor creates assets for the rich. Co-operative credit goes to the well to do families and so do the extension services. World Bank finances investment in tubewells which though nominally registered in the irrigation group of the poor are in fact owned by the rich landlord who charges an exorbitant rate for the use of water by the poor. Government purchase agencies buy from the merchants though established to buy from the poor farmers and thus pass the advantage of higher price to those who have. Police whose duty is to provide security only oppress and exploit the poor and create in them a sense of fear. Justice at the court is too costly for the poor to avail of.

If aid and programme for the poor only exacerbate disparities, what then is the way out? In the view of the authors what is required is a fundamental change in the land ownership pattern which can only be brought about by drastic land reforms – a low ceiling on the ownership of land and co-operative farming by the poor; but who would usher in these reforms/ Not certainly the corrupt bureaucracy and political elite holding the reins of power. These can be brought about only by the organised and the awakened poor themselves. A revolutionary solution indeed! Sooner or later, the pent up anger of the poor must burse open and tear asunder the exploitative and oppressive economic and social order. This may appear to be a vigilant solution but is the present order without violence - an order which condemns the poor and dispossessed to slow but sure violence of needless starvation?

But till the hungry and poor wake up, the rich must exploit them, the police must oppress them, the political elite must dupe them, the donor agencies must give aid in their name and the researcher must find in them fascinating material for study!

The plight of the poor who belong to the religious minority – the Hindus – is specially worse. They are the most vulnerable and the helpless and are the easy victims of the Muslim land grabbers. They are the last to get the assistance – if at all – from law and administration. There plight is indeed pathetic. During the liberation war, they hid themselves in the temporary camps set up in India. On return they found their land grabbed and their houses looted. They died of shock.

Nine months stay in a village in Rangpur district, living in the manner of a village family in a hut and acquaintance with Bengali language which enabled them to converse with the villager in their own language, enabled the authors to be 'Insiders' and give an intimate picture of the villagers – Akathar Ali, the Diwani is the village leader, his brother Hussain the political activist and the link between the village and the outside world consisting of the elected council, the co-operative and the thana officials; Nafis Haji Mohmmed the landlord, the land grabber and the exploiter; Abu, the marginal farmer; and Hari, the landless, who dies of starvation. The author also describe their wives and children. The wives must toil, produce children, get emaciated in the process and yet get beaten by their husbands who are free to marry and divorce as they please since their religion allows them to do so. The lot of the Muslim women may appear to be better than that of the Hindu women since the Muslim law allows a daughter half of what the son inherits. But parda, polygamy and divorce make their lot worse than that of Hindu women. Muslim religion teachers brotherhood and bans interest on loans. But it hardly helps the Muslim poor. Not charging interest turns out to be a cruel hypocrisy when the poor are made to part with the produce of their mortgaged land at half the market price! The poor can only pray Allah to give them a better life in heaven but here in this world the poor must put us with their lot since Allah has sanctioned the riches of the rich and the poverty of the poor.

We in India seem to know very little of what happens in our neighbouring country. How many of us know that a lakh of Bangladeshi died of hunger in the famine of 1974? And do we know exactly why Bangbahdhu Sheikh Mujibur Rahman was assassinated and why his assassination went upwept, unhonoured and unsung? Bangbandhu had promised that rice and sugar would be available at half the price after Pakistani exploiters wer removed. In actual fact, prices soared up several fold – putting rice and sugar beyond the reach of poor. Aid poured in Bangladesh which came to be identified as the international basket case but bulk of the aid was swallowed by the corrupt kiths and kins who surrounded him and with whom he came to be identified. His errors were compounded by the insinuations of the religious fundamentalists who found fault with him that he wore a Hindu coat, was dressed like Lord Ganesh and did not utter the Arabic greeting Khuda Hafiz at the end of his lecture. He was tarred as a collaborator with Hindu India which was responsible for the rise in the prices of rice and jute which were smuggled out of India.

When would Bangladesh get a leader who would find a balance between Bengali nationalism and Muslim religion, break the stranglehold of the rich, the landed and the powerful and provide work and the morsel of rice for the poor whose toil and energy can provide enough rice from the rich land even for the burgeoning population? This itself could provide the motivation for a smaller family since assured living would give hope to parents that their children would survive. Even the illiterate Bangladesh women were, according to the authors, enthusiastic about the use of the family planning methods and neither religion, nor illiteracy nor male domination could come in the way.

We in India might consider ourselves to be more fortunate than people in Bangladesh. But the lot of our poor people cannot be said to be much better than that of the poor in Bangladesh. The lessons of this intimate Study of Bangladesh are applicable to the Indian situation as well. We also need revolutionary solutions to break the stranglehold of the rich and the powerful and provide a ray of hope to our teaming millions below poverty line.

'A Quiet Violence – View from Bangladesh Village' by Betsy Hartmen and James Boyce, Zed Press, 57 Celendonian Road, London first published 1983, second reprint 1986.

Chapter - 5

Secularism Reconsidered

In his address to the recent Congress Session at Tirupathi, the Prime Minister invited a national dialogue on the subject of 'Secularism'. More specifically, he wanted all concerned to keep politics scrupulously apart from religion and in that context suggested a clear cut identification of parties which because of their religious connotations should not be allowed to participate in the democratic political process.

The Prime Minister's suggestion is very timely because while secularism has been proclaimed as one of the cardinal features of our constitutional and political system, in actual practice, the concept of secularism has remained vague and undefined. Each has his own definition of secularism, and as a result, secularism has become like a well worn hat which has lost all shape!

Secularism is hardly a concept of Indian origin. It has hardly any relation to our historical past or the genius of our people. Secularism has essentially been a Western concept and has its relation to the history of the 'Reformation' movement. The British monarch challenged the pretentions of the Pope in matters temporal and declared that he rather than the Pope would be the source of authority in secular matters. Thus, was a clear cut sepration brought about of the state from the church, and the secular realm from the religion. This historical origin of religion bears no relation to India because India had no such institution as an organised church claiming authority over kings and monarchs.

Secularism in India has been the sequel of India's partition on a religious basis. If Pakistan was formed on the basis of religion, and was a Muslim State, India could well have declared itself a Hindu State, since religion was the basis of partition which was accepted by our leaders like Jawaharlal Nehru and Sardar Patel. However, these leaders specially Pandit Jawaharlal Nehru, were not prepared to accept the logic of the partition, but were insistent that the principles for which the Congress stood would continue to be the legacy of independent India. The Indian National Congress had claimed when it led the fight for freedom that it represented the entire nation of many religions and faiths, despite the dissident claims of the Muslim League. Though partition marked the defeat of the Congress claim, it did not want to disown or dilute the heritage of Indian nationalism. Moreover, even after partition, a large number of people belonging to non-Hindu religions specially the Muslim religion continued to be the citizens of India. Thus, though Pakistan became a theoretic state, the Indian State did not want to identify itself with any particular religion. The Indian Constitution, therefore, proclaims no religion as the state religion. On the other hand, it expressly provides religious freedom to all the citizens of India. The Indian Constitution forbids discrimination on the grounds of religion or faith. This means that the state treats all citizens as equal and gives them equal opportunity. At the same time, the citizens should look upon themselves as equals, without any feeling that they are citizens belonging to this religion or that.

Consistent with the Constitution, the Representation of the People's Act provides that there should be no appeal to religion in times of election. Taking into account this stipulation, the Bombay High Court unseated a number of Shiv Sena candidates elected to the Parliament and the Assembly on the ground that they appealed to the voters on grounds of religion.

While this is so, the fact remains that religion and caste have played a crucial role in India's electoral process. Firstly, parties with express religious denomination like Indian Muslim League, Hindu Maha Sabha, and the Akali Dal have felt free to participate in the elections in our Secular Democracy. The time has come, therefore, to consider whether parties with clearly religious denomination should be debarred from participating in the elections.

But the matter does not end there. All parties including those with nationalistic pretentions have always kept religion and caste in view while setting up candidates or appointing elected members to various positions like those of Ministers or even higher positions of authority.; The voters are thus made to believe that they must vote for the candidates of the religion or caste to which they belong. Secularism, in the ultimate analysis, is the state of mind and that state does not exist either in the minds of the voters or the candidates or the parties which set them up. It is this which has made Secularism in India a fraud and deception.

From politics, religion and caste considerations enter into administration. Whenever communal riots take place, demand is made that police forces should be representative of all the religions and castes. Communal disturbances, it is argued, cannot be avoided or controlled unless a police force of a particular religious or caste composition is in position. The implications of such thinking are highly dangerous because it strikes at the root of the professional character of the police force and the civil services. If this line of thinking is allowed to go unchallenged, it will spell the doom of the whole administration itself. Administration has necessarily to be impartial and objective. It has to be trained and equipped to be so. Then alone will it inspire the confidence of all. If this concept is given a go by, administration will be a medley of castes and religions which cannot be relied upon in times of trouble.

Therefore, what is required of all parties in political and related matters, is an unflinching commitment to the concept of citizenship alone to the exclusion of other competing claims.

Sometimes, Secularism is considered synonymous with 'Sarvaa Dharmaa Samabhavaa', that is equal attitude of respect to all religions. This no doubt, is a concept consistent with the tradition of telerance of this country, as also the tolerance of the Hindu religion. The Hindu religion has preached '*Ekam Sat Vipra: Bahuda Vadanti*' that is, truth is perceived in different ways by different scholars. The idea of the entire world as one family has been the ideal of the Hindu thought. Throughout the centuries, people persecuted in different countries of the world, have found a safe heaven in India. The Jews persecuted in different parts of the world lived with complete security in this country. The Parsis persecuted in Iran, found a safe heaven in the land of Gujarat. The Syrian Christians are the oldest Christian Community in Asia. In modern times the Tibetans hounded out of their own country by the Chinese have been living in peace at Dharmashalas headed by their spiritual leader Dalai Lama. This tradition of tolerance is consistent with the humanistic outlook of the modern times, specially of a the leaders of Indian freedom movement like Mahatma Gandhi and Pandit Jawaharlal Nehru.

But in practice, the concept of 'Sarvaa Dharma Sam Bhavaa' has degenerated into people in authority visiting shrines of all religions! These visits are shown on Television, as though they form part of cocept of secularism. Secularism stands for separation of religion from the State and not bringing all religions into State activities. This is what has become of secularism in India which has thus lost all clarity. When VIPs visit temples, churches, mosques and gurudwaras as part of their official activities and when these visits and cremation ceremonies with priests chanting hymns, functions are shown prominently on national T.V., the difference between preaching and practice becomes known to all and pronouncements regarding secularism look hollow. Of course, every individual including those in authority are free to follow their personal faith or participate in rituals if they are so inclined; but surely secularism requires that these are strictly treated as personal occasions and not public functions.

Nor is it clear whether the concept of secularism is promoted by treating some communities permanently as minorities. In democracy there are no such permanent minorities at all; to allow such feelings to persist or to encourage them in contrary to Secularism. The cause of secular democracy is not promoted by continuation of policies to give special treatement to minorities. Thus, the setting up of Minorities' Commission or the special police force of or for the minorities, or providing reservations for minorities are the surest means of perpetuating the pschosis of minoritism and destroying the concept of secularism. Secularism is an attitude of mind and the perception of one self as the member of a minority community is detrimental to the growth of citizenship. It also appears very strange that while a small community like Parsi never claims special minority status, the claim is stridently made by another community much larger in number.

The special treatment to minorities not only creates a non-secular attitude amongst minorities, certain sections of the majority community i.e. the Hindus also get the feeling, rightly or wrongly, that there are discriminations against them in their own country. Thus, they feel that the birthday of prophet Mohammed is declared a holiday, but the birthday of Lord Ram is not. This is considered a slight to Hindu religion. Indeed it is doubtful whether declaring public holidays on religious occasions is secularism at all. It is much better to have general holidays only a Independence Day and Republic Day and may be on the birth anniversary of Mahatma Gandhi, the father of the nation, but holidays on religious festivals should be replaced by providing certain number of holidays to all people which they could avail of, if they so desire, for observing religious rituals or celebrating religious festivals in the manner they desire.

It is also necessary to see that religion is connected with culture and way of life of people. Insisting on removal of every single vestige of religion from public life in the name of secularism, is bound to prove counter productive. For example, every day the All India Radio starts with the programme called 'Vandana', a programme of bhajans. 'Secular fundamentalists' may consider this a religious activity and therefore, not entitled to find a place on the All India Radio which is a public sector organization. Religious rituals like breaking the coconut or Bhoomi Puja are universally conducted on ceremonies relating to inauguration of construction of public buildings or releasing of ships, etc. (it is doubtful whether such ceremonies should be held at all). It would be churlish for anybody to insist that such religious rituals should be banned on public occasions. The statue of Saraswati is often installed at the entrance of Universities or educational institutions. Should this be considered inconsistent with secularism/ In several offices the lower level functionaries observe religious pujas on some days and even distribute prasad to all the members of the office. Should this be banned? The drivers, the drivers of public vehicles often display the photographs of deities and would not start the vehicle without performing pooja. Should drivers of public vehicles be banned from doing so? Obviously, there should be some sense of proportion in applying all ideas including secularism.

Finally, Secularism does not mean abandonment of the moral basis of political, social and economic order nor does it mean eliminating influence of religion on human behaviour. The recent developments in the communist countries shows that such efforts are bound to fail. Moreoer, values are precious in social life and religions can play a useful role in preserving social values. Without these for many people, life becomes a journey on an uncharted sea. Secularism should not mean an emasculation of a people or cutting them asunder from the roots of their traditions.

Even though we call ourselves a secular republican democracy, unfortunately, the concept of secularism is totally garbled in the minds even of those who hold positions of authority. No wonder there is complete confusion in the minds of the common people. Moreover, there is no clear cut code of secularism nor any programme for its propagation. It is high time that this is done. Otherwise, secularism would be mistaken for other concepts, which however good in themselves are at variance with the concept of secularism. The confusion surrounding the concept of secularism should be removed by a categorical and clear cut definition by the National Integration Council of the concept of secularism and the code of conduct it involves. It may then form the text for educating students in all the educational institutions and indeed for educating all the citizens of the country through a multimedia programme of adult education.

Chapter - 6

The Message of Swami Vivekananda

Swami Vivekananda was the chosen disciple of the mystic, Shri Ramakrishna Paramhansa. India has produced many religious and spiritual leaders through the centuries. But Swami Vivekananda was a religious leader with a difference. He was the Messaiah of India's resurgence who gave a call to his countrymen, particularly the youth, 'to awake, arise and stop not till the goal is reached.'

Swami Vivekananda electrified the World Parliament of Religions held in Chicago on September 11, 1893 by the message of tolerance and broadmindedness which has been the heritage of India's civilization and culture. But when he returned to India, the message that he gave to his countrymen was different. It was a call for action. He found that while the West was full of energy and positive action which created life of prosperity in those countries, India was supine and lifeless and the masses of the Indian people were steeped in poverty, squalor and ignorance. He, therefore, asked the young people of India to take up the mission of helping their fellowmen to take up the life of action. It was a message of the dissemination of the 'Rajyogi' of the West to drive out the 'tamas' which had darkened India.

It was with this aim in view that he set up the Ashram at Belurmath near Calcutta and started the order of 'Ramkrishna Mission' and its counterpart for women 'Sharada Mission' to take up the life of social service.

It was because of the concern of Swami Vivekananda for the upliftment of entire people of India that he stood for the doctrine of equality or samata. He wanted to drive out the castes and sub-castes and rituals which tended to divide the people of India and made them the victims of superstitions. He believed that the common people of India had immense potential which had not developed because they were exploited and uneducated.

Swami Vivekananda's views on education derived from his concern for rejuvenation of India. He did not want education for mere clerical jobs in the service of the colonial rule. He rather wanted that education which would makc people self-reliant and capable of meeting the needs of the society.

It is because of his vision of India that Swami Vivekananda though a religious man was essentially a great patriot who provided inspiration to even great leaders like Mahatma Gandhi and Pandit Jawaharlal Nehru.

Swami Vivekanda's message of national resurgence is still relevant today, when India seems to be in dire economic straits and at the mercy of the International Monetary Fund and the World Bank. The solution to India's problems today is the same that Swami Vivekananda had given a hundred years ago. It is his message of self-reliance.

It will be appropriate in the anniversary year on the meditation of Swami Vivekananda on the rock of Kanyakumari, that all Indians, particularly the youth of India, will remember the message of Swami Vivekananda. He wanted the youth of India to be strong in physique and capable of hard work, and launch upon their path of future life with a sense of idealism and dedication and burning patriotism in the service of the motherland.

Chapter - 7

Science and Sprititualityy

(Presidential address delivered at the International Conference on Science and Spirituality organized at B.V.B. Pune on June 5, 2009 by the International Forum of followers of Gurudev Ranade for Philosophical Research)

Jawaharlal Nehru, the first Prime Minister of free India was known as a rationalist, a man of science. He wanted his fellow Indians to develop a scientific temper. Yet in later years of his life, under the influence of Vinoba Bhave, he started saying that India should combine science with spirituality. Both are essential and should go hand in hand with each other. They are not only, not mutually contradictory or incompatible with each other but are indeed mutually complementary and supplementary.

Science is an enterprise of the intellect while spirituality is the cry of the heart, or cride Coeur", a quest of the soul. Science explores the external world while spirituality explores our inner being. Human beings, over centuries, have been engaged in both those explorations.

The external world, which science explores consists of the '*Panchamahabutas*' – the five basic elements viz. *Prithvi, Aap, Tej, Vaayu* and *Aakaash, Prithvi* or earth is one on which we human beings and animals live, move and have our being. It is out of the earth that grow grass, crops and trees which provide nourishment for animals and human being so is essential for their survival. In the bowels of the earth are deposited metals and minerals, coal and hydrocarbon resources. Our body itself is called 'Kshetra' and a part of the earth itself as conceived by the poet who said "Dust thou art and to dust thou returnest" Science has explored all those and out of those exploration have evolved a whole range of sciences – Physics, Chemistry, Botany, Biology, Microbiology, agricultural sciences, veterinary sciences, medical sciences etc.

"Aap" or water occupies a larger portion of the world and human body than earth itself. Water is the first requirement for the survival of the human beings and animals. That is why in Sanskrit it is called *Jeevan* or life itself. Water is available in the form of rain from the clouds, flowing streams and rivers, wells and subsoil water below the aquifers and the vast seas and the oceans in which the rivers flow. Science has explored water in all those forms and out of the exploration are born a variety of science like meteorology, hydraulic sciences, oceanography etc.

"Tej" or energy is pervasive. It provides the power for producing heat and movement. Wood, coal and hydrocarbon (petroleum) provide thermal energy, and water provides hydropower. Latest addition is the atomic energy. But above all is the solar power so essential for photosynthesis without which crops and trees cannot come to fruition. The greatness of the solar power is that it is renewable. So are the wind power and the wave power. Science has explored all those sources of energy.

"***Vaayu"*** i.e. air or wind are also pervasive. Without oxygen in the air human beings cannot survive. A number of gases in the atmosphere have positive or negative effects on human being. Science has explored all these elements in the atmosphere.

Finally **"*Aakash*"** or space is all around us. Space exploration has given birth to the latest scientific exploration which has enabled human being to realize that the universe is far vaster than what we had imagined. The medieval religions believed that the objects in the space are heavenly bodies which don't move. They also thought earth does not move and is created by God. Copernicus visualised the sun centered universe and Galelio confirmed this theory through the telescopic observations for which he had to be at the receiving end of the wrath of the religious orthodoxy. Now human being have landed on the moon and are thinking exploring the resources on Moon and the Mars. These seems to be no end to scientific explorations.

Human beings have applied the principles and theories of science to produce technology to serve these own ends. Technology has put at the disposal of human beings a wide range of tools, engines and machines. Transport is the most outstanding example. From the age of horse drawn carriages and bullock drawn ploughs we arrived at this age of fast moving automobiles, locomotives, railways and aeroplanes and now the spaceship. Man can move faster than sound. Tractors have replaced bullock to till the soil. Telephone have facilitated distant communication. The latest tools at the disposal of humanity are the computers and the mobile phones, which have ushered in the new information age. Nano technology is another new dimension.

Science which has provided technology for better living has also been the base of highly sophisticated defence and war technology. Science and technology have placed at the disposal of human beings a veritable cornucopia, an abundance of goods and services which have greatly enriched human lives. Human beings are enjoying richer, better and fuller life. At the same time with science and technology, human being have produced weapons of mass destructions which can completely wipe out human lives. Some of the worst examples of death and destruction are provided by the scientifically and technologically most advanced nation viz. USA. If reduced to ashes Nagasaki and Hiroshima – two towns in Japan at the end of world War II with the first and only use of atom bombs in the name of saving world from communism, USA resorted to carpet bombing with Naplan bombs which defoliated Vietnam, killing millions of farmers. And more recently, alleging that Iraq is in possession of weapons of mass destructions – allegations which turned out to be lies – USA let loose a war of 'shock and awe' on that helpless country destroying its infrastructure and the heritage of architecture of the ancient Babylion civilization preserved in Baghdad's national library and museum.This has made humanity wonder whether science and technology are a blessing or a curse.

Science and technology are blessing in that they have raised material standards of living of human beings, have provided not only necessities but all kinds of comforts and conveniences. But human desires are insatiable and pursuit of material goods and service is unending. Satisfaction of material needs does not necessarily lead to happiness and peace for mankind. Rather hedonism leads to restlessness, cut throat competition and even mutual rivalries. At some stage, human beings realize that materialism can not be the "be all and end all of life". When this stage comes, human beings do not hesitate to abondon materialism in search of higher things of life. This is what Buddha and Mahavir did 2500 years B.C. Both of them were born in royal families and lived in affluent surroundings. And yet Buddha on being touched by the sorrow caused by penury, illness and death, decided to give up his comfortable life, left his young wife and child and his palace to understand the basic causes of human suffering and how to overcome it. After years of penance, he had his spiritual awakening under the *bodhi* tree in *Gaya.*

Pursuit of the 'higher things of life' is what is called spiritualism. Spiritualism takes many forms. Firstly, it is in the form of realization of the 'higher values' of life. These 'higher value' are articulated in many way. One articulation is the trinity of 'Satyam, Shivam, Sundaram'- truth, goodness and beauty. Another is '*Satya and Ahimsa'* – Truth and Non-violence - which were the sheet anchor of Mahatma Gandhi's life. Co-operation, friendship and peace are the watchword of Indian culture conveyed by the prayer – "*Om Sahanaavavatu Sahanau bhunaktu, Sahaviryam karvavahai, Tejaswina Va dhitmastu Maa vidhvishavahai.* Yet another is the concept of equanimity of mind" i.e. the attitude of a *Karma Yogi,* a *Stithpradnya'* doing his duties, irrespective of happiness or sorrow, victory or defeat.

The values of life enable us to distinguish between right and wrong. In our tradition '*Kaama, Krodhaa, Lobha, Mohaa, Mada and Matsara'* namely viz. Lust, Anger, Greed, Temptation, Pride and Envy are the six bad things to be abjured and have to be overcome, if we are to attain happiness. On the other hand '*Daya, Kshma, Shanti'* – Compassion, Tolerance and Forgiveness and Peace are the right attitudes – for an individual as well as the humanity.

Values provide the basis for a moral life. Thus, a Sanskrit Vachana Says, '*Paropkarah: Punyaay Paapaya Parpidnam'* Blessed are those who do good to others and cursed are those who harm others. Bhagwan Buddha laid down the eight fold path of good moral life – right thought, right attitude, right conduct and right action, avoiding extreme actions and behaviour.

Reverence for nature is another value of Indian civilization and culture. We should live in harmony with nature and not by exploiting it. Trees, Rivers and mountains are objects of worship. The same kind of feelings is towards animals like cows. Even snakes are worshipped on *Nagapanchami* day which is celebrated as festival. There are very much in tune with todays concerns for environmental preservation.

Another value is concern for "the poorest, the lowliest and the lost" Mahatma Gandhi enjoined us to serve *"Daridra Narayana'*. The poor are the embodiment of the Lord. Service to them in another form of spiritualism. Mahatma Gandhi looked after the laper. Mother Teressa spent her life in the service of the poor.

Yet another concept of spiritualism is 'Mukti' or emancipation from the bondage of life. Indian concept of life enjoins us to give up at some stage of life, all attachments to material pleasure, even to our own kiths and kins. Alone in all civilizations, Indian civilization has conceived, the four *Ashramas* or stages in life viz. *Brahmacharyashramaa* – the stage of a student, *Grihastashrama* – the life of a householder, when a person performs all duties of a householder including bringing up children and looking after the material interest of his family. *Vaanprasthasramaa* – the early stage of detachment when one leaves the scene of active life and resorts to secluded life in places nearer the nature and finally *Sanyasaashram* - i.e. a complete recluse.

At these later stage of life the goal or what Gurudev Ranade had to call the Sumum bonum of life is 'God realization'. The easiest form of God-realisation is Bhakti or devotion to God through daily *Prathana(* prayers) and *pooja (*worship), *Namsmaran* (reciting Gods name, visits to temples, participation in Bhajans and Kirtans and pilgrimages to holy places of worship. But the higher quest or *Sadhanaa* is for the realization of the ultimate. *Upanashidic* rishies tell us that our identity is not our body and the limbs of the body which help us to live our daily life. Rather it is the inner soul – Atma – which is imperishable, which cannot be annihilated by weapons nor burnt by fire. (*Nainan Chindanti Shastraani, Nainan Dahati Pavakah)* This atma is a fragment of *Paramatma* or *Parabhrahma, Chaitanya* which is imparishable. – *Anaadi* (without beginning), *Anant* (without end), *Nirgun* (without any outwards manifestations). *Niraakar* (without any shape of form). *Avyakta* (not capable of being expressed), *Amurta* (not manifest), *Amartya* – (immortal). The merging of the self in the universal self require *Sadhanaa* or spiritual dedication.

Can science and spirituality blend with each other? If so in what way? It is not easy to answer this question. But it may be said that science without spirituality might be meaningless while spirituality without science can be blind (*Andha Shraddhaa).* Can both be harmonized ?

Chapter - 8

Remembering Jawaharlal Nehru

On 14th November 2012, the nation will be observing 123rd birth anniversary of Jawaharlal Nehru, a great patriot who was at the forefront of national struggle for independence and who as the first Prime Minister of free India for the initial seventeen years after independence became the builder of modern India.

Aftermath of Partition

Even before the attainment of independence, Nehru headed the interim Government and had to grapple with the horrible. aftermath of partition, communal riots, killings and consequences of mass exodus across the border. Nehru and Patel were blamed for hastily accepting partition in the face of the opposition of Mahatma Gandhi and not properly anticipating the consequences of partition and preparing the administration for dealing with them. Perhaps in the situation as it developed, partition and formation of Pakistan as an independent nation had become inevitable and the two leaders felt that their was no alternative but to accept and face the inevitable. And Nehru faced the situation bravely. While Pakistan was found on the basis of Jinnah's two nation theory, Nehru never accepted it and assured the Muslims who had not migrated to Pakistan that their future would be safe in India. He even, in his typical courageous manner personally entered the streets to stop the communal frenzy. A separate Ministry of Relief and Rehalibitation was formed to provide succour to the refuges who had crossed the border leaving all their belongings behind.

Building institutions of Democracy

The second immediate task was to provide stability to the new born nation, setup basic institutions of democracy, define long-term goals and set the government moving towards the attainment of these goals. This required single minded determination and ceaseless action. Nehru laboured for long seventeen years to perform those tasks.

A new nation needs a written constitution. A constituent assembly was setup to undertake the immensely important task. While several other nations, sought the help of foreign experts and advisers, India did it on its own. India did not lack experts in constitutional law and related subjects in diverse fields of economics, politics and administration. The drafting committee under the Chairmanship of Dr. B.R. Ambedkar admirably performed their task of giving unto the people their own constitution. The Government of India Act 1935 no doubt provided the administrative framework. But the idea of ideological content of democracy, fundamental rights, independence of judiciary, directive principles, federal structure with a strong centre, values of libery, equality, fraternity and social posture had to be provided as the keynote of the constitution. In that task, Nehru played a key role while Sardar Patel took care of the administrative backup needed by a democratic polity in the shape of all India services and giving them a measure of security. It goes to the credit of both Patel and Nehru that they did not take a vindictive attitude but absorbed the existing all India services including policies, on the ground that they were the instruments of repression of the national movement for the colonial rulers and for putting them in jail for long years. That was the mark of their statesmanship. Within years, the constituent assembly finalised the constitution and was adopted by "We, the people of India i.e. Bharat".

But constitution only provides the framework. It can be a live document only if those at the helm of affairs make it meaningful to the people. Parliamentary democracy has to be functional. Nehru nurtured Parliamentary institutions. In his days, the parliament functioned for almost half the days in a full year. Nehru made it a point to remain present during question hours or when important matters came for discussion. He attentively listened to the debate including the criticism of the opposition and personally replied to the debate in a detailed manner. He gave great respect to the Speaker and bowed down before taking his seat. This was the respect he showed to parliament – very few successive Prime Ministers did so.

The Constitution is for the people. But the people had to be held together. A Constitutional document by itself cannot do so. Nehru with his immense popularity amongst diverse people of India in different parts of the country and his visible presence despite being a busy Prime Minister made him a symbol of national unity. Rajaji who became his relentless critic in later years of his life, admitted in the obituary tribute to him that he was thousand times more popular than any one of them! He addressed mass meetings in which he did not indulge in demagogy but engaged in conversation with people sharing their grief and joy.

With his immense popularity he could easily have become a dictator. One party leadership or personal rule came to many new born countries of Asia and Africa. But Nehru never faultered or wavered on the path of democracy.

Mahatma Gandhi wanted the Congress Party to be dissolved after independence so that new parties could come into existence on basis of clear-cut political ideology. But Nehru did not follow his masters's advice but deftly used the Congress Party's heritage to remain the ruling party of India both at the centre and in the states during his life time. The arrival of other parties including the local or sectoral parties was a phenomenon of the political scene of India only after he left.

Nehru moulded the Congress party according to his own thinking. After Patel passed away he became the undisputed single leader of the party.

Nehru was blamed for not building up the opposition. Nehru did not accept this accusation. He said he could not be expected to build the oppbsition parties. But he never put down the opposition during his time even when the Communist Party came to power in Kerala, though despite his unwillingness, he suspended the elected Namboodripad Government and imposed President's rule under the pressure of his daughter Indira Gandhi who became Congress President. Even though opposition remained weak in his time, it had articulate leader in Parliament like J.P. Kripalani, Minoo Masani, Nath Pai, Atal Behari Vajpayee and Hiren Mukherjee whose views were taken note of by the Prime Minister.

Reorganising the States

The nation had to be held together but the nation state has also to be built to consolidate the national polity. The first task was to integrate the various political entities in the structure. The most important such entities were the former princely states running into thousands, some of them very large like Hyderabad state ruled by the Nizam. It is to the lasting credit of Sardar Patel that he accomplished the task of integrating former princely states in the India union with consummate skill and a mixture of 'carrot and stick' in short period of five years. In the task he was ably assisted by his Secretary V.P. Menon. Nehru did not have much role to play in the immense operation.

Only Kashmir he kept for himself perhaps because he was a Kashmiri. But he messed up the Kashmir issue. He relied too much on Shaikh Abdulla who let him down. He had to be removed and kept in custody in South India for many years. This was a blot on his record as a democrat and Nehru knew it. In last years of his life, he tried to make amends for his treatment of his friend and political ally by bring him back. But the Sheikh never gave up his wayward ways.

When Pakistan tried to take Kashmir by sending hordes of tribal warriors who indulged in killing as they advanced towards Srinagar, the vacillating ruler of Kashmir hastily signed the instrument of accession. Nehru quickly sent troops by air who beat back the invaders out of the valley. But Nehru stopped short of taking the area beyond the valley including Gilgit and Baltistan northern territory despite the willingness and ability of the Army to liberate that part as well. Instead he stopped the operation and on the advice of Viceroy Mountbatten, he approached United Nations with complaint against Pakistani invasion. But the Security Council dominated by erstwhile colonial powers let him down and Kashmir became a festering sore and remains so to do this day. Many feel that Nehru should have left Jammu and Kashmir to Sardar Patel, who could have handled it in a much more decisive fashion.

Nehru's hesitant approach was seen in regard to Goa as well. The French volunterily left their possessions but Portuguese refused to do so despite persuation by Government of India. Patel felt that it was a matter of couple of hours to liberate Goa but Nehru hesitated fearing that it will hurt the image of India as a peaceful nation. But after many years it was by an armed invasion that Goa got liberated and Nehru could not escape the criticism of the Western Powers that he had strayed away from peaceful approach though they themselves never hesitated to use military force.

The British had set up huge provinces like Bombay and Madras which put together, people belonging to different languages. The Motilal Nehru Committee report in 1927 recommended organisation of states on linguistic basis. The Congress party was committed to this idea and its provincial Congress Committees corresponded to the idea of linguistic provinces. However, Nehru as Prime Minister decided to postpone the reorganization of provinces (called states in the constitution) since he felt that the newly established nation state had yet to stabilize itself and could not be entangled in the intricate problems involved in such reorganisation. It will open up Pendora's box. The first priority for him was security, stability and development and reorganisation could, for him wait. But he did not reckon with strong linguistic urges for separate identity. The first such claim was of the Telugu people Potti Shriramalu sat on indefinite fast for the formation of Andhra to be carved out of Madras Province and set up as a separate state. Nehru did not yield and Potti died after fasting for 61 days. The event caused conflagration in Andhra area. Bezwada railway station was burnt. Nehru realised that demand for Andhra had to be conceded and a separate Andhra Pradesh was born as a new state. This provide the beginning of the process of reorganisation of states on linguistic basis. Nehru appointed Fazal Ali Commission to look at the issue comprehensively. They made their recommendations some of which proved controversial. For example, they did not recommend Maharashtra with Bombay as its capital though Marathi people and leaders were bent upon it Nehru thought of Bombay as central territory but that made him so unpopular with Marathi people that they defeated Congress in poll. Nehru saw the writing on the wall and conceded the demand of Marathi people.

Foreign Policy

India as an independent sovereign nation required formulation of its foreign policy. As a member of United Nations it needed to play its role in world affairs External relations had to be established by setting up embassies and high commissions in different countries of the world. These had to be staffed. A new service called Indian Foreign Service had to be setup. Above all, goals of Indian foreign policy had to be defined. None was more qualified to do all this than Jawaharlal Nehru. Over years he had links with several countries and had participated in international gatherings. London was no longer India's window to the world. New Delhi had to have its own outlook and perspective. Nehru throughout his lifetime Prime Minister was also the Foreign Minister. Nehru defined the principle parameters of Indian foreign policy. They were (1) End of colonilism – supporting the Afro Asian countries to emerge to freedom and building Afro Asian Solidarity. (2) Pursuit of world peace and (3) to realise 1 and 2 develop a policy of non-alignment steering clear of the two superpowers United States and USSR and their power blocks in which the world was divided. The idea of non-alignment was that India would not be tied to the apronstrings of world powers. America did not like this independent posture. It wanted India to side with it and be a member of the military blocks in different parts of the world like NATO, CENTO and SEATO. John Faster Dules, the secretary of State of Isenhower presidency, described Nehru's foreign policy as 'immoral'. America cold shouldered India and set up Pakistan as a counter weight by assisting it economically and militarily. It accused India of siding with USSR by not condemning its actions like invasion of Hungary. Despite all this, India was able to establish its image as a peace loving country, taking independent position on international issues. Some critics feel that as a democracy India should have sided with America. One has only to see what happened to Indonesia under Suharto, Pakistan under military dictators and Iran under Shaha Reza Pehlvi to realise the consequences of being a satellite of USA.

As a strong advocate of Afro Asian Solidarity, Nehru put his weight behind United Nation's membership of China under the communist rule despite strong opposition of the US. He enunciated five principles (Pancha Sheel) of friendly relations with China but China betrayed this friendship when it attacked with large number of troupes in the north-east boundary of India, threatening even Assam. Fortunately China pulled back after 'teaching India a lesson'. This gave a set back to Nehru's foreign policy and defence policy. USSR refused to help India saying that China is a brother communist country and Nehru had to seek American help. Nehru was accused of naivete in dealing with China and living in the false hope conveyed by the slogan 'Hindi Chini Bhai Bhai'. Nehru himself admitted that he was 'out of touch with reality'. As a matter of fact Nehru never trusted China. In one of his fortnightly letters to Chief Minister he had clearly stated that China under the communist role may be a threat to India. His conviction grew stronger as years passed by. As brought out by Inder Malhotra (IE, Oct'3, 11) Nehru told C. Parthsarthy ambassador designate to China – "Don't trust Chinese one bit. They are arrogant, deceitful, hegemonist and thoroughly unreliable lot. Be extremely vigilant in Bejing and don't fall for any blandishment Chines may offer. It is all deceit'. Clearly Nehru was not in fool's paradise what he did not anticipate was such a large scale invasion by China. Nehru could no longer follow Mahatma Gahdhi's advice that India should have 'smallest possible army'. India started military buildup and became a large purchaser of weapons and armaments from the western countries.

Planned economic development in Mixed Economy

Nehru clearly defined his economic policy. The laissez faire approach of the British days had to be given up and purposeful planned development had to be undertaken. He set up the Planning Commission and the National Development Council for the purpose. India would be a mixed economy consisting of those sectors viz. public, private and co-operative. Public sector would gain the commanding heights of the economy. He talked of 'socialist pattern of society' clearly distancing himself from doctrinaire socialism implying wholesale social ownership of means of production but underlining equity – both economic and social. This was consistent with the directive principle of the constitution that means of production would not be concentrated in few hands and fruits of development must be widely disseminated. There was reversal of Nehru's approached in 1991 when India went for liberalisation and privatisation. Nehru's policy was blamed for 'license permit raj', and for stifling private entrepreneurship leading to low rate of growth of 3½ %. Actually after stagnation era of the British rule, Nehru's policy was a clear break. Foundation were laid for future development by bringing into existence institutions like IITS, IIMs and a chain of National Science Laboratories. Nehru wanted science and technology as the basis of development. He emphasized dissemination of scientific temper amongst people at large. He fully supported Dr. Homi Bhaba in the development of nuclear science and establishment and development of Tata Institute of Fundamental Research.

Nehru the Administrator

It is often stated that Nehru was a statesman with a vision but not an administrator like Sardar Patel. This is to be less than fair to him. Nehru was a "thinking administrator". What is the essence of good administration? It is formulating a comprehensive framework of policy and setting up administrative and institutional structure to implement the policies. Nehru's framework of policy was truly comprehensive not equalled by any of his successors.

He recorded his personal notes on files, expressing his views and giving a sense of direction to administration. I have seen his note running into more than ten pages giving his views on the subject of administrative reforms. Subsequent Prime Ministers rest content with initiating to register their approval to the proposals put up before them. Truly he embodied the mind of Government. I have heard many of his addresses at important national conferences and meetings including the meetings of NDC attended by Union Ministers and Chief Ministers of State. He never read speeches written by civil servants but delivered them extempore. They were full of insights, original thinking and new initiatives. His formal letters to Chief Ministers show how deeply, carefully and in a practical manner he had analyzed various problems and challenges facing the country, the alternative approaches of dealing with them and the choice the nation and government had to make.

If amongst all the developing countries India is looked upon as a successful example of development through democracy, it is because of the path laid down by Jawaharlal Nehru.

Chapter - 9

Relevance of Mahatma Gandhi

The years that have passed since the death of Mahatma Gandhi have shown that the Mahatma is relevant, not only to India, but to all of humanity. His life and thought have become a source of inspiration to movements in all the continents of the world. Wherever and whenever there is injustice, exploitation and discrimination, a fall in moral values or outbreak of violence, people have derived solace and inspiration from the Mahatma to counter these evils.

Thus, to mention only a few examples, the Rev. Martin Luther King, who fought for the rights of the black in the US, Nelson Mandela who spent 27 years in jail in his fight to end racial discrimination in South Africa or Chief Albert Luthuli who was expelled from his own country to fight for the same cause, Lech Walesa, the leader of the Solidarity movement which overthrew the Soviet hegemony in Poland and Aung San Su Ky who, despite being elected as the democratic leader of Myanmar, is held captive by the military rulers of that unfortunate country, are all disciples of Mahatma Gandhi.

In our own country, Vinoba Bhave who undertook a nation wide *padyatra* for his *Bhoodan* movement aimed at distributing the surplus land of the landlords among the landless, *Lok Nayak* Jayaprakash Narayan, who led the national protest movement against the autocratic Emergency rule imposed by Indira Gandhi, the leader of the *Chipko* movement in the Himalayas, Shri. Sunderlal Bahuguna and last but not the least, Baba Amte, who put the despised lepers on their own feet and gave them a sense of self-reliance are all eminent Gandhians.

What is it in Mahatma Gandhi's life and teachings which seems to be universal in their application transcending the barriers of time and space?

Mahatma Gandhi was a saint in the tradition of *Bhagwan* Buddha of 2500 BC and Jesus Christ. Like them, he showed the path of compassion, tolerance, love, truth, peace and non-violence.

But he was not only a saint. He was also a valiant leader of masses of people who fought steadfastly for political freedom and social equality. From early years as a young man, till his assassination at the age of 79, in his life-long struggle, he led several movements and struggles.

For him, moral principles were not just for individual salvation. They were also instruments for political economic and social transformation. Karl Marx inspired Communist thought to put an end to the inequality and exploitation of Capitalism. But he, like Adam Smith, the father of the free market economy also envisaged the concept of the economic man rather than the moral man.

For Karl Marx, moral values were a product of the system of economic relationships. For Mahatma Gandhi, on the other hand, moral values had their own inherent strength and what he aimed at was the creation of a moral force which could put an end to exploitation and injustice in any form.

Gandhiji was not a bookish scholar or philosopher. He had read only a few books such as John Ruskin's *Unto the Last.* But what he read, he deeply reflected upon and if convinced of any idea or principle, he would translate it into practice. For him, there was no dichotomy between theory and practice, concept and action.

That is why Gandhiji did not develop a monolithic philosophy contained in a definitive work such as Karl Marx's *Das Kapital*. Every idea that he put forward, or every principle that he preached, he had already tested in the crucible of experience. It is only then that he placed these ideas before the people and mobilized mass support for them.

Of the most important ideas that he put forward was that of non-violence. When he launched his first non-co-operation movement in 1919, he had no hesitation in winding it up as soon as he got reports that the Chauri Chaura police station was burnt and reduced to ashes with all the policemen inside.

When, as a aftermath of partition, there was communal violence all over the country, he did not participate in the independence day celebrations but went far away to Noakhali (now in Bangladesh), moving bare-foot from house to house, extinguishing the flames of violence.

That is why Viceroy Mountbatten described him as a one-man army on a mission of peace. But Gandhiji's non-violence was not that of a timid person; it was non-violence of the brave. He would not bow down meekly before injustice, Gandhiji had once observed that free India would have the smallest army in the world. But when the marauders infiltrated into the Kashmir valley and indulged in rape and looting, he did not oppose the decision of the Government of India to send the army to the Kashmir valley to drive out the intruders. Gandhiji would have been alarmed at the violence that the world has witnessed during the last 50 years. World War II ended with the US letting loose atomic bombs on the Japanese cities of Hiroshima and Nagasaki. No doubt, World War III has not yet broken out, but bombardment of Vietnam and the use of long range missiles against Iraq and Serbia have taken a heavy toll of human life and American thinkers like Samuel Huntington are talking of the *Clash of Civilizations*. Russia has indulged in relentless bombing on Chechnya, taking tool of civilian lives. The world has not yet learnt the lesson that violence solves no problem and vicilized humanity should solve the problems through peace and goodwill and that in the ultimate analysis, all wars should end and all armies which are instruments of coercion and violence should be disbanded. While insisting on a comprehensive test ban treaty (CTBT), the US is in possession of thousands of nuclear weapons and missiles on ready alert.

Gandhiji stood for communal harmony. He was acutely aware that people of different religions live in India and he wanted them to live with feelings of brotherhood towards each other. He was an intensely religious person and was deeply attached to Hinduism but he respected all other religions. His evening meetings started with prayers of all religions.

Free India adopted the constitution in which people of all religions were given freedom to pursue and propagate their own religion. The state itself had no religion but would protect the religious freedom of all people. This was the concept of the secular state embodied in our constitution. However, despite this, religious conflicts have occurred from time to time and took a high pitch after the demolition of the Babri Masjid on the fateful day of Dec. 6, 1992. People of India should never forget Gandhiji's message of communal harmony if India has to progress with the united efforts of the people in the years to come.

Gandhiji insisted on moral values in politics. He felt that politics without principles has no purpose. He insisted on the purity of means no less than the purity of ends, because he believed that no matter how good are the ends, they would not remain good if the means to attain them were bad.

For him, freedom was the goal, but it had to be accomplished through a non-violent movement and furthermore, freedom itself was not the ultimate goal, but the means of improving the lives of masses of people, of "wiping every tear from every eye."

That was the pledge which Nehru, his disciple, gave when he became the first Prime Minister of India. But over the years, especially after Nehru's death, the moral standards of Indian politics have sharply fallen. Politics is used for the pursuit and perpetuation of power and power has become an end in itself. Misuse of power for the pursuit of private and partisan interest has become widespread, and no wonder corruption and nepotism have become rampant.

From Bofors onwards, Indian public life has been mired in scams and scandals of vast proportions. India has been ranked as one of the most corrupt countries of the world.

If Gandhiji had been alive to see all this, what would he have felt? Was this the free India for whose existence he had dedicated his life? Gandhiji is not present in our midst to wipe out corruption, but only his ideal of clean public life can save India from the slippery slopes of corruption.

Gandhiji belived in political and economic decentralization. He wanted the village *Panchayat* to be the basis of the Indian polity. His was a bottom-up and not a top-down approach. But framers of the Indian constitution did not accept his ideas. The chairman of the drafting committee Dr. Ambedkar went to the extent of saying that *Panchayats* were dens of narrow mindedness.

Afraid of the fissiparous tendencies, the constitution makers went in for a strong union. Even the states remained comparatively weak. *Panchayats* had to find a place in the directive principles of the constitution.

A few years after independence, it was realized that development work in a large country like India should be undertaken through the grass root level *Panchyati Raj* institutions. The 73rd amendment of the constitution gave *Panchayati Raj* institutions a constitutional position, yet these institutions cannot realize their full potential without alert public opinion in the village communities. The Gandhian workers in the countryside should undertake the task of strengthening the democracy at the ground level by creating alert public opinion.

Mahatma Gandhi wanted to promote economic decentralization through *Khadi* and village industries. He felt that they alone can generate adequate employment opportunities and sustain the traditional skills of the village artisans. They would bring the production and consumption of goods in close proximity with each other.

This Gandhian pattern of economic decentralization was fully justified and amplified by the famous economist Schumacher in his well known book *Small is Beautiful.* But Nehru was enamoured of the modern westernized concepts of industrialization and went in for mass production rather than production by masses, as envisaged by Mahatma Gandhi.

The age of information has once again opened out opportunities for decentralized economic activity. Thus, the Gandhian concept of decentralization seems to hold relevance for the 21st century.

Gandhiji must also be considered to be the harbinger of the modern movement of environmental preservation. As far back as 1927, he warned against indiscriminate exploitation of the natural resources in the name of raising the material standards of living. He said that nature has enough for fulfilling the human needs but not for meeting human greed. For him, unlimited consumerism was totally unjustified and could not lead to human happiness. Thus, Gandhiji must be considered to be the originator of the modern concept of sustainable development.

Gandhiji's thoughts on education and health were also equally revolutionary in character. Gandhiji wanted education to be related to the reality of life. We have forgotten this basic principle with the result that the education that we impart is said to be utterly useless because it does not create economic self-reliance and alienates the products of the educational system from the society. Gandhiji, like Rabindranath Tagore, wanted education to be imparted in the mother tongue. Acquaintance with English has got the better of understanding the subject.

In his ideas of health, Gandhiji laid emphasis on proper diet, environmental sanitation and a healthy style of living. By promoting junk food, tolerating squalor and insanitation and unnatural ways of living and depending more on allopathic systems of medicine to cure illness, we have exacerbated out health problems.

Gandhiji's ideas of non-violence, social harmony, political and economic decentralization, sustainable development and proper balance between the spiritual and material aspects of life have much relevance to happy human living in the 21st Century.

Chapter - 10

The Legacy of Mahatma Gandhi

Mahatma's Causes

Mahatma stood for causes for which he struggled throughout his working life. They were – Freedom, Unity, Equality, Self reliance and deccutralisation. They were related to each other. Though these causes were, 'ends', he was equally concerned with means' to achieve those ends. The means had to based on the principles of 'Truth' and 'non-violence'.

Such was the magnetic influence of his personality, his thoughts and actions that he was able to attract the supporet and co-operation of a galaxy of towering personalities of his time – Rabindranath Tagore, Motilal Nehru and his son Jawaharlal Nehru, Sardar Vallabhbhai Patel. Maulana Abul Kalam Azad, Rajendra Prasds Rajgopalachari, Subhashchandra Bose and many others from different parts of the country, despite the fact that they differed in many ways from him on various occasions and for various reasons. Equally he was able to inspire to masses of people in India to participate in his struggles.

Struggle for Freedom, Non-violent, Non-co-operation

Freedom meant firstly political freedom, emancipation of India from the British colonial rule. His struggle for freedom stemmed from his sense of self respect and dignity not only of himself but of every individual. This assertion of self respect began in South Africa where as a young lawyer he was thrown out of the train on a cold platform of Gitz Mortiz Burg station, despite the fact that he had a valid first class ticket on the ground that the first class was reserved only for the whites. Gandhi, would not accept this tyranny and injustice even though Indians in South Africa had meekly succumbed since they did not have the courage to oppose the powerful racist government of the white people. But young Gandhi mobilised the Indian people, gave them courage and determination to assert their self-respect and join his struggle against the racist rule over next twenty years. He was not able to see the end of the racist rule but a beginning was made which ultimately culminated in the end of 'apartheid'. Nelson Mandela who spent a long period of more than twenty years in jail drew his inspiration from Gandhi who became a Mahatma. Indeed Gandhiji became an inspiration to all the oppressed people of the world. Martin Luther King, the leader of African-Americans, was also his follower, carried on his struggle in America for ending racial discrimination there and culminating in the election of Obama, an Afro-American, as the President of that country.

Gandhiji assumed the leadership of the Congress party after the demise of Lokmanya Tilak. He launched three mass movements the non-co-operation movement in the twenties., the civil disobedience movement of the thirties and the Quit India Movement of the forties which ultimately culminated in India's freedom although accompanied by tragic partition of the country.

Lord Meghnad Desai in his book 'Rediscovery of India' has criticised Mahatma Gandhi for his agitationist approach, for launching on non-co-operation movement spurning the offer of Morley Minto reforms aimed at "progressive rerealisation of self government." He feels that co-operation with the first govt led by Ramsey Macdonald of Labour party of England would have been to the advantage of the Indian people. Gandhiji and Nehru wanted 'Sampoorna Swaraj' which as declared by Tilak was 'the birth right of the Indian people". A clarion call for "Sampoorna Swaraj" was given at the Lahore Congress in 1929 by the young President Jawaharlal Nehru. Indian people led by Congress could hardly have accepted limited freedom under the tutelage of 'British Government. The 'Quit India movement' became inevitable when Viceroy Linlithgo unilaterally decided that India would join the British government in its war against Germany without consulting the Indian people. The Prime Minister Winston Churchill contemplatusly dismissed India's claim for freedom saying that the charter of freedom after world war II would not hold good for India. It was US President Francklin Roosevelt who supported Indian right for freedom.

Gandhiji used the techniques of non-co-operation, non obedience and 'Satyagrah' and mass movement to fight the colonial rule. Were these techniques relevant in Independent India ? Dr. B.R. Ambedkar in his address to the Constituent Assembly categorically stated that neither coercion though non-violence nor violent movement would be all right when Indian constitution has provided constitutional means available to every citizens for safeguarding his or her fundamental rights. But despite Dr. Ambedkars warnings, legacy of Gandhian techniques of opposing government by 'fasting' continued. Potti Shri Ramalu carried on fast unto death for the birth of a separate state for Andhra (Telugu) people. When Sri Ramalu sacrificed of life, Nehru had to concede the demand leading to coming into existence of Andhra Pradesh out of erstwhile Madras province. This started the process of reorganisation of states in India on linguist basis. Recently Anna Hazare successfully used the Gandhian techniques of fasting for compelling the Government to concede his demand for forming a joint committee of civil society and government to formulate on revised Lokpal Bill.

Unity and Communal Harmony

Gandhiji realised that unity of the Indian people was a precondition for a successful national movement against the powerful British rule. He realised that religious divide, especially among Hindus and Muslims, and divisions within the Hindu Society on grounds of castes and outcastes made Indian people incapable of a united struggle and a national effort. He, therefore, gave importance to bridging the communal and caste divide. Gandhiji was prepared to go to any length to achieve this. He supported the retrograde Khilafat Movement to get Muslim participation in the freedom movement. He did succeed in this with the support of Muslim leaders like Moulana Mohammad Ali and Shaukat Ali. But once he suddenly wound up the movement after the Chaurichura Police Station was burnt, the Muslims deserted congress. Another nationalist Muslim leader was Mohammad Ali Jinnah, Sarojini Naidu once called him the symbol of Hindu-Muslim Unity. He was the lawyer of Lokmanya Tilak when the British charged him with sedition. But the same Jinah parted ways with Congress after the Nagpur session where he was hooted out, blaming Gandhi for introducing religion in politics. The allegations were not incorrect, witness his support to Khilafat movement against Jinnha's advice and his concept of 'Ramraj' as the ideal of after independent India and all religion prayers sung at his Prarthana Sabhas in the evening. The real reason for leaving Congress was that Jinnha was a lawyer who spoke in conferences and did not like mass movements. He ate beef, did not do Namaz five times a day and had a Parsee wife – hardly an example of a devout Muslim and yet he had the Muslims desert Congress to join Muslim League which was recognised by the British as the representative of the Muslim community. Gandhiji claimed that Congress represented the entire people of India including Muslima. Jinnah made the claim for a separate nation for the Muslims called Pakistan. The last minutes effort of Mahatma Gandhi to persuade Jinnah give up his demand for partition, by offering him Prime Ministership of a united India failed when he contemptuously spurned the offer. Gandhiji had made a public statement that the vivisection of India would be over his dead body but he could not keep his word and partition did come into existence forming two independent nations.

Behind the coming into existence of Pakistan as an Islamic nation was the pernicious two nation theory advocated by Jinah which was accepted by majority of the Muslim people. Congress often blamed the British for deliberately creating divide between the Hindus and Muslims. But the fact remains, that such a feeling of separate identity did exist amongst the Muslims. Though Muslims and Hindus joined together in the revolt of 1857, the Muslim modernist Sir Syed Ahmed Khan (1817-1894), the founder of Aligarh Muslim University, clearly stated in a speech delivered at Patna that 'In India there are two prominent nations which are distinguished by the names of the Hindus and Musulmans. At the same time as common inhabitants of India, the two should have mutual co-operation, sympathy and love". On the other hand if we show 'mutual disunity, animosity and illwill for each other, we would only destroy ourselves." However, Jinnah who become an undisputed leader of the Muslims in 1940s book an extreme approach.

Rational Jinnah chose to give a strident expression to Muslims separatism, 'Hinduism and Islam' he told the British represent two distinct and separate civilisations and are as distant from one another in origin and manner of life as the nations of Europe. The concept of 'one Indian nation is a 'misconception'. The hope that Hindus and Muslims can evolve a common nationality' is an empty dream. However, a large population of Muslims, almost as many as in Pakistan formed as separate Muslim nation, continued to live in India as equal citizens of the Indian Republic and of the Indian nation. Jinah spurned the approach of the Congress to present a united front of people of India. He dubbed Congress as essentially a Hindu party. This approach and mindset inevitably led to the partition of India. Future events like the end of East Pakistan and the birth of Bangladesh, the internecine conflicts in Pakistan and rise of Islamic terrorism, not only falsified Jenahs's formulations but brought immense grief to Muslims in Pakistan and elsewhere.

Mahatma Gandhi's view was an advocate of 'Hindu-Muslim' unity. He asserted that millions of Hindus have sought after it. The member of each community vied with each other in accomodating memebrs of sister communication. They respect each others religion feelings. No trace of suspicious lurked in anybody's heart.'

Even after partition Mahatma Gandhi continued to struggle for Hindu-Muslim unity. While India was celebrating the birth of freedom in the nation's capital, Mahatma was moving barefoot in Naukhali in Bengal dousing the flames of aroson and violence let loose by communal orgy. He wanted India and Pakistan as to live in harmony and went on fast for making India give Pakistan its due share of assets,. After it was withheld by Nehru and Patel (Prime Minister and Deputy Prime Minister) on the ground that the resources would be used for military attacks on Kashmir and elsewhere. The govt of India had to succumb but such was the anger of Hindu extremism, that Nathuram Godse who was its embodiment shot at Mahatma at prayer meeting in Birla House. The Mahatma died for the cause of communal harmony with the name of Shri Ram on his lips.

Caste cleavages in Hindu Society

Another great hindrance to the unity of India was the existence of castes and sub-castes amongst Hindus arranged in a hierachial order with outcastes or untouchables denied even basic human dignity and access to drinking water from common wells and lakes. Dr. Ambedkar with his higher education in American and British Universities took the leadership of the untouchables particularly Mahars – the sub-caste to which he belonged. He strindently demanded a separate electorate for the outcastes (scheduled castes) at the Round Table conference convened by the British, who ever ready to 'divide and rule' readily conceded. Gandhiji was determined to retain the untouchables whom he called 'Harijans' within the Hindu fold. He went on indefinite fast. After 21 days of fasting, Gandhiji's health became critical and such was the pressure on Dr. Ambedkar that he had to agree to the compromise formula viz. though there would be no separate electorate for the scheduled castes, they would have reserve seats, a practice continued even after India become a free democratic Republic under its own Constitution. Reservations were to last for 15 years but continued indefinitely through constitutional amendments.

Against this background it will be interesting to understand the outlook of these tall leaders. In his address at the conference on 'Annihilation of caste', Dr. Ambedkar made a frontal attack on that institution 'Caste'. It is a hierarchy, he said, in which divisions of laboures are graded one above the other. This prevents individuals to take positions on the basis of 'trained capacities'. In the existing social order of Hindus, they are compelled to stick to the social status of their parents. This results in frustration and unemployment and comes in the way of social efficiency. Caste is a harmful institution in as much as it involves the subordination of man's natural powers and inclination to the exigencies of social rules. Hindu society has become only 'a collection of castes'. Dr. Ambedkar felt that the remedy is not just 'intercaste dinning' but 'inter-caste marriages' as well. He cited Buddha to vindicate his stand that the authority of 'Sastras should be rejected.

Gandhi took serious note of Dr. Ambedkar's views. But he asserted that 'caste has nothing to do with religion'. He admitted that caste comes in the way of spiritual and national growth. He was a favour of intercaste marriage. But he uttered a word of caution. "Old prejudices have to be overcome with patience."

After attainment of independence, an interim government was formed. A new constitution had to be framed. Gandhiji prevailed on Congress to invite Dr. Ambedkar to be the Chairman of the Drafting Committee. Dr. Ambedkar performed his task with distinction which elicited the admiration of the entire Indian nation. He spoke like 'a wise democrat'. (the term used by Ramachandra Guha in 'Makers of Modern India') when he addressed the Constituent

Assembly. He commended the constitution as placed before the Assembly as workable, flexible and strong enough to hold the country together both in peace time and war time.

Policies of Independent India

Mahatma Gandhi had definite ideas regarding the economic, political and social system in free India. Every citizen and family, every community must feel free and not in anybody's bondage. This meant maximum decentralization, not cocentration of power in those who run government at the centre and in the states. In his words, 'Independence must mean independence of the people of India and not those who are ruling over them. The rulers of India would have to be servants of the people ready to do their will. Independence must begin at the bottom. Every village must be a Republic or Panchayat having full powers. Every village has to be self-sustained and capable of managing its affairs even to the extent of defending itself against the whole world. In the structure composed of innumerable village communities, there will be, every widening never ascending circles. The outermost circumference will not wield power to crush the inner circle but will give strength to all within and derive its own strength from it."

When Indian Constitution was being framed Gandhiji was not there to guide the deliberation of the Constituent Assembly. He was snatched away by the bullet of an assassin less than six months after the attainment of independence. However, some members did ask for the Gandhian model for our Constitution instead of the Westminster model. But this was not accepted. The chairman of the drafting committee of the Constitution Dr. Ambedkar totally opposed the concept of village as a self governing republic. 'What is the village' he said in course of address to the Constituent Assembly but a sink of localism, a den of ignorance, narrow mindedness and communalism. I am glad that the draft constitution has discarded the village and adopted individual as the unit'. All that was conceded was a directive principle of the Constitution laying down that 'village panchayats shall be promoted as unites of self-goverment.

That provided the basis for the establishment of three tier Panchayat Raj instituons as recommended by the Balwantrai Mehta Committee appointed by the then Ministry of Community development enthusiacally supported by Jawaharlal Nehru, the Prime Minister. He wanted panchayat, co-operative and the school to be the basic instituions in every village. The three tier panchayatraj institutions viz. Panchayat at village, Pancyahat samities at Block level and Zilla Parishad at the District level were established in diferent states of India through Acts possed by their Legislative Assemblies. Rajiv Gandhi wanted to go further and introduce an amendment of the constituion to make panchayati raj institutions the third tier of Parliamentary democracy. He did not succeed in this but his successor Narasimha Rao succeded in getting the 73rd amendment passed to provide a constitutional base to Panchayati Raj institutions.

An articulate advocate of Gandhian model was Jayprakash Narayan, one of the ardent followers of Mahatma Gandhi and Vinoba Bhave. In 1959 he published a tract. 'A plea for restructuring of Indian polity' in which he advocated an alternative political system for India based on the revival of village panchayats and replace the topdown model of Parliamentary democracy by one working from village panchayats upwards – an elaboration of Gandhiji's idea of 'oceanic circles.' The foundation of our polity should be self governing, self sufficient, urban-rural local communities. The highest political institution of the local community should be the Gram Sabha of which all adults should be members. The selection of the Pancyahat should be by general consensus of opinion in the Sabha. The Sabha and Panchayat should see that the village becomes self sufficient in matter of food and clothing as soon as possible. They should so plan that there was no unemployment in the village and every family reached a minimum level of living. Self government to be real should be about essential problems of life.' The gram panchayats would be integrated into Panchayat Samiti. It would be elected by Gram panchayats not by their members. The District Council will be formed by integration of Panchayat Samitis, and district councils should come together to create the State Assembly. The State Assembly is a like manner would bring into being the Lok Sabha.' These should be the underlying principles of our constitution. All this remained a utopia. !

Jawaharlal Nehru, the chosen heir

With the blessings of Mahatma Gandhi, Jawaharlal Nehru became the first Prime Minister of free India. Mahatma preferred him to his elders – Sardar Vallabhbhai Patel, a fellow Gujarati and C. Rajgopalachari whom he had described as his 'conscience keeper'. Ramchandra Guha has succinctly given the reasons why Gandhiji chose Nehru despite profound differences in their outlook – 'Nehru venerated Gandhi', the older man in turn showered more affection on his disciple than on his four biological sons. The two men differed in temperament and altitudes to modernity. Nehru was indifferent to religion. Gandhi believed deeply in his own version of god (his 'inner voice' mine) Nehru thought that industrlisation was the only solution to endemic poverty. Gandhi called instead for the renewal of village economy. Nehru believed in mass production in modern factories, Gandhi believed in production by masses engaged in village industries – Charakha being the symbol Nehru had great faith in the powers of modern state to uplift and reform society. Gandhi was sceptical of state power, trusting instead in the conscience and will of individuals and communities. Hence, his concept of 'trusteeship'. Beyond these differences were fundamental similarities. Both were patriots in the most inclusive sense who identified with all of India rather than with a particular caste, language, region and religion. Both abhored violence and preferred democratic government to dictatorship. All this and Nehru's own independent appeal to the young led Gandhi to anoint him as he has political successor. Nehru, Patel nor Rajaji challenged Gandhiji's choice. Patel worked as Deputy Prime Minister and Home Minister and within a short period till his death in 1950 he made an enduring contribution to India's unity by integration of all princely states including Hyderabad but not Kashmir which Nehru kept to himself with tragic consequences Kashmir remains to this day a festering sore. Many believe that had Nehru left Kashmir to be dealt with Patel like all other Princely states, the result would have been different.

Rajaji had great affection for Nehru though he become an inveterate critic of Nehru's economic policy and founded a new party – the Swatantra Party which opposed Nehru's Statism which gave rise to licence permit raj. Despite his trenchant criticisms of Nehru's policies, he paid a mourning tribute to Nehru on his death in 1964. "I have been fighting Nehru all these years over what I consider faults in public policies. But I knew all along that he alone could got them corrected – A beloved friend has gone the most civilised person amongst us all."

Nehru's Economic policies

Nehru tried to find a via media between totalitarianism in Communist countries and unbraided capitalism in western countries. He evolved the concept of planning in a mixed economy. The economy should be self-sufficient. Economic development cannot be left to the vicissitudes of the market forces but needs to be deliberately planned with optimum use of the natural and human resources based on science and technology. The mixed economy should consist of three sectors – public, private and co-operative. The public sector should hold the commanding heights of the economy in defence industries, heavy industries like steel, coal and heavy engineering and new technological industries like electronics. Planning should give a sence of direction to the entire economy. The Industrial Policy Resolutions of 1948 and 1956 reflected this.

Rajaji feel that the planned economy approach had given rise to 'license permit raj'. In making his case for Swatantra Party he said, "The Swatantra party stands for minimum government and minimum state interference, for minimum taxation, for minimum interference in private and profesional affairs of the citizens and for minimum regulation in industry and trade.' As against was Nehru's socialism which has led to state central of everything. The license 'permit raj' has stifled entrepreneurship and private initiative He wanted corruption and inefficiency of permit-licence raj to go. Gandhiji would have approved of Rajaji's approach.

It required two decades after Nehru's death for a realisation that what Rajaji had asked of Nehru, deserved to be recognised. It needed Narsimha Rao's Congress government who appointed Dr. Manmohan Singh as his Finance Minister, to quietly wind up the Nehruvian model and go in for 'economic reforms' to dismantle the licence permit raj and go in for marketisation, privatisation, liberatlisation and globalisation.

Non-violence and world peace

Like his mentor, Nehru stood for non-violence and world peace. But when Jinnah sent tribal marauders to invade Kashmir and take it by force, Nehru had to send the army to drive out the invaders. Gandhiji approved of this action. Gandhi wanted India to have the smallest possible army. Nehru also concentrated on development than on defence. But when China invaded India's northern boundaries in 1962, Nehru had to go in for strengthening the armed forces and the process has gone all along till today. Gandhiji would have been distressed by the violence and armed race on the sub-continent. But would be have found out a non-violent, peaceful alternative?

After world war II, no third world war has taken place. But innumerable bloody conflicts do take place all over the world. This sub-continent is no exception. The strife torn world has started looking at the life work and thoughts of Mahatma Gandhi to usher in a era of world peace.

(The quotations in this article are from 'Makes of Modern India' an compilation by Ramchandra Guha with excellent bio-graphical and background notes)

Chapter - 11

Celebration of Festivals

— By Dr. P.R. Dubhashi

Festivals are a part of the way of life of the Indian people. No other people in the world celebrate as many festivals as the Indian people. Festivals are connected with our myths and legends.

They are celebrated throughout the year in tune with changing seasons. We as a people are observing them over the years – as many as we can remember.

The annual cycle of festivals begins with *'Yugadi'* on *Chaitra Shudha Pratipada* when the new year starts. It is known as *'Gudhi Padwa'* in Maharashtra when *'Gudhi'*, a silver pot hung on the top of a pole with a garland around is raised on the top of the house. Every house, humble no less than a majestic one, raises the *Gudhi*, a symbol of the commencement of the new year. Then follows *'Rama Navami'* the day of the birth of Lord Rama. The *jeshtha pournima* is called *Vat Pournima.* On this day women praying for their husbands. The commencement of *'Chaturmaasa'* comes in the month of *Shravan* The *'Shravani Somwar'* (Mondays of *Shravan*) is observed with *Pooja*. It is, during this season that festival *'Naag Panchami'* is observed. During the festival Naga 'King Kobra' is worshipped offering milk. Men collect milk from house to house with cries of *'Nagobala dudh dya'* – give milk for Nagoba. Follows *'Janmashtami'* or *'Gukulashtami'* the birthday of Lord Krishna. Then comes *'Ganeshotsav'* the festival of Lord Ganesha, the benign god of wisdom, who is described as *'Sukhkartaa – dukhharta'* - one who showers happiness and removes unhappiness through his blessings. The Ganesh festival is observed over one and half day to 10 days- according to practices of different peoples. After *Ganeshotsava* the rainy season ends.

The autumn season starts with *Navaratri* culminating in *Vijayadashami*. On this day Goddess Durga vanquishes the buffalo demon and is called '*Mahishasura Mardini*'. This day is marked by '*Seemolanghan*', crossing of boundaries for new achievement. *Apta* tree leaves are exchanged as token of gold. The Mysore *Dasahra* festival was made famous by the Mysore royal dynasty. It attracts thousands to Mysore from all over the country. Dasahra is followed by Diwali the festivals of lights – all houses are illuminated with earthen lamps. Deepawali celebrates the vanquishing of *Narakasura,* another demon by Lord Krishna. Deepawali is the most beloved of all festivals. Then starts the winter season with the festival of *Makar Sankranti.* Then comes the spring season marked by the festival of *Holi* with *'Holika Dahan'* killing of ill faith symbollised by lighting and burning of wooden sticks.

All these seasons are celebrated in different parts of the country with their own speculations. For example, Dasehra is celerated as '*Durga Pooja*'in Bengal when it is celebrated over several days. '*Onam*' is a special festival of Kerala. *Sankranti* is celebrated as Pongal festival in Tamil Nadu.

Though all there are family festivals, they become social functions. For example, Pandals are erected during *Ganapati Festival'* where people congregate to publicly celebrated the *Ganesh* festival. Similar pandals are erected for *Durga Pooja'* in Bengal. Lokmanya Tilak took a lead in making *Ganesh festival*, a public festival. He wanted to make the festival, an occasion for public gathering against the British rule. Cultural programme like '*Powadas*' or patriotic songs were arranged for bringing about public awakening.

Festivals are occasions for culinary delights at home. '*Shrikhanda*', a sweet made of curd (*Dahi*) is prepared on *Janmasthami* day. Coconut sweets are prepared on *Nagpanchami* day. On Dasehra, *Basundi* – a sweet made of milk. Diwali offers in every home a veritable feast of various types of sweets like *Laddus, Wadis, Anarsa (*a sweet of *gur*), *Chirota* etc. Children specially enjoy the sweets but grown up are not far behind.

Recent years have unfortunately marked distinct deterioration in observing the festivals. The 'touch of Midas' to the festivals has become a curse. For example during *Gukulahtami or Janmashtami* '*Dahi Handis'* pots of curds are hung and erected several feet high on many streets and children are lured to erect pyramids to catch hold of *Dahihandis.* The *Dahihandis* are so high that while catching them many accidents taken place, some accident prove fatal. The judiciary had to intervene to put a restrictions on practices dangerous to life of children.

Ganesh festival lead to traffic bottleneck, especially on the final immersion day when hundreds of processions carrying the idol for immersion slowly move through the streets holding up all traffic and unsettling the normal life over thirty hours ! The participants in the procession shout- '*Mangal Murti Morya, Pudhchyaa Varshi Lowkar ya*' 'Benign God Ganapati please come early next year' to beating of drums. The deafening sound leads to heavy sound pollution. The trouble to the old and seek can only be imagined. The Diwali crackers are another example of severe sound and air pollution. Such public celebrations during festival days far from promoting devotion degenerate into unholy indulgence in wayward behaviour. Lakhs of rupees are spent to induce children to participate in *Dahihandis* or bursting of crackers.

Such type of celebrations is entirely incompatible with smooth and ordinary public life which is needed in modern times. We need to put a stop to such noisy indulgence in excesses and polluting practices in the name of celebration of festivals. These make a mockery of the purpose of festival and destroy the sanctity and cultural values of our festivals. Society needs to be educated to stop indulgence in environmental and sound pollution in the name of celebration of festivals.

Chapter - 12

Conferring Rights on Citizens - Laws and their Implementation

I - Policy Contradictions

UPA Government at the Centre dominated by the Congress Party has followed during the last nine years a dual policy. On one side, a policy of marketisation, privatization, liberalization and globalization which has lead to growing inqualities and dispartities between the 'haves' and 'have nots', rapid urbanization marked by large number of slums and shanties with abominable conditions of living, rising consumerism and its concomitant hedonistic values destroying the moral fabric of the society and leading to rampart corruption as witnessed in Commonwealth Games scam, IPL scam, 2G scam and coal scam. To mitigate, as it were, these unsavoury consequences of the policy of liberalization, the Government has taken, under the influence National Advisory Committee headed by Congress Party President Smt. Sonia Gandhi, a number of legislative and administrative measures to 'confer' rights on the citizens – "right to get information" from public authorities, right to free education to all disadvantaged children under age of fourteen, right of employment and of food security. There is an inherent contradiction between these two sets of policies, one concentrating on 'growth' and the other on distribution of fruits of growth to disadvantaged by 'conferring' rights on people. Recently Smt. Sonia Gandhi, categorically stated, while speaking to a reporter. that these rights given by UPA (Congress) would help "it to get a third term after 2014 general elections. These measures to give to people rights is our USP ! She spoke as though she was the bountiful ruler and the people supplicants !

The contradictions have led to disturbing consequences- fall in the rate of growth, continuous spiral of inflation, fall in employment opportunities, acute disparities with billionaires flouting their wealth and rise in poverty in depressed sectors of the economy. Crimes like rape and murder have defaced India that adversely imparted tourism and the flow of foreign investment, widening external trade deficit and continuous fall in the value of rupee vis-a-vis dollar creating further fears of exacerbating inflation.

II – Resolving Contradictions

Social scientists and social thinkers, no less than Government need to make an indepth analysis of the economic situation full of contradictions and suggest measures to resolve them. This has to be done with reference to the economy and society as a whole as well as to specific segments.

In resolving these contradictions, differences of approach of the Finance Ministry and the Reserve Bank of India came out in the open. The Finance Minister tried to pressurize the then RBI Governor Subbarao to reduce interest rate to stimulate investment while the RBI resolutely resisted arguing that this could not be done in the face of inflationary pressures. Finance Minister and the Prime Minister showed little concern on the disastrous affect of inflation on the lives of the common people and did not announce comprehensive measures to effectively cut inflations.

Government is accused of working under 'corporate' pressures from abroad. Effort on the part of government to open more and more fields of the economy to foreign investment have not produced much visible result. For example, in the retail distribution field, Government expected to attract big multinational firms like Wallmart and Tesco to open branches in India but this has not happened because the investment in US seems to have become a more attractive destination. The fact seems to be that while the US economy got out of the recession which struck US economy in 2008. India which escaped it in 2008, seems to have landing in it in 2013 and governments seems to have no clue.

The Prime Minister has recently stated that, 'globalisation is irreversible'. But this does not mean that Government should helplessly allow the economy to go into drift in the face of continuous spiral of inflation and deficit in external balance of payment. Political parties and people have started accusing Government of lack of governance and 'policy paralysis'. Most people fear that a Congress led government with a decreased majority in Parliament and subject to pressures of the so called allies and supporting parties and several state government run by non-UPA parties, will not be able in last year of its tenure Assuming it will not call for general elections earlier, it will not be able to take any decisive steps towards the introduction of so called more "economic reforms".

As regard the policy of giving rights to people, it is necessary to state that it is not the government that confers on people the various rights on people. It is the Constitution of India Republic which is the fountain head of the fundamental rights of the citizens – rights like freedom of speech, expression, and assembly and right to peaceful life and liberty. Moreover, the Directive Principles make it obligatory for the state to ensure to citizens the right to an 'adequate means of livelihood' and promote social order in which justice, social, economic and political will inform all institutions of national life; and the operation of the economic system would not result in concentration of wealth and means of production to the detriment of the common people.

It is clear from what is stated in Part III and IV of the Constitution that it is not a question of conferring right on citizens but of the obligation of state to fulfill its obligations as defined in the Constitution. It is not as though the 'rulers' are conferring rights on the 'ruled' as a matter of favour for which the ruled should feel indebted to the Government and re-elect it for the third time to 'rule'.

In this paper it is proposed to briefly analyze the measures taken to confer rights of people mentioned above and examine the extent to which the various legal and administrative measures to 'confer' rights on people have actually worked out in practice.

III. Right to Information Act

The Act enacted in 2005 intends to provide for a practical regime of right to information to citizens to secure access to information under the control of public authorities in order to promote transparency and accountability of the working of public authorities. It envisages the constitution of Central and State Information Commissions to whom citizens can approach for securing information.

That such an Act became necessary is a measure of distrust between public administration and the citizens for whom it exists. It was natural that such a distrust should exist during the British rule. Suppressing the freedom movement was necessary to ensure continuity of British rule. Matters relating to such measures had to be kept confidential. But after the attainment of independence such confidentiality had lost its raison detre. The Indian Republic brought into existence under the Constitution is based on the concept of supremacy of the people and the accountability of the government and public administration to its citizens. This implies that the administration should be on open book and confidentiality could exist only to the extent absolutely necessary in a few matters such as those relating to the Defence and Security of the country. Even in such matters, confidentiality has to be limited and should not be used to cover up wrong actions and misdeeds of public authorities. After all, we promised unto ourselves Welfare State and not a Police State as it existed under the British rule. But these assumptions proved wrong. Even under the British rule, large initiatives were taken to set up Railway network and nationwide postal service, a well organised District Administration all over the country, mapping up all land through surveys, establishment of Universities and educational institutions, public hospitals and health services, large irrigation dams and canals like the Sakkarbarrage and Ganga Yamuna canal. All this could not have being accomplished without participation of the people. On the other hand, the promise of the end of the Police. State was not kept after independence by elected governments and confidentiality clause was used to hide the misdeeds of politicians in power and some civil servants colluding with them. People increasingly felt that matters of pubic interest were kept hidden. The feeling against government was fuelled by social workers like Anna Hazare who went on fast and activists like Aruna Roy who mobilized public opinion in the country against misuses of power in administration while executing public works programme. They insisted that people had the right to know expenses incurred and cases of their misuse and demanded information regarding the actions of public authorities. The Government had to respond to these agitations. Maharashtra State was the first to pass an act giving the right to information to the people followed by the Central legislation on the subject. Central Right to Information Act was passed on October 12, 2005.

Some argue that the Act has became on effective tool to make public authorities and government accountable to the people and fight corruption. Following are a few examples (1) The assets of Ministers, bureaucrats and judges have been made public. (2) The amount spent by Ministers and Officers on foreign trips have been made public. (3) The selection process of UPSC and State PSC and IITS has come under public scrutiny in order to ensure fair play. (4) Some scams have been exposed. However, it should be pointed out that it were the audit reports of CAG under Shri. Vinod Rai which exposed huge scams like 2G, Coal and Commonwealth Game seems. The credit goes to CAG rather than the effect of action under the RTI Act. Smt. Aruna Roy has claimed that the Act has changed the power equation between Indian citizens and Government. It has became a tool for people to exercise their authority. It has forced local authorities, State Government and Central Government to disclose information to them earlier denied. It has ended the culture of exclusion and secrecy and replaced it by openness and inclusion. She had however, admitted that the lack of political will and bureaucratic resistance tend to threaten the needed action under the Act.

Government have often argued that the Act has led to 'policy paralises'. The Government has been reluctant to disclose nothings on files. Judged had been reluctant to disclose their assets. Political parties have been reluctant to be brought under the ambit of the Act. Eternal vigilance of the citizens is needed to curb these attempts to escape the provision of the Act.

It is not as though the working of the Act has been smooth. It leaves much to be resolved. There are far too many glitches in the implementation of the Act. In states, several positions of Information Commissioners are vacant, Consequently thousands of cases are pending. Very little budgetary provision was made during the first five years after the Act was passed. In cases where the departments concerned should have suo-motto offered information to the citizens, misleading, confusing, incomplete, delayed and wrong information is given. Moreover, there is lack of proper implementation mechanism for the implementation of penal orders passed by the Information Commissioners. This has taken heavy toll of the effortiveness of the Act. Punitive action against officers who fail to carry out orders of Information Commissioner and appeal authorities is stymied. The state information commissioner do not use their powers to compel the government to follow their acts. They simply pass the blame on Government. In some cases activists who brought up cases under the Information Act were killed. In Maharashtra State alone nine RTI activists were killed and 44 attacked in the last eight years. Gujarat come second with 34 attacks including three murders. Delhi, Bihar, Uttar Pradesh, Haryana, Andhra Pradesh and Karnataka followed with ten reported attacks. The culprits were not brought to book.

IV. The Right of Children to Free and Compulsory Education (RTE) Act.

This Act was enacted in 2009 to ensure free and compulsory education to all children between the age of 6 to 14. It was not as though conferring such right on citizens by Union Government was necessary. Such right was already there under the Constitution. What was necessary for Government to perform its duty as laid down under article 41 of the Constitution to make provision for securing the right to education. Article 45 of the Constitution specifically states that the state shall endeavour to provide, within a period of ten years from the commencement of the Constitution, for free and compulsory education for all children until they complete the age of fourteen years. It is the State which failed in performing its duty. The Constitution recognizes the limits of the economic capacity of the State in performance of its duty. But it is the Government headed mainly by the Congress which failed to accord high priority to education in its plans and programmes. The Kothari commission prescribed that six percent of the national income should be devoted to education. In actual reality, it is hardly one per cent. But instead of making adequate provision for education, the Union Government have enacted law to 'to confer right of education'

The State and local governments like Municipalities and Zilla Parishad have not paid adequate attention to the improvement of the quality of their schools and ensuring good quality of teaching staff and good infrastructure.

As a result a number of private schools have proliferated and families even from poor strata of society whose children are entitled to get free education in these schools prefer to pay huge fees to send their children to private schools. Many of the newly proliferated private school, were English medium schools. Children even from poor families with illiterate parents want to send their children these schools bearing the financial burden. The fever of English medium schools has caught on, even from the primary stage. Imposing English medium on children whose parents speak to them in mother tongue is a bizarre contradiction and even a monstrosity vitiating the very purpose and process of education.

The new Act which make it compulsory for the private schools even those receiving no government grant, to provide 25% free seats to disadvantageously placed families. Government claimed that all these years, the poor were exploited by private schools by charging them higher fees. Now Government has come as a Good Samaritan for the poor giving them free seats in private schools. But as whose cost? The Private schools which get no Government grants would have to bear the burden. The Government promises to reimburse the private schools to a limited extent. The promise still remains on paper. The Act was introduced without fully straying the implications and the process of implementation of the various provisions of the Act. State Government have yet to make any actual financial provisions, putting the private schools in a State of financial jeopardy. The Government brazenly suggested that the private schools should approach private donors without considering for a moment the implications.

Apart from the uncertainty in the release of grants, is the question regarding eligibility. Only the Primary school entrants under 25% free grants would be entitled for partial reimbursement. But what about the situation where the nursery schools are the entry point? The Act does not cover these schools, leaving the entire burden of free seats in nursery school on private institutions. This is the surest way of pushing them in financial jeopardy. It has been suggested that that the Act should cover pre-primary stage schooling which has become universal. But there is no response from Government so far and no action.

The Union Government which has enacted the law has left the implementation entirely to the State. But the State administration from State Secretariat level to the level of local government is in a state of confusion leaving the private schools to the mercy of their arbitrary dictates issued from time to time. Piecemeal actions rather than a comprehensive integrated action is what is taking place. This is inevitable when Acts are passed in a hurry with concern for political gain.

A survey showed that 25% of quoto has not been filled as stipulated under RTE even in State schools. The picture is particularly dismal in urban centres.

For example, according to a recent survey in Brihan Mumbai Corporation area, not a single admission was given under RTE. Pune fulfilled only 50%.

At the alter of equality, the selection procedures based on 'merit' followed by several schools over the years have become illegal. The admissions made by schools at any stage on selective basis are banned. One of the well known schools from Pune, 'Jnan Prabodhini' selcted 'merited' students based on tests for its admission to fifth standard. The school claimed that the very objective for which the school was established was to select merited or gifted students and give them education to make them future leaders of the society in various fields of life. However, the local education officers cancelled their admissions as repugnant to the new Act. The school appealed to High Court which turned it down declaring that the admissions made by them were null and void. The school intends to appeal to the Supreme Court which in principle has already upheld the constitutional validity of the Act.

The Act palpably meant to be 'children' or 'student' friendly, has banned any terminal examination till the 8th Standard. Students would automatically be promoted. It is widely reported that this has led to students not taking their studies seriously. Consequently they have problems in facing examinations from 9th standard onward, since they are ill prepared. Such complaints have come not only from the institutions and teachers but from the parents themselves. But the 'authorities' have rushed through the Act assuming they know the best. When practical problems such as those mentioned above arise in course of the implementation of the Act, the Centre chooses not to hear and puts the entire responsibility on the State Government, local government and the school authorities.

Those who engineered the Act went on the assumption that school authorities, teachers and even parents are inimical to children and throw unnecessary stress on them. All disciplinary procedures are a taboo under the Act. Education of children of course has to be joyful and creative experience for children. But studious habits and discipline should be inculcated from childhood. If these are given a go by, the students will suffer in later life and society will degenerate.

The Act has laid down high standard of infrastructure facilities for schools like well appointed, building, class rooms, office rooms, toilets, ramps for disabled students, furniture, drinking water facility, playground with boundary wall etc. as well student-teacher ratio (less than 30 at primary level and 35 for secondary). The authorities accuse the private schools of amassing money starving their schools of necessary infrastructure facilities. But they forget that the worst culprits in this respect are government, municipal and local board schools. In fact, the Authorities instead of imposing the Act should have first made adequate provisions for the schools. That would have been a sound beginning of educational reform. But the Government wants only 'credit' for their achievements and not real reform. In a recent survey in Pune it was found that 95% of schools in Pune District do not comply with the ten infrastructure parameters under RTE Act.

There is no adequate administrative machinery in the education department to deal with the various provisions of the Act and monitor their implementation.

V. Right to Employment

The State of Maharashtra was a pioneer in introducing the scheme of guarantee of employment on public works in rural areas. The scheme was at the initiative of late Shri. V.S. Page, a prominent politician, who became the Speaker of Maharashtra State Assembly. The scheme provided employment in rural areas and was widely appreciated. Other states were free to follow the example of Maharashtra. But the UPA in government overlook them by introducing the Mahatma Gandhi Rural Employment Guarantee Act 2005 in (MG NAREGA) promising 100 days work each year to every rural household. It was stipulated that wage payments should be made within 15 days of work. It was believed that the scheme was responsible, to a great extent in bringing the Congress back to power with a decisive mandate in 2009 general elections and hence was looked upon as a key welfare legislation.

One flaw noticed in course of the implementation of the Act was delay in payment of wages. Wages amounting to Rs. 2500/- 25% of wage payment across the country have been delayed over 15 days. Of this Rs. 125/- crore, day of payment were delayed for more than 90 days. The Union Minister for Rural Development Shri. Jayram Ramesh has proposed amendment to the Act according to which if the payment is not make within the stipulated period a compensation at the rate of ¼ to ½ of total wages (depending on number of days) will be given to the beneficiary. The State will have to take responsibility of their functionaries and in case of delay at any step, the compensation amount will be recovered from the responsible functionary agency.

This is another example of the Union Government introducing into a scheme, that too through legislation, which legitimately belongs to the state government and for whose implementation the Union Government is entirely dependant on the state machinery of administration. The states, many of which are run by the 'opposition' parties, rightly object to such initiative by the Central Government as intrusion into the sphere of the state and thus inconsistent with the constitutional principle of federalism.

It is also doubtful whether a law was needed in a matter which, is no more than just one scheme for administrative action as a part of the programme of rural development.

One criticism of the implementation of the Act was poor quality of assets created. This was bound to happen when employment guarantee schemes were not integrated with rural development programmes as a whole. The Union Government now wants linking of the NAREGA with Pradhan Mantri Gram Sadak Yojana (PMASCY) as well as with programme of construction of rural godowns even provision of public toilets.

The weakness in the implementation of the scheme is its poor administrative infrastructure. The existing administrative infrastructure was found to be inadequate and unable to ensure good quality progress and timely payment of wages. The scheme provides for only 6% of the scheme for administrative expenses which has been found inadequate.

Maintenance of assets created under the scheme also leaves much to be discard. This is what happens when a separate employment scheme is tagged on to the regular programmes of rural development.

It could be argued that expansion of a comprehensive Rural Development programme would generate more income and employment. A separate scheme of emplyment on rural works as hardly appropriate.

The academicians V.M. Dandekar and Neelkant Rathi in the path breaking book on Poverty in India had recommended such a scheme for the poor. They had recommend a works programme to generate employment, since unemployment and under employment widely prevailed in rural areas. But even at that time a view was held that focus should be on a comprehensive programmes of agricultural and rural development which would generate income and employment on a sustainable basis. A separate ad-hoc works programme hardly goes with a long term approach and process of development.

NAREGA, it is a argued, has created problems for agricultural economy by artificially jacking up wage rates and making it difficult to get labour since it is diverted to easy work under Narega scheme. On the other hand, some activists have pressed for increase in wage rate under NAREGA scheme applying the provisions of Minimum Wages Act.

There have been complaints of large scale leakages and corruption in the implementation of the NAREGA programme. These have not been adequately dealt with.

VI. Right to Food Security

The idea of subsidized distribution of food especially for disadvanged i.e. those below the poverty line has been there since the days of scarcity of food during world war II, when a system of rationing of food grains at less than market level prices was introduced. The rationing system was, from the beginning, marked by corruption in the form of bogus ration cards and diversion of food meant for public distribution to market which allowed the shopkeepers to profiteer at the cost of the common man. In early days after independence when food was scarce, the public distribution system, despite its shortcomings and defects, continued. However, after India started producing sufficient and even surplus food grains, raison detre for distribution through rationing did not exist. Yet in the name of welfare, public distribution continued for several years. Some state like Tamil Nadu did well in establishing public distribution system run on an enduring basis. In more recent time. Dr. Raman Singh, Chief Minister of Chattisgarh earned the name of 'Chavalwala baba' for a successful scheme of rice distribution specially for the tribal areas.

However, superseding the initiative of several State Governments, the Union Government in order to take credit decided to give Right to Food Security to people through legislation. Though this was an election promise of the ruling Congress Party given in 2004 and again in 2009 when it came to power, it took concrete steps only in 2013 to introduce food security as right to people. It tried to rush through in ordinance just before Parliament was scheduled to meet which met with wide criticism. The Food Security Bill was then brought before Parliament on a priority basis. Several Chief Ministers specially Narendra Modi, Gujrat Chief Mnister wrote to Prime Minister pointing out several deficiencies in the bill and asking the Prime Minister to call for a meeting of the Chief Ministers before the matter was finalized by Parliament. This was an eminently reasonable suggestion since public distribution was always handled by the State Governments. But the suggestion did not prevail and the Bill was placed before Parliament. The BJP, the opposition party having criticized the bill as vote security (not food security bill), did not oppose the bill which was unanimously passed.

The Bill sought to provide 5 Kg of food grains, per person per month covering 75% of rural population and 50% of urban population i.e. 67% of India's total population, wheat at Rs. 2 per Kg and. Coarse Gram at Rs. 1/- per Kg. and Rice at Rs. 3/- per kg.

Prime Minister described the measure as an example of UPA Governments people oriented approach of Government UPA Chairperson Sonia Gandhi made her rare participation in the debate making an impassioned plea for support of opposition. She dismissed the problems of finding resources for the scheme stating that it was the business of Government to raise needed resources. The opposition fell in line without raising amendment. Both government and opposition had to face 2014 Lok Sabha elections in March !

However, in Parliament the members of opposition as well as economist like Ashok Gulati raised several points regarding inadequacies of the Bill (1) The scope of the bill in terms of coverage of population provided for, was less than 90% coverage in Chattisgarh. Some members pressed for universal coverage. (2) 5 Kg per person per month was inadequate. The average consumption of cereals in the country is 10.7 Kg. That means consumers will have to go the market for more than haft their needs, (3) 5 Kg cereals per person cannot solve health and nutrition problems. Clean drinking water, better sanitation and nutritious items of food like milk, fruits, vegetables, oil, eggs, fish and meat are also essential. All these food items will have to brought from the open market. (4) The cost of ensuring food security would place enormous fiscal burden on an economy already suffering from huge fiscal deficit. The food subsidy already high, will increase by Rs. 33,000 crores additional outlay. There will also be additional financial burden on the states for implementing the scheme. (5) Rising fiscal deficit will add to inflationary spiral which has already gone out of control making life miserable for the common man. (6) Administrative problems involved in implementation of the scheme are not properly spelt out. Government efforts to procure and store food grains required under the scheme would need to be augmented. The implementation of the scheme would depend on distribution system which mainly consists of private retail trade. Except in a few states, effective public distribution system does not exist. Entrusting food security to such a system would lead to leakages and corruption.

Accordingly to Global Hunger Index of the World, hungry people were estimated at 842 million of which 210 million are in India. No doubt food security for India's hungry is essential. But it is doubtful whether the Food Security Act will adequately meet the problem.

VII. Conclusion

The various rights 'conferred' by the Congress Government were clearly aimed at securing political gains. The Prime Minister and the President of the Congress Party, buoyed by its record of conferring rights on people, recently claimed that the Congress would come back to power for the third time, winning the 2014 Lok Sabha elections. There confidence received a set back when the Congress made a poor show in recent Assembly elections, where it lost Rajasthan rejected after a landslide victory for BJP and could not snatch back Madhya Pradesh and Chhattisgarh. In national capital it could not even cross a single digit number. Obviously the common people do not feel benefitted by 'right'. On the other hand corruption and inflation seem to have taken a heavy toll of their daily lives.

Merely putting rights on the statute book does not satisfy the people. The rights should actually be enjoyed in daily lives. That requires effective implementation of laws regarding the so called 'rights' conferred by the Government on the people.

Post script – Conferring rights on people did not enable UPA to come back to power; to the contrary, Congress sunk to lowest ever number of 44 seats in Parliament – not even 10% of seats required for it recognition as the opposition party. The New Prime Minister, heading the NDA Government spoke in sarcastic tone about the NAREGA but was compelled to provide larger financial provisions for the programme in the face of rural unemployment and agriculture distress. The other rights regarding education, information and food also remained in tact.

CO-OPERATIVES - III

Chapter - 1

What is Co-operation? Objectives, Methods and Performance

Co-operation is an economic organization of individuals who get together in a participative process for arranging performance of services to meet their felt needs. These needs may vary. Thus, consumers may get together to provide for themselves goods and services to meet their family needs. Farmers may get together for arranging the sale of their agricultural products or for the supply of inputs like seeds and fertilizers needed for agricultural business. Industrial workers may get together to provide employment for themselves by organising the production or manufacturing of goods and services. People in need of residential accommodation may get together in a housing co-operative to acquire sites and build houses. The people in need of credit at times of need – whether farmers or urban middle class people or industrial workers may come together to form a credit co-operative where they deposit their savings arising out of thrift and borrow at times of need, out of the resources of that society.

Objectives

The basic objective of all these co-operative is the same viz. to provide services through self-help and mutual-help. The co-operative form of organization eliminates exploitation of the consumer by the trader, the worker by the employer, the borrower by the lender and the tenant by the landlord. Thus, the consumer is both the seller and the buyer. The Consumer Society procures goods and services in the market as at a low price as possible and makes them available at fair price to the members since both the buyer and the seller are the same. There is no scope for middle man's profit. If the services are rendered in an efficient manner, the co-operative through the co-operative method is able to obtain goods and services and supply them at a lower rate than in the market because of the elimination of the margin between the seller's price and the buyers's price. In the same manner when the farmer procures seeds, fertilizers and pesticides, the co-operative form of organization enables him to obtain good quality seeds and fertilizers at a lower price than what would be otherwise available from the dealers in seeds and fertilizers. Similarly the farmer's marketing association would be able to make it possible for the farmers to get much better price for their products than if they were to sell them through the Dalals and agents in the market who would be interested to pay the farmer as low price as possible as and sell it as high a rate as possible to the purchaser of the agricultural products. Thus, the private enterprise creates a wide gap between the producers's price and the consumer's price. It is well known that while the farmers get very unreasonably low price for vegetables, fruits, etc. the consumers in the urban areas pay through their noses.

Similarly the sugar factories and dairy co-operatives by making the farmers also the industrialists are able to provide a price for sugarcane or mil which the private manufacturer would never give. Thus, it is the co-operative which is able to give a better price for sugarcane or milk to the farmers as the case may be.

In a housing co-operative the landlord and the tenant are the same and there is no scope for charging of excessive rent by the landlord to the tenants.

It is this non-exploitative element of business that constitutes the main rationale of the co-opereatie form of organization from the social point of view. It is this character of co-operative form of organization that makes it particularly beneficial to the small man whether small farmer, the small consumer or the individual worker who has nothing but his labour to sell. That is why co-operative is rightly called the 'shield of the weak and not the sword of the strong'.

The application of the principle of co-operation amongst co-operative would make it possible for linking up farmers's co-operative with consumer co-operatives or industrial co-operatives. Since such links are also to be developed on the non-exploitative basis it would be possible to develop through vertically and horizontally lined co-operatives, a non-acquisitive and non-exploitative economic order. If cooperation among co-operatives is fully developed, it would pave the way for achieving the dream of all co-operators viz. the establishment of a 'co-operative commonwealth'. India has developed a variety of co-operatives in different sectors. But since the principle of 'cooperation among co-operatives' is not developed, we have still a long way to go to attain the dream of 'co-operative commonwealth'.

Method

Co-operation is an economic democracy. Democracy is cardinal principle of co-operation. Co-operation method is, therefore, the democratic method. Co-operation is not just the collection of capital. It is an association of human beings. It is because of this basic principle of co-operation that the decision making process is co-operative has to be democratic. Education is another principle of co-operation and hence the co-operative methods have to be educative.

The co-operative democracy derives its authority from the Central Body of members. The Board of Directors or the Committee of Management of a co-operative is responsible for the day-to-day management. But it is answerable to the General Body and must report. General Body its performance. The General body also approves the budget and the annual programme. The audited accounts of the society are also to be placed before the General Body. Very often the General Body degenerated into rituals. Members do not attend the meetings. The Board of Directors does not consider it necessary to place all the facts concerning performance of the society before the General Body. This kind of working falls short of the co-operative method of working explained above.

Performance

It is often said that the performance of the co-operative enterprise cannot be equal to that of a private enterprise. That this is fallacious statement is seen from the fact that amongst the fertilizing manufacturing enterprises in the country the co-operatives viz. IFFCO and ISPC are considered to be the most efficient; there plant utilization has been even above 100 percent. These two enterprises have generated surpluses much bigger than fertilizers enterprises in the public sector. Criteria for performance include optimum utilization of resources, minimization of cost per unit of production, or maximization of returns per unit of investment. It is necessary for a co-operative also to have high performance with reference to these criteria. To be sure these are not the only criteria for judging the performance of the co-operatives because the co-operatives fulfill broader social objectives as well. The benefit of co-operatives accrue to the weaker sections of the society. They also serve social purposes. For example, the sugar factories as well as the co-operative dairies have done a great deal for developing backward rural areas in which they are located by providing a variety of services including those in the field of education and health. They have created rural entrepreneurship and have had considerable spreads-affect and economic diversification.

The economic and social performance of co-operatives would be of a high order if they are properly managed. It is, therefore, extremely important that the Managers and staff of the co-operatives are of a high caliber. They should be selected on the basis of their qualifications and experience and they would be given an opportunity to act in the most efficient manner. In some co-operatives there is undue interference by members of the Board of Directors. In such cases, the work of the Managers leaves much to be desired.

Conclusion

The first five year plan observed that the co-operative sector gives a sense of direction, balance and value to the national economy. At the present time when there is a wave of marketisation and privatization, it is necessary to bear in mind this statement regarding the place of the co-operation in our five year plans. Efficient and socially oriented co-operative can give great strength to the economic progress of our country, particularly to the progress of the disadvantaged sections of the society. There are many types of co-operatives of the weaker sections which have yet to make much headway. Thus, the labour contract co-operatives of workers can have a great role. They can be used for construction of major projects without the involvement of exploitative contractor system. Similarly where private enterprises or public enterprises become sick, they should be taken over and run efficiently by workers co-operatives with our causing retrenchment or unemployment.

Chapter - 2

Should Multi-State Co-operatives be Registered as Companies Under the Companies Act?

Dr. V. Kurien, Chairman, National Dairy Development Board, has submitted a proposal to the Government of India for the amendment of the Indian Companies Act for facilitating establishment of Multi-State Co-operative Companies.

The Government of India has elicited the views of the National Co-operative Union and the State Co-operative on the proposal. The proposal also came up for discussion at the meeting of the General Council of the National Co-operative Union of India held on 27th December, 1992, as also the later at the XII National Co-operative Congress which concluded on 20th March, 1993. However, at the meeting of the Congress, there was no scope for detailed discussion on the proposal to consider and weigh the pros and cons and arrive at a consensus.

The rationale for the proposal is briefly as follows

The Co-operative Act as it exists in most of the states, was devised at a time where co-operatives were small and local, and dealing with very limited functions of agricultural credit. Today, very large co-operative engaged in highly sophisticated economic functions extending over different states and even the export market have come into existence.

The current Co-operative Societies Act is not congenial for the functioning of technologically oriented enterprises with advanced economic functions in a competitive environment, with large dimension of activities extending beyond the boundaries of the State and even the nation as a whole.

In the context of the current new economic liberalization policy, co-operatives of a large size engaged in Multi-State business and export trade are called upon to compete effectively.

In the wake of the new economic policy of liberalization, the Government has removed the shackles on private companies. Large cooperative, however, still suffer from the restrictions of the current Co-operative Act in force in different states. The proposal for a more liberal co-operative law as suggested by the Committee set up by the Planning Commission has not yet been finalized. Indeed most states have been reluctant to go in the direction. Hence, it is proposed that the large multi-state co-operatives engaged in complex economic functions may be registered as co-operative companies. Among these large co-operatives would be the Federal co-operatives such as the State Co-operative Marketing Federations and NAFED or large Multi-state co-operative like IFFCO and KRIBHCO (both fertilizer manufacturing enterprises in the co-operative sector). The National Engineering Co-operative engaged in the manufacturing of sugar plants and machinery also falls in the same category. Apart from providing such machinery for domestic enterprises, it is exporting such machinery to South-East Asia, SAARC and African countries.

While the need for removing the shackles of co-operatives in the text of the new economic policy is to be appreciated, it is necessary to take care that the remedy proposed would not be worsen than the disease.

I am afraid that the proposal to bring large Multi-State Co-operatives within the ambit of the Company Act, would be the case of that sort.

Firstly, it would immediately create a divide within the co-operative fold. While large co-operatives already successful in their business, using modern management practices will get the nomenclature of a company, a large majority of the co-operatives serving the small man whether the small or marginal farmers, or artisans, or fishermen, or urban consumers, or householders would be left to work under the traditional co-operative law. It is they indeed, who need support and encouragement to develop on the lines of modern business organizations. With large successful co-operative becoming companies, the impression already prevalent that the word 'co-operative is synonymous with backward business, will only get confirmed.

It is a characteristic feature of the co-operative business, that various co-operatives form a part of an integrated structure with vertical and horizontal links. Cooperation amongst co-operatives has been recognized as a principle of cooperation. These concepts of integrated functioning and cooperation amongst co-operatives will receive a big setback when successful co-operatives with Multi State jurisdiction assume the company form of organization. For example, even though IFFCO and KRIBHCO are large size co-operatives engaged in business, their membership extends even to the primary credit co-operatives in rural areas. The whole objective of setting up a fertilizer co-operatives in the co-operative sector was to serve the farmers organised in vast rural areas through primary cooperatives. These links may get snapped if large majority of co-operatives are in primary sector, but the large co-operatives who are expected to serve in the co-operative sector are organised as companies. Similarly, NAFED may be engaged in export trade, but the entire business of export trade has to be linked with the generation of surplus as produced by the farmers who are members of credit and marketing co-operatives at the primary level. The division within the co-operative fold is fraught with grave consequences detrimental to the development of the co-operative movement as an integrated movement.

As it is, the large co-operatives have a tendency to grow on capitalistic lines undertaking profitable business through purely commercial operations without any mutual links with the primary base of the cooperatives. Such commercial operations without co-operative connections, would not really serve the co-operative cause. The large co-operatives registered as companies will soon lose their co-operative identity and character and work purely like private enterprises with profit maximization as the sole objective of business. They will be governed more by interest of the 'shareholders' than 'members'; they will be concerned more with return on capital than dividend on participation in transactions. The distinct nature of co-operative form of organization and indeed the co-operatives character of the enterprise will itself be lost in the framework of the Company Law.

It is, therefore, important that the large multi-state co-operatives retain their co-operative identity and have organic links, horizontal and vertical, with other co-operatives and in that process land leadership and strength to the entire co-operative structure.

The proper course of action, therefore, is to take steps for radical change in the co-operative Law on the lines suggested by the Committee of the Planning Commission. The Committee on co-operatives Law and Finance appointed by the Government of Maharashtra, under my chairmanship, had also proposed radical change in co-operative law consistent with the work of co-operatives as autonomous organizations. The policy of liberalization is a right opportunity for the co-operative movement to strive for its own liberalization by insisting on a simplified framework of co-operative Law such as the one proposed by the Committee of the Planning Commission. True in Sweden, the co-operatives work not under the co-operatives Law, but a general simple law relating to any economic organization because they do not have a separate co-operative Law. India has a tradition of a separate co-operative Law, and all that is required now is to drastically simplify this law as recommended by all the expert opinion on the subject.

If the State Governments do not agree to these changes, it is high time that such change is borught about through constitutional amendment. If through such an amendment, Panchayati Raj institutions have become a part of the Constitution today, there is no reason why co-operatives also should not find place in the constitutional polity. We would confer the status of autonomous economic organizations on the co-operatives in the country. If in the current economic crisis co-operatives survive, as autonomous economic organizations, then they are likely to succeed and thrive.

Chapter - 3

Dr. Ambedkar's Philosophy and the Principles of Co-operation

Dr. B.R. Ambedkar was an economist, a political scientist, a lawyer and an educationist, above all, was rebel against an unjust social order.

Born in a Mahar family in Maharashtra in indigent circumstances, thanks to financial support extended by the benevolent Sayaji Rao Gaikwar of Baroda, he reached the highest level of academic achievement in the foremost institutions of higher learning in U.K. and U.S.A. and yet on return to his own country, young Ambedkar was at the receiving end of the same social disabilities and humliliations which were the lot of the untouchablities in India for centuries. Not only did Dr. Ambedkar rebel against such treatment but he made his life's mission to liberate his people from all the unjust social order. The culmination came with the great moment at which he led hid people from the fold of the orthodox Hinduism into Buddhism which Dr. Ambedkar felt, embodies a moral order based on humanism.

The basic principles of this moral order, Dr. Ambedkar has enshrined in the preamble of the Constitution of India which he had privilege of shaping in his capacity as a Chairman of Drafting Committee. These were justice, social, economic and political, liberty of thought, expression, faith, belief and worship, equality of status and opportunity and fraternity between all the members of the society.

In his address to the Constituent Assembly Dr. Ambedkar had emphasized that all these basic values were interconnected. Thus, there could be no liberty without equality, but equality cannot survive without liberty, justice could only be based on liberty and equality, finally, there could be no fraternity among the people without liberty, equality and social justice.

Dr. Ambedkar was not a co-operator in any formal sense of the term. And yet it in obvious that there is kinship between Ambedkar's philosophy and the principles of co-operation. Thus, the first cooperation principles is of democracy. Democracy and liberty are inseparable. Then comes equality. No person could be excluded from co-operative membership on the basis of caste, creed and community. The admission of members to co-operative is thus based on the principle of equality. Unlike a Joint Stock Company where voting strength is related to ownership of share capital and therefore inevitably implies inequality based on ownership of wealth and resourses, the voting in a co-operative society is based on the principle of 'one member, one vote'. Dr. Ambedkar's concept of fraternity is reflected in the co-operative philosophy of self help and mutual help. By helpint each other, all members of co-operative hope to reach a higher level of living. Co-operatiion stands for justice because the benefit from the co-operative enterprise are not in proportion to the ownership of share capital but in proportion to participation.

The co-operative movement can derive great moral strength from the principles and phiolosophy of Dr. Ambedkar.

Chapter - 4

Co-operation for a Better World and Better India

The declaration of the year 2012 as 'co-operative year' is an appropriate opportunity for co-operators in India to make a critical appraisal of the state of co-operative movement in India and plan future course of action on the theme 'Co-operation enterprises Build a better world'.

The very birth of co-operative movement in the world was for creating a better world for the weaker sections of society who were not getting a fair deal in the new economic and social order ushered in by the industrial revolution and its concomitant, the capitalistic economy. Power and capacity to direct was concentrated in the hands of a few capitalists while the workers in factories, where was concentrated the production process with new machines and technology, were getting a raw deal in the shape of long hours of work, low wages, poor working conditions ands various other forms of exploitation. The industrial revolution first came to Britain during 1760 to 1820 and slowly spread to other countries in Europe, US and later to Japan and later to other Asian and African counrties. The workers organised themselves in Trade Unions to fight for their rights and improve their wages and working conditions. The other form of organisation which was aimed at bettering their livelihood and get out of the clutches of capitalistic exploitation was co-operation. The workers were forced to buy at higher prices the wherewithals of life from the 'truck shops' run by the factory owners. The workers in Rochdale in Lacashire in North England came together and decided to set up their own consumer co-operatives where they could get essential articles of good quality at fair prices. Through intensive discussions and deliberations, they formulated the principles governing the practices of their co-operative enterprises which over year were refined and accepted by the co-operative movement all over the world viz. democratic member control, open membership (open to all those who are in need and are prepared to fulfill those needs through participation in co-operative action), limited interest on capital and distribution of dividend in proportion to participation, member education and co-operation amongst co-operatives These principles were adopted by co-operatives all over he world.

Another form of co-operatives organised by workers were industrial co-operatives where workers were themselves owners of enterprises and worked them on the basis of co-operative principles. The industrialist turned philanthropist, Robert Owen established co-operative community of his workers in England and spread the gospel to USA.

Another situation where co-operative organisations came to rescue was when farmers in Prussia were emancipated from the stranglehold of landlords known as Junkers in Prussia in the erstwhile feudal order. The emancipated farmers were in need of finance hitherto supplied by landlords even though at heavy interest and with several condition attached. Raiffeisen, a burgomaster in Prussia, took the lead in organising farmers co-operative credit societies which worked successfully. This Roiteison model provided a pattern for co-opearative credit institutions in India and other Asian countries.

A further evolution of co-operative credit institutions took place when co-operative credit was linked to co-operative supplies for agricultural business eg. seeds, fertilisers and insecticides, co-operative marketing and co-operative processing.

The co-operative movement spread to other countries in Europe like Denmark (known for dairy co-operatives), Sweden (known for consumer co-operatives), other countries in Asia like Japan (agricultural co-operatives) and Israel (collective farming). Thus, co-operative movement became a world movement.

The co-operative organisations in India were setup during the British rule itself. Deccan Agricultural riots of 1870 and 1880 as a consequence of the farmers suffering from exploitative money lending by Savkars (money lenders). Farmers attacked them and burned their books. The British regime looked for some way of providing relief to farmers. They passed laws to control the activities of money lenders. They sent Sir Frederick Nicholson to Germany to study the workers of co-operative credit institutions. He came back with the message – 'Find out, Raiffeison in Indian villages'. His message became the basis of co-operative evolution in India.

After independence co-operatives got a boost. The first Prime Minister of free India Jawaharlal Nehru wanted to 'Convulse India with co-operation' and making co-operative a basic rural institution. The Rural Credit Survey Committee set up by Reserve Bank of India in 1981 recommended a three tier system of co-operative institutions and a crop loan scheme linking credit with marketing and processing. It provided the blue print for rapid co-operative development in the rural economy in post-independence India. The same approach was successfully accepted in the field of dairies. The Amul Dairy under the leadership of the late Kurian was a conspicuous success and became a model for replication. Co-operatives were also found useful in the field of housing for lower and middle income groups. Apex institutions like NABARD and NCDC were set up to give shrift support to agricultural co-operative credit and marketing and processing.

In all this evolution of co-operative principles practices and institutions were basic values such as 'selfhelp and mutual help', 'each for all and all for each', simplicity and elimination of exploitation in all forms.

II – Defects in co-operation

The rapid revolution of co-operation over three or four decades of planning, was accompanied by several weaknesses entering into the co-operative system. The policy of 'massive state participation was recommended by the 'Rural Credit Survey Committee'. Their argument was that co-operatives of the weak have no chance to survive and succeed against the entrenched landlords, money lenders and traders in the rural economy without massive state support - both policy support and financial support. While state support did help to accelerate the growth of co-operatives, it led over years to 'governmentalisation' and 'politicisation of the co-operative movement and its concomitant fall in management standards – leading to mismanagement and even corruption. Co-operative office bearers have forgotten the simple life style of pioneers like Vaikunth Mehta/ They live like 'co-operative barons'. Nor is their any proper understanding of co-operative principles and values which distinguish co-operative enterprises from capitalist enterprises. There are no intellectual leaders of the stature of Prof. D.R. Gadgil. As a result co-operative movement has lost its ideological and intellectual foundations. Mahatma Gandhi called co-operative 'a moral movement'. It is no longer so.

III – Effect of Policy of liberalisation

While co-operative movement has fallen from the edifice of high values, it has also lost the policy support from government from 1991 onwards. Government have vigourously followed the policy of marketisation, privatization and liberalisation. Co-operative found no place in this new policy. The so called 'co-operative leaders' have themselves come under the influence of the new policy. They do not feel concerned that major co-operative institutions like State Co-operative Banks and District Co-operative Banks built over yerars through sustained effort have fallen on evil days and co-operative sugar factories, the pride of co-operative movement in

Maharashtra have fallen sick and are getting privatised. It is sad to see the so called co-operative leaders themselves taking initiatives in privatising co-operative sugar factories.

The new policy of liberalisation, privatisation and globalisation led to acute disparities between rural and urban areas and reckless exploitation of natural resources like land, minerals, forests and spectrum space in the interest of rapacious businessmen and builders joining hand with corrupt politicians in power and venal civil servants. This development is not in national interest. More than 2,00,000 farmers have committed suicides during the era of liberalization. Co-operative credit and marketing institutions have failed to come to their rescue. The money lender has come back on the rural scene with the support of politicians in power. Government packages of help has proved ineffective. There has been a relentless spiral of inflation which has hit hard the common man. Instead of building up a network of co-operative institutions in the field of agricultural credit, marketing, storage processing and consumer distribution, Government is looking to entry of multinationals in retail trade to deal with the problems of farmers and consumers. The proposal met with stiff resistance.

IV – Plan for rejuvenation

If co-operative movement has to be rescued from its desperate straits and reconstruct its position in national economy, a major effort for rejuvenation of the co-operative movement is called for, on the twin basis of (a) elimination of leadership and management shortcomings and (b) a forward looking plan for its all round development without state support. A big educational and organisational effort is needed in the direction. The co-operative movement should make an earnest effort to work out a plan and programme of action for the rejuvenation of the co-operative movement. The plan should include changes in (1) Co-operative law (2) Co-operative policy (3) Co-operative organisation and (4) Co-operative management and leadership.

Co-operatives often complain about excessively restrictive provisions in co-operative law (these keep on increasing) which intrude on the autonomous functioning of the co-operatives. They forget that co-operatives often themselves invite such restrictive provisions by their malfunctioning. Co-operative laws are passed by the state legislatives and enforced by officials of co-operative department. With the passing of the 97th amendment of the Constitution made on January 12, 2012 (there was hardly any informed discussion in Parliament on this amendment nor much in the states), the State Laws will have to be amended by the legislative Assembly to fall in line with the provisions of the 97th amendment. This should finally settle the problem of the restrictive provisions of law.

But far more intractable problem is the political domination of the co-operative institutions, 'Political neutrality' is or ought to be a principle of co-operation. Here in India, specially in Maharashtra co-operatives are major instruments in the hands of politicians and and are looked upon as a stepping stone to rising political career. This makes co-peratives victims of political fluctuations and warfares. When the Chief Minister of Maharashtra superseeded the State Co-operative Bank, it was considered an affront to the N.C.P. the alliance partner in its Government.

The federal structure of co-operatives requires higher tiers to lend support the tiers below. Here each tier goes about in its way and vertical linkages are lost. Nor are there horizontal links leading to 'co-operative always co-operatives' which is also a principle of co-operation. As a result of absence of vertical and horizontal links, co-operative organisation as a whole is weakened and cannot fulfill its potential.

The new policy of liberlisation and globalisation initiated in India in 1991 has completely by- passed the co-operatives. 'Amul' had strikingly shown how farmers can be organised through co-operative and get high returns to their milk delivered to co-operative. But instead replicating that in other states and for other crops like fruits and vegetables, the present Government expects the multinationals like Walmarts and Tescos who are invited to enter into retail distribution in to do so. If there is not enough godown and storage capacity in rural India, it is a sad commentary on the successive Five Year Plans and their achievements.

Let us hope that in the International Year of Co-operative we will give thorough look at co-operative law, organisation, management and leadership and bring about root and branch changes.

ECONOMICS - IV

Chapter - 1

Restructuring of The Indian Economy : Penumbra of Ambiguity

The Finance Minister has made statements on his economic reforms – both on the floor of the Parliament and in the recent Congress Session at Tirupati. These have been characterized, not without reason, as examples of double-think and double-talk. Certainly, the Finance Minister has the responsibility to explain the rationale of his economic reforms to the nation, and to obtain for it as a wide measure of agreement as possible in all sections of the society. But this cannot be accomplished by projecting partisan or one sided versions nor by creating ideological ambiguities which might well serve to confound rather than clarify.

In the first instance, the Government should not be in a hurry in claming success for the new economic reforms. To be sure, the Government has gained temporary reprieve and has been able to save the country from external bankruptcy. But at the same time, the Government must make the entire nation realise that the real task only lies ahead because it is yet to be accomplished. The foreign exchange reserves which had reached all time low of Rs. 2,300 crores in June, 1991 have no doubt climbed to Rs. 15,000 crores. But this has been accomplished by increasing India's debt from $ 70 billion to $80 billions. This would only increase the liability of the nation in the years to come. Nobody can vouchsafe for the nation's ability to service or repay the huge debt in the years to come with its present level of economic performance. The real challenges before the nation is whether the nation's capacity to repay such a heavy burden of external debt could be built up in the years to come. This would be the crucial test of the new economic policies.

In meeting this grave challenge, we must understand why the foreign exchange crisis in June 1991 assumed such serious proportions that resort had to be had to the transfer of gold from the vaults of the Reserve Bank of India to the Vaults of Bank of England and Banks in Zurich. Economist I.G. Patel described this event as a matter of shame. This was followed by a savage compression of imports by the Reserve Bank imposing 200% cash margin for foreign exchange required imports. The third step was the devaluation of Indian rupee by more than 20% in two stages.

While emergency measures had to be taken by the Government to stall imminent bankruptcy, the bankruptcy itself was building up for quite sometime in the eighties and was the result of policy changes introduced in the second half of the last decade. In a hurry to take India in the 21st Century, the past policy of economic self-reliance based on import substitution was abandoned in favour of export led growth. The new policy encouraged imports in order to promote exports. The import of capital goods, electronics and synthetic goods led to the rapid rise in imports from Rs. 14,000 crores in 1984-85 to Rs. 35,000 crores in 1989-90. While imports increased by 21%, exports increased only by 17%. This was inevitably reflected in the soaring trade deficit of Rs. 7700 crores in 1889-90 and Rs. 10,600 crores in 1990-91. This was against the background of cumulative external debt of $ 70 billion and debt service ratio of Rs. 27%.

Faced with such a situation, instead of introducing financial disciplines and reducing indebtedness, the Government resorted to short term commercial borrowings at heavy rates of interest to service debt and bridge the gap between borowing and repayment of outstanding debt. This led to a massive increase of private crudit from $330 million in 1970 to $ 21000 million in 1999 and $ 54000 million in 1991. For 40 years India was living beyond its means by getting aid on concessional terms but it was only in 1980s that India began to rely on concessional loans and NRI to finance over consumption.

During 1991, while commercial borrowing was of the order of Rs. 3050, serving of debt was of the order of Rs. 4,600 crores i.e. a negative balance of Rs. 956 crores. This was a sure sign that the country was indeed caught in a debt trap.

Despite this history, instead of candidly admitting facts, an attempt to place the entire burden of responsibility of crisis on the government of the opposition parties may appear to be only a political exercise. Such an approach would not enable the nation to draw a proper lesson from the past experience.

The change in our policy from import substitution to export promotion was based on the facile assumption that increased imports by themselves would lead to adequate increase in exports. We do not know that the latter would depend on competitive prices of our products, our ability to satisfy a demanding and discriminating consumer market of cash rich – economies requiring high uniform quality and timely deliveries, not to mention our ability to counter the lobbies even in these markets in favour of domestic producers, despite their preachings of benefits of free market economy to the developing countries.

Nor is it correct to assume in a facile manner that devaluation by itself would lead to improvement in the trade balance. Already, the export price advantage of devaluation has been washed away by increasing domestic prices. All that has resulted from devaluation is that our country is required to pay more in terms of rupees for all its imports of essential commodities like petroleum and edible oil, further fuelling the fires of inflation.

It has also been realized that the external debt crisis moves in a tandem with the internal debt crisis caused by phenomenal increase in deficit financing and public debt. The latter again is the result of economic profligacy in the latter half of the last decade. Between 1983-84 and 1990-91, the gap between government expenditure and current revenue increased annually by 16.2%. Most governmental expenditure came under non-development heads. In 1990-91, 72% of the Central Government expenditure of Rs. 106,717 crores was spent on non-plan heads. The budget deficit during 1983-84 was of the order of only Rs. 1470 crores. It increased to Rs. 3745 crores in 1984-85 and to whopping deficit of Rs. 10,982 crores in 1989-90 and to Rs. 11,430 crores in 1990-91. The growth in inflexible commitments to interest payment, defence expenditure and subsidies were given as the main reasons for increase in deficit financing. The interest payment rose by 21.7% annually, defence by 14.2% and subsidies by 21.2% reaching by 1990-91 to Rs. 21.850 crores. Rs. 15.750 crores and Rs. 12,121 crores respectively. The increasing interest payment reflected rapid increase in domestic public debt which reached 55% of Gross Domestic products.

The large fiscal imbalance has led to excessive liquidity in the economy. This has inevitably generated severe inflationary pressure, leading to double digit inflation.

The Finance Minister claims that the fiscal deficit has been reduced from 8.3% to 6.5%. but is not quite clear how this has been accomplished. No doubt, abolition of export subsidy as also reduction in fertilizer subsidies has provided substantial savings in public expenditure. But while the Finance Minister has appealed to the public to tighten the belt, there has been no major attempt to do this in Government itself. Over the years, many white elephants and holy cows have flourished in the domain of public expenditure in India. The government has been carrying the burden of expenditure due to organizational obsolesce. The government must learn from what Mrs. Margaret Thatcher did in U.K. to reduce public expenditure. She undertook an extensive exercise of 'value for money analysis throughout the entire a gamut of public expenditure. Recently, there has been a report on the substantial savings in expenditure of defence established in United Kingdom which nevertheless has not reduced the efficiency, but has served only to enhance it. The Finance Minister has tried to reassure the public employees that economy in public expenditure would not result in retrenchment of staff but only redeployment. But redeployment must be such to improve the productivity and performance of government. Our government would do well to follow the 'scrap and build technique' of Japan, where old organizations in Government which do not serve the purpose any longer or have become dysfunctional are scrapped and replaced by new organizations for performing new tasks which have become relevant in the new context. Here again comprehensive approach is needed. Many organizations in the central government have lost their relevance in the context of the new policy like DGTD, Chief Controller of Imports and Exports, many portions of the departments of Industry and Commerce dealing with licensing and the Planning Commission itself.

In England the unpleasant task of pruning public expenditure was performed by Sir Dennis Rainer, Joint Director of Marks and Spencer. Government of India must find her own agent to undertake this unpleasant but necessary task.

Instead of undertaking such a comprehensive exercise for pruning public expenditure on a rational basis, the Finance Minister, in hurry to bring down deficit from 8.3% of GDP to the predetermined figure of 6.5% of GDP has chopped allocations to 'soft' social sectors like prevention and control of pollution, rural sanitation and water supply, waste land development, promotion of non-conventional energy sources, biomass development etc.

Devaluation and reduction in public expenditure were only the initial measures which have been followed by many others which constitute the new economic policy. These other measures include reduction of the scope of public sector to only 8 areas as against ony 17 so far, elimination of industrial licensing except for a list of 18 items, shift of emphasis of MRTP from controlling the size of investment by large business houses to controlling unfair or monopolistic practices, reform of the financial system, and removal of the clause by which financial institutions could convert their loans into shareholding, automatic approval for foreign technology agreements in a list of high technology areas, automatic approval to import of capital goods where their cost is covered by foreign equity and permission to foreign direct investment up to 51% in a list of high priority industries. These are all the measures for deregulation of industries and the globalisation of the economy.

The Finance Minister asserted on the floor of the Parliament in his reply to the debate on the budget that all the measures which constituted the new economic policy stemmed from the manifesto of the Congress Party rather than the prescriptions of the World Bank and the international Monetary Fund. At the same time, he also stated that India as a founder member of these institutions has a right to approach them during times of stress and when a country avails of financial support of these two institutions they have to accept the conditionality attached to loans given by these institutions. The acceptance of these conditionalities, Government claimed, does not amount to an abridgement of the sovereignty of the country, as alleged by some of the opposition parties. It was also argued that there was nothing wrong in the acceptance of such conditionalities if they were necessary for the economic and financial turn around.

It is now well known that all the recent economic reforms have been based on the 1987 World Bank Report – "Indian industrializing economy in transition", and the November'90 Report "India as strategy on trade reforms". The first report cited above suggested economy wide improvement in efficiency in resources allocation by gradually replacing restrictive, discretionary, opaque, complex and 'difficult to understand and difficult to administer' system of regulatory control and protection with an allocative mechanism that relies on the market system of external and internal competition. This report has also recommended replacement of high tariffs and quantitative restriction on imports with moderate and uniform tariffs. The report conceded that such reforms would not doubt upset marco economic balance and render a significant portion of the domestic industry uncompetitive but the reports assured that the phased implementation of trade reforms and appropriate fiscal and exchange rate policies would assure restoration of macro economic balance. The economic policies of the past had created a situation in which despite high level of investment growth of the industrial sector was disappointing, India's share in the world market was declining, and parts of the industrial sector were inefficient and technologically backward, thanks to the sheltered market in which they functioned. The creation of an dynamic, efficient and internationally competitive industrial sector, the report suggested required replacement of the protective regime with one based on moderate uniform tariff of average of 20% and elimination of quantitative restrictive imports on all items. The report also recommended restructuring of enterprises and removal of impediments to such restructuring. All firms should be allowed to readjust their operations and restrictions on exit and labour displacement should be removed. The report also recommended devaluation of the order of 22%. The report criticized the 'false concept' of self reliance of the past based on import substitution regardless of cost emphasis on heavy industry, protection and control which led to a high cost economy.

The close congruence between the prescriptions of the World Bank and the International Monetary Fund and the new package of economic reforms is evident and yet to deny the connection between the two and a insist on a entirely domestic origin of the new policies would only put in jeopardy the very credibility of the pronouncements of the government. A candid admission of the influence of the World Bank institutions, obviously under the control of only surviving super power, would prepare the nation much better to put the effort required to get the country out of the situation which has made it inevitable for the country to accept the conditionalities.

Of the same category is the insistence at the Congress party is Parliament and at the recent Tirupati Session that the Government has not deviated from the Nehruvian Model, while at the same time abandoning every single component of the model. Nehru, throughout his 17 years of Prime Minister always instated on non-doctrinaire and pragmatic approach to policies, and it is doubtful if, were he to be alive, would follow the 'Nehruvian model'. Nehru himself would have asked the country to change the model if such a change served the national purpose and delivered the goods.

While swearing by the Nehru Model, an impression is created that the Nehruvian model has failed to deliver the goods. This again is not true. As explained above, the present crisis is not the result of following the Nehruvian model. Rather it is result of the abandonment of the model in the late eighties. The Nehruvian model had given the country slow but steady growth based on self-reliance, though in course of its implementation it finally led to the emergence of the 'low growth economy'. But all this was the result of the rigidities of the complex controlled economy. However, the controls were not a necessary part of the Nehruvian model. Controls were only the means and never the objectives.

It is necessary for the country to clearly and dispassionately reflect on what went wrong with the Nehruvian model, and to what extent its various components have or have not served the national purposes. This would be a much better exercise than what is happening today, namely, giving up the essentials of Nehruvian model but swearing by it on the public platforms, all the time.

Nehru wanted development and abolition of poverty through planning in which the state would play a leading role. Nehru did not want the economic fortune of the country to be left to the vicissitudes of the market forces but rather be the result of deliberate and conscious planning for the optimum use of the natural and manpower resources of the country. He felt that such planning resulted in a faster rate of economic growth, its equitable distribution and greater self-reliance. Planning achieves many things which the market cannot. Firstly, planning stands for purposive arrangements of the future. It is based on an attempt to forecast the future trends in relation to predetermined objectives. Secondly, these objectives are defined not in terms of the present level and distribution of purchasive power, but in terms of what is needed by the nation as a whole and by the masses of the people. Thirdly, it stands for collective decision making of the nation. Behind it is the concept of 'India-incorporated'. It reflects the common determination of all the components of the nation. All these ideas cannot be dismissed as unfriendly to the market and therefore deserving summary rejection. In Japan there have been planning for many years based mainly on forecasting. The role of Ministry of International Trade in Japan in foreign 'Japan incorporated' is also well known. Japan's spectacular economic performance has been the result of the combined efforts of the government, business, and workers in Japan. There is no reason why these time tested ideas relating to the growth of the nation should be totally abandoned. In this context it is pertinent to take note of Japan's view that 'the World Bank and IMF should encourage more developing countries to engage in government backed industrial planning, in other words to emulate some of the policies that Japan used in the 1950, 1960s and 1970s to attain its dominating economic present'. (Indian Express, April 28, 1992).

For many years, the concept of 'indicative planning' has been projected as one which does not replace market, but rather works with it. Such a system of planning has been tried in France with advantage. It also exists in Japan. In his address to Indian Merchant Chamber, Bombay, Dr. Saburo Akita pointed out that 'Planning in Japan was not the exclusive work of Government economists but included participation by a broad spectrum of people including representatives from industry, labour, media and academia.'

Economist like Amartya Sen have emphasized that the institution of market is not appropriate in fields like education and health. Secondly, market does not lead to optimization unless certain preconditions are fulfilled, and these include, among others, perfect knowledge and innumerable buyers and sellers of products and services. Several economists have emphasized that these conditions do not obtain even in developed countries much less so in India. It, therefore, cannot be assumed that free market by itself can lead to efficient allocation of resources. As Dr. Akita pointed out in his lecture cited above 'It is not true that market economies are necessarily superior to centrally controlled economies. Market mechanisms are not infallible'.

Nor is it correct that private sector is necessarily efficient. These are any number of examples of thoroughly inefficient private enterprises and efficient public and co-operative public enterprises.

Moreover, how do we measure efficiency? Profit is not the only measure of efficiency; nor can any one say that social benefit counts for nothing. The issue has recently been raised by Dr. Kurien of NDDB. If availability of liquid milk to consumers in the country is a desirable objective, then it makes little sense to insist that private milk enterprises should also be allowed entry in the milk sector. As has rightly pointed out, such an entry would lead to diversion of milk to manufacturing of milk products rather than to the consumption of the poor in the cities. Profit is not always synonymous with social benefit.

Attributing economic efficiently to market alone also overlooks the fact that efficiently is a product of human resource development. The connection between markets and efficiency is stated in abstract at the macro level. It is based on the concept that in a market economy any organization which is less efficient than the optimum, will incur losses and will be pushed out of the market. Only those firms with efficiency higher than the average would survive. But large firms use their resources for controlling and manipulating the market and hold it to ransom.

Efficiency is the product of ability to work and willingness to work. Ability is the result of education and training and attitude to work is the result of system of incentives and motivation and culture of a people. It is true that the examples of erstwhile Soviet Russia and Eastern European countries show that even after 70 years of so called socialist incentives and motivation, they do not really work. Pursuit of self interest is the dominant motive and the incentive system in the economy should encourage such pursuit in the interest of an efficient performance of the economy. Yet to rule out all non pecuniary motivations and replacing them by hedonistic motivations alone, is unlikely to be the right prescription for a developing society.

The public sector, no doubt, has failed to come up to the expectations of Pandit Jawaharlal Nehru. Instead of being the commanding heights of the economy, they have come to depend on budgetary support. But the condition for efficient performance of the public sector enterprises was operational autonomy. If this conditions not fulfilled, public sector enterprises cannot be expected to perform efficiently. Unfortunately, the politicians and the bureaucrats have not always stood by the autonomy of the public sector enterprises. Loan melas and write off of loans are two clear examples of meddling with the public sector banks with disastrous results. Planning without excessive control regime and public enterprises without erosion of their autonomy would still deliver the goods.

In hurrying with liberalization, it would be hazardous to overlook the role of the state and its agencies. The Government will have to play a crucial role in building up physical and social infrastructure of development. It also have to create a climate in which the private sector could act, remove any barriers that may arise and to indicate general directions.' (M.V. Kamath – 'India and Japan : Lessons to Learn Gomantak Times, April 24, 1992)

The Nehruvian model envisaged that the State would play a leading role in the process of development. It would be 'a welfare state in action'. It would set up a machinery of development administration which would be an agent of change. If these expectations were not fulfilled, it was because of deterioration in political standards way below what existed soon after independence. The state became in the words of Gunner Mydral a 'soft state' what is worse, there was a precifitous fall in moral standards. Corruption, black economy and criminalisation of politics raised their ugly head in the post Nehru era. Even Nehru had noticed deterioration in moral standards only a few years after he assumed office as Prime Minister and drew pointed attention of the Chief Minister to this phenomenon in his fortnightly letters. He appointed a Committee under K. Santharam to suggest measures to stem the tide of corruption. But when Indira Gandhi publicly declared that corruption is a world wide phenomenon, corruption gained a new legitimacy in India. And now ugly shadow of Bofors looms large on the public life of the country. The State cannot play its role unless there is a tradition of clean public life and those who control the leavers of power are held accountable to those who place them in power in the first instance. Officers of the IAS, the highest Civil Service of the country, were considered above corruption in the early days after independence. Today many of them as members of even the higher judiciary in the country have become suspect in the eyes of the people. How can State in such conditions play the role assigned to it in the Nehruvian model?

The combination of a command economy and corrupt machinery of the State can be disastrous. That is why liberalization of the economy has been hailed as a liberation from the tentacles of the State machinery.

Nor is the idea of self reliance to be faulted per se. Indeed it should continue to be sheet anchor of our policy, if India is to escape the strangle hold of the new economic imperialism. The Finance Minister wants to forget about the East India company. But the new Multinational companies are not necessarily different from the erstwhile East India company in terms of their attitudes as is shown by the attitude of the Union Carbide Company notoriously connected with the Bhopal Gas tragedy. The attitude is the same to make use of the raw materials and the market of the backward countries and exploit the backward people. The multinational companies would bring capital and technologies, but only if these subserve their interest. If they import capital and technology for producing soft drinks and potato chips, the country may not benefit all. Here again the concept of profit may not be in consonance with social benefit.

It is necessary for India to bear in mind the experience of Latin American countries in following the prescriptions of the World Bank and International Monetary Fund. Countries like Brazil and Turkey which followed the World Bank prescription, had to undergo very painful process of adjustment which involved the fall of their standard of living by 10%. People of India, already with low level of living, might not be able to survive such a fall. If India suffers from stagflation in the wake of the new policies or if already a low standard of living of the people is further sacrificed at the altar of the free market, the result may be disastrous. It is necessary, therefore, for the nation to be on the guard and continuously monitor the impact of the new policy.

The nation was gripped in a financial crisis despite the fact that there was no real economic crisis. The nation had the good fortune of three successive good monsoons. This was an extraordinarily lucky circumstances. However, such good luck cannot continue for all time. In a country where climatology has six years of seasonal cycle, drought years are bound to follow good monsoon years. Already the shadow of drought has loomed large on the vast areas of the country in states of Maharashtra, Gujarat, Madhya Pradesh and Rajasthan. This will not only worsen the economic scenario, put severe pressure on public expenditure at a time when government is keen to reduce it as a part of the package of economic reforms. Drought management cannot be left to the market. The British followed the liaises faire policy resulting in mass starvation. Here is yet another example of the inadequacy of the market mechanism in dealing with serious socio-economies problems.

The real task of the country is to develop its own productive capacity and not getting some loans from the World Bank or the International Monetary Fund. This would require much greater efficiency in production in fields, factories and offices and a wide spread dissemination of work ethic. These must have a place of priority in the new package of economic policy reforms. The nation is capable of making any sacrifices provided it is confident that those who are at the helm of affairs mean what they say and make sacrifices first before they ask the nation to tighten the belt. Unfortunately, this is not happening. The recent event of a vast amount of Rs. 600 crores of bank money being placed at the disposal of a stockbroker shows how carelessly public money is being utilized.

The nation must get out of the ideological ambiguities and must be shown the clear path of self-reliant economic growth.

Chapter - 2

What Makes Countries Rich or Poor?

These, then, are the main factors invoked to understand why nations differ in wealth. The factors are multiple and diverse. We all know, from our personal experience, that there isn't one simple answer to the question why each of us becomes richer or poorer: it depends on inheritance, education, ambition, talent, health, personal connections, opportunities, and luck, just to mention some factors. Hence, we shouldn't be surprised that the question of why whole societies become richer or poorer also cannot be given one simple answer.

Within this frame, Acemoglu and Robinson focus on institutional factors: initially on economic institutions, and then on the political institutions that create them. In their words, "while economic institutions are critical for determining whether a country is poor or prosperous, it is politics and political institutions that determine what economic institutions a country has." In particular, they stress what they term inclusive economic and political institutions: "Inclusive economic institutions...are those that allow and encourage participation by the great mass of people in economic activities that make best use of their talents and skills and that enable individuals to make the choices they wish." For example, in South Korea but not in North Korea people can get a good education, own property, start a business, sell products and services, accumulate and invest capital, spend money in open markets, take out a mortgage to buy a house, and thereby expect that by working harder they may enjoy a good life.

Such inclusive economic institutions in turn arise from political institutions that distribute power broadly in society and subject it to constraints.... Instead of being vested in a single individual or a narrow group, political power rests with a broad coalition or a plurality of groups." South Korea recently, and Britain and the US beginning much earlier, do have broad participation of citizens in political decisions; North Korea does not. Inclusive economic and political institutions provide individuals with incentives to increase their economic productivity as they think best. Such inclusive institutions are to be contrasted with absolutist political institutions that narrowly concentrate political power, and with extractive economic institutions that force people to work largely for the benefit of dictators. The ultimate development of inclusive political institutions to date is in modern Scandinavian democracies with universal suffrage and relatively egalitarian societies. However, compared to modern dictatorships (like North Korea) and the absolute monarchies widespread in the past, societies (such as eighteenth-century Britain) in which only a minority of citizens could vote or participate in political decisions still represented a big advance toward inclusiveness.

From this striking dichotomy, the authors draw thought-provoking conclusions. While absolutist regimes with extractive economic institutions can sometimes achieve economic growth, that growth is based on existing technology, and is nonsustainable and prone to collapse; whereas inclusive institutions are required for sustained growth based on technological change. One might naively expect dictators to promote long-term economic growth, because such growth would generate more wealth for them to extract. But their efforts are warped, because what's economically good for individual citizens may be bad for the political elite, and because economic growth may be best promoted by political institutions that would shake the elite's hegemony.

Why Nations Fail offers case studies to illustrate these points: the economic rises and subsequent declines of the Soviet Union and the Ottoman Empire; the resistance of tsarist Russia and the Habsburg Empire to building railroads, out of fear that they would undermine the landed aristocracy's power and foster revolution is especially relevant today. The likely future trajectory of Communist China, whose growth prospects appear unlimited to many Western observers do not appear to Acemoglu and Robinson, who write that China's growth "is likely to run out of steam."

In their narrow focus on inclusive institutions, however, the authors ignore or dismiss other factors. I for example - the effects of an area's being landlocked or of environmental damage, factors. Even within the focus on institutions, the concentration specifically on inclusive institutions causes the authors to give inadequate accounts of the ways that natural resources can be a curse. True, the book provides anecdotes of the resource curse (Sierra Leone cursed by diamonds), and of how the curse was successfully avoided (in Botswana). But the book doesn't explain which resources especially lend themselves to the curse (diamonds yes, iron no) and why. Nor does the book show how some big resource producers like the US and Australia avoid the curse (they are democracies whose economies depend on much else besides resource exports), nor which other resource-dependent countries besides Sierra Leone and Botswana respectively succumbed to or overcame the curse. The chapter on reversal of fortune surprisingly doesn't mention the authors' own interesting findings about how the degree of reversal depends on prior wealth and on health threats to Europeans.

Two major factors that Acemoglu and Robinson do mention, only to dismiss them in a few sentences, are tropical diseases and tropical agricultural productivity:

Tropical diseases obviously cause much suffering and high rates of infant mortality in Africa, but they are not the reason Africa is poor. Disease is largely a consequence of poverty and of governments being unable or unwilling to undertake the public health measures necessary to eradicate them.... The prime determinant of why agricultural productivity—agricultural output per acre—is so low in many poor countries, particularly in sub-Saharan Africa, has little to do with soil quality. Rather, it is a consequence of the ownership structure of the land and the incentives that are created for farmers by the governments and institutions under which they live.

These sweeping statements, which will astonish anyone knowledgeable about the subjects, brush off two entire fields of science, tropical medicine and agricultural science. The well-known facts of tropical biology, geology, and climatology saddle tropical countries with much bigger problems than temperate countries.

A second weakness involves the historical origins of what Acemoglu and Robinson identify as inclusive economic and political institutions, with their consequences for wealth. Some countries, such as Britain and Japan, have such institutions, while other countries, such as Ethiopia and the Congo, don't. To explain why, the authors give a just-so story of each country's history, which ends by concluding that that story explains why that country either did or didn't develop good institutions. For instance, Britain adopted inclusive institutions, we are told, as a result of the Glorious Revolution of 1688 and preceding events; and Japan reformed its institutions after Meji revolution1868; but Ethiopia remained absolutist. Acemoglu and Robinson's view of history is that small effects at critical junctures have long-lasting effects, so it's hard to make predictions. While they don't say so explicitly, this view suggests that good institutions should have cropped up randomly around the world, depending on who happened to decide what at some particular place and time.

But it's obvious that good institutions, and the wealth and power that they spawned, did not crop up randomly. For instance, all Western European countries ended up richer and with better institutions than any tropical African country. Big underlying differences led to this divergence of outcomes. Europe has had a long history (of up to nine thousand years) of agriculture based on the world's most productive crops and domestic animals, both of which were domesticated in and introduced to Europe from the Fertile Crescent, the crescent-shaped region running from the Persian Gulf through south-eastern Turkey to Upper Egypt. Agriculture in tropical Africa is only between 1,800 and 5,000 years old and based on less productive domesticated crops and imported animals.

As a result, Europe has had up to four thousand years' experience of government, complex institutions, and growing national identities, compared to a few centuries or less for all of sub-Saharan Africa. Europe has glaciated fertile soils, reliable summer rainfall, and few tropical diseases; tropical Africa has unglaciated and extensively infertile soils, less reliable rainfall, and many tropical diseases. Within Europe, Britain had the further advantages of being an island rarely at risk from foreign armies, and of fronting on the Atlantic Ocean, which became open after 1492 to overseas trade.

It should be no surprise that countries with those advantages ended up rich and with good institutions, while countries with those disadvantages didn't. The chain of causation leading slowly from productive agriculture to government, state formation, complex institutions, and wealth involved agriculturally driven population explosions and accumulations of food surpluses, leading in turn to the need for centralized decision-making in societies much too populous for decision-making by face-to-face discussions involving all citizens, and the possibility of using the food surpluses to support kings and their bureaucrats. This process unfolded independently, beginning around 3400 BC, in many different parts of the ancient world with productive agriculture, including the Fertile Crescent, Egypt, China, the Indus Valley, Crete, the Valley of Mexico, the Andes, and Polynesian Hawaii.

The remaining weakness is the authors' resort to assertion unsupported or contradicted by facts. An example is their attempt to expand their focus on institutions in order to explain the origins of agriculture. All humans were originally hunter/gatherers who independently became farmers in only about nine small areas scattered around the world. A century of research by botanists and archaeologists has shown that what made those areas exceptional was their wealth of wild plant and animal species suitable for domestication (such as wild wheats and corn).

While the usual pattern was for nomadic hunter/gatherers to become sedentary farmers, there were exceptions: some nomadic hunter/gatherers initially became nomadic farmers (Mexico and lowland New Guinea) while others never became farmers (Aboriginal Australia); some sedentary hunter/gatherers became sedentary farmers (the Fertile Crescent) while others never became farmers (Pacific North-west Indians); and some sedentary farmers reverted to being nomadic hunter/gatherers (southern Sweden about four thousand years ago).

Acemoglu and Robinson use one of those exceptional patterns (that for the Fertile Crescent) to assert, in the complete absence of evidence, that those particular hunter/gatherers had become sedentary because, for unknown reasons, they happened to develop innovative institutions through a hypothesized political revolution. They assert further that the origins of farming depended on their preferred explanation of institutional innovation, rather than on the local availability of domesticable wild species identified by botanists and archaeologists.

Among arguments to refute that widely shared interpretation, Acemoglu and Robinson redraw in their Map 5 on page 56 the maps on pages 56 and 66 of archaeobotanists Daniel Zohary and Maria Hopf's book *Domestication of Plants in the Old World*, depicting the distributions of wild barley and of one of the two hybrid ancestors of one of the three wheats (which Acemoglu and Robinson misleadingly identify just as "wheat"). They take these maps to mean that "the ancestors of barley and wheat were distributed along a long arc" beyond the Fertile Crescent, hence that the Fertile Crescent's unique role in agriculture's origins "was not determined by the availability of plant and animal species."

What Zohary and Hopf actually showed was that wild emmer wheat is confined to the Fertile Crescent, and that the areas of extensive spread of wild barley and wild einkorn wheat are also confined to the Fertile Crescent, and that the wild ancestors of all the other original Fertile Crescent crops are also confined to or centered on the Fertile Crescent, and hence that the Fertile Crescent was the only area in which local agriculture could have arisen. Acemoglu and Robinson do themselves a disservice by misstating these findings.

My overall assessment of the authors' argument is that inclusive institutions, while not the overwhelming determinant of prosperity that they claim, are an important factor. Perhaps they provide 50 percent of the explanation for national differences in prosperity. That's enough to establish such institutions as one of the major forces in the modern world. *Why Nations Fail* offers an excellent way for any interested reader to learn about them and their consequences. Whereas most writing by academic economists is incomprehensible to the lay public, Acemoglu and Robinson have written this book so that it can be understood and enjoyed by all of us who aren't economists.

Why Nations Fail should be required reading for politicians and anyone concerned with economic development. The authors' discussions of what can and can't be done today to improve conditions in poor countries are thought-provoking and will stimulate debate. Donors and international agencies try to "engineer prosperity" either by foreign aid or by urging poor countries to adopt good economic policies. But there is widespread disappointment with the results of these well-intentioned efforts. Acemoglu and Robinson pithily diagnose the cause of these disappointing outcomes in their final chapter: "Attempting to engineer prosperity without confronting the root cause of the problems—extractive institutions and the politics that keeps them in place—is unlikely to bear fruit."

June 7, 2012 Jared Diamond Book Review

Chapter - 3

Ethics Versus Profits

With the collapse of the socialist economy in the erstwhile Soviet Union and the Eastern European countries, the ideology of the free market economy has been left without a rival. Socialism was considered to be a alternative to capitalism and to free market economy. But 70 years of socialism have proved it to be a 'God that failed', and with this capitalism or free market economy has come to assume an undisputed sway over the minds of people around the world.

The free market ideology is based on the assumption that profit motivation is an engine of economic progress. Adam Smith, the father of the Science of Economics, wrote in his treaties 'Inquiry into Wealth of Nations', that pursuit of self interest by every individual ultimately redounded to the public good. In the pursuit of self interest, every economic agent, be he a producer, a consumer or owner of a factor of production, seeks to maximize his private profit. Thus, every owner of the factors of production, whether land, labour, capital or enterprise, seeks to get maximum return to himself. The producer who combines all the factors of production to produce goods and services, seeks to maximize his profit. The consumer seeks to get maximum satisfaction from the money that he spends on the variety of goods and services. The decisions of all the consumers, producers and factors of production to maximise their own self interest, ultimately lead to optimum returns from the economic resources of the nation. In a famous sentence Adam Smith said, 'the butcher, the baker and the brewer produces meat, bread and wine not to meet the wants of the people, but to earn a good profit for himself and thus fulfill his own self interest. But in pursuing his profit he serves the society'. The competition between various factors of production and various firms, producers and enterprises ensures that non can earn undue profit at the cost of others. Thus, pursuit of private profit by all, lends to optimum utilization of resources and best returns to all concerned.

At the bottom of this theory of economic motivation is the assumption that man is an economic animal, and the motivation which governs his actions are economic. This assumption ignores altogether the fact that human beings have motivation other than pecuniary in character. It is this assumption that led John Ruskin to state that 'Economics is a dismal science'. However, the fact of the matter is, man is more than an economic animal and is often governed by higher considerations and motivations though the latter undoubtedly seem to have suffered a retreat with increasingly powerful hedonistic motivations governing attitudes and decisions of human beings. But even then, it is a imperfect view of human beings to ignore non-egoistic and non-material motivations of human beings such as caring for the family, concern for the weaker sections of physically handicapped, commitment to social good, love for the nation, and spiritual attainment. These are other factors which tend human beings to replace egoistic motivation with altruistic motivations.

These altruistic motivations are ignored when the economist advocates the merits of a free market economy based on motivation of private profit. Those who tend to admire profit motivated economy, seem to feel that money is a measure of everything, that material goods are the be all and end all of life and wealth is synonymous with welfare. The protagonists of this view are the worshipers of the Mamnon. Like Midas they want to touch everything with the hope that it would turn into gold. But Midas came to grief because of his excessive greed. After all a human being is far more precious than gold. The goal of human life is happiness which mere wealth may not bring. Money is, no doubt, needed for obtaining the necessary where withals for a healthy life. But if carried beyond a point, the mindless pursuit of material possessions can only bring unhappiness and misery to individuals as well as the society as a whole. This is being increasingly realized by thinking people all over the world.

This was of course realized by Gandhiji long back. He warned against unlimited pursuit of material goods. He used to say that every businessman and industrialist must look upon himself as a trustee of the society and use the money earned by him for the benefit of the society. He further said that while Nature can cater to the needs of human beings, it cannot satisfy his greed.

The wisdom of Gandhiji's philosophy is now recognized. In ceaseless pursuit of material goods, the acquisitiveness of man has tended to the threat the life supporting system of Nature. The most precious gifts of Nature are being squandered away. Air and water are polluted. The green-house effet is tending to obliterate many nations. The chloro fluro carbon has polluted the environment. The black forest in Germany is being destroyed by acid rains. The indiscriminate mining has destroyed the forest wealth. The industrial waste has polluted precious waters of the rivers and seas and destroyed the fish and other sea life.

All this done in the name of developing profit-making enterprises, but it is forgotten that the private profit can be antagonistic to social benefit. Why would any business or industry be allowed to earn profits at the cost of Nature which ultimately provides the life supporting system of humanity?

It has to be understood that human beings are a part of the ecological system. If the ecology is damaged, human life cannot survive for long. Economic development merely based on private motivation can prove counter productive. Degradation, depletion or destruction resources, like soil, water, flora and fauna can have disastrous consequences for human survival.

It is rightly said that we do not inherit the earth from our ancestors. We rather borrow it from future generations. The present generation specially in the affluent countries has no right to be blind by profit motivation so as to destroy the human civilisation in the years to come or damage the quality life.

Economist John Kenneth Galbraith has rightly said that our profit motivated system has led to private opulence, but to public poverty. The profit motivation has systematically led to a neglect of the social infrastructure, such as public parks and gardens and clean environment. Human aspects of life are neglected and public assets fall into decay.

Profit motivation also leads to wasteful expenditure. High pressure salesmanship and multi-media advertisements by manufacturers and salesmen of ever increasing new range of products leads to the revolution of rising expectations. The consumer then tends to buy goods which are clearly superfluous as compared to those which are essential for healthy life. The consumer will buy a colour television and remain glued to it rather than buy books and enrich the mind.

Economic text books say that consumer is a sovereign, and the producer produces goods and services to meet the needs of the soverign consumer. But as Galbraith has pointed out, this process has been reversed. Thanks to high pressure salesmanship of modern time, the consumer is made to buy those goods and services which the producer wants to sell. The worst examples are those advertisements which tend to promote cigarettes for women not to talk of men, though, it is by now well established that smoking is a great danger to life. Profit making tends to promote alcoholic drinks rather than milk. Young men and women become victims of profit motivation when they resort to drugs of various sorts. Deaths of innocent people by adulteration of liquor have been chronic in our country in recent times. This is what happens when profits drive out ethics.

Profit motivation tends to destroy human relationships. The poet wants us to reflect on ;what man hath made of man'. Private motivation tends to make us blind and makes us forget that while some people are wallowing in luxury, others are without bare necessities of life. Indian luxury hotels stand side by side without abominable slums.

Private profit motivation also ultimately leads to a flourishing black economy arising out of illegal sale of foreign currency, smuggling of gold or illegal transactions in land as also corruption by people in public authority. The flourishing black economy and corruption are the bitter fruits of hedonism which seem to have gripped the minds of our people who are the inheritors of a great civilization that has treated 'the whole world as our family.'

Time has, therefore, now come for all of us to once again examine the moral basis of our economic order. There is no justification for a economic order based on private profit if it ultimately renders a large number of our fellowmen houseless, uneducated, and undernourished.

On the world scale, profit making as the sole motivation of life would only lead to perpetuation of the old economic order in which rich countries exploited the poor countries. It will also lead to a worldwide threat to human survival.

It is high time that we realise that private profit motivation and unbridled pursuit of self-interest must give way to a concern for fellow human beings, for the gifts of nature, for peace of mind, and for social justice and solidarity.

Chapter - 4

Wither Economic Reforms

The massive rebuff suffered by the Congress party in recent Andhra Pradesh and Karnataka elections would have undoubtedly make the Prime Minister and his advisors undertake an agonizing reappraisal of the new economic policy of liberalization which he initiated three years ago.

For sometime, the World Bank and the International Monetary Fund as also several economic experts and advisors, have developed the feeling that the policy of liberalization has somewhat slowed down, that there are still miles to go and so the pace of liberalization should be stepped up and economic reforms vigourously followed up to their logical conclusion.

However, the success of the policy would depend upon the understanding and the support of the people. Encomiums of the World Bank and experts from abroad and the awards from Europe and Japan to the Finance Minister for his outstanding performance are not enough. The policy must ear the appreciation of the people of India.

The people through their verdict in the recent elections, have shown that they cannot be taken for granted, that their economic sovereignity cannot be eroded at the dictates of the World Bank and they could defeat the party in power at the centre with a vengeance unless the consequences of the economic reforms on their well being are taken into account.

Unfortunately, no attempt has been made to explain the liberalization policy, its dimentions and the implications to the people of the country. For example, there have been no discussion of the policy at the local levels like panchayat samitis or panchayats. Economists may argue that the economic policy is technical in nature and it is beyond the pale of understanding of the common people. However, it must be realized that economic policy is too important a matter to be left to economists alone. People who are at the receiving end are vitally concerned with it and the policy makers are accountable to them for its consequences.

The logic of the new policy of liberalization is based on the sanctity and efficacy of the market – on the belief of the economists that market alone provides for a rational allocation of resources. In a free market, enterprises whose market costs are less than market prices enter, survive and succeed, whereas those whose market costs exceed market prices have to suffer exit. Everything should be decided by the calculus of profit and loss – says the logic of free market. All decisions as to what to produce, how much to produce, for whom to produce, where to produce and when to product have to be determined by the market signals. This does not take into account the fact that the market reflects and existing distribution of purchasing power, and if it is inequitable, the market will not produce and supply essential goods and services which are required by a large majority of the people, many of whose are below the poverty line. Nor does the primacy of the market theory take note of the fact that the market has its imperfections, that there are many people outside the market mechanism and that many essential goods and services of the nature of public consumption like safe drinking water or education and health services cannot be left to be provided by the allocative mechanism of the market.

The beginning of the new economic policy was the imposition of fiscal discipline, which was a good idea. The habitual tendency of budgetary deficits had to be curbed. The Finance Minister had made a commitment that the fiscal deficits will come down from 8.6% to 6.5% of GDP. The deficit can be reduced by cutting down public expenditure and mobilizing public revenues. The World Bank way of cutting down public expenditure was by abolishing subsidies and raising of prices of public utilities and services. In pursuit of this policy, the Finance Minister abolished sugar subsidy, reduced food subsidy and raised railway fares and the prices of petroleum products and cooking gas successively and with cascading effect. Even the banks have started charging for their services in order to reduce their deficits. People are required to pay the price of all these measures. Essential articles like food grains, sugar, tea and milk have become expensive for the common man. An ordinary cup of tea now costs Rs. 2/- to Rs. 3/- and the six of the cup has become smaller! Rice cost Rs. 10/- a kg and urad dal Rs. 32/- a kg. Government goes on issuing announcements that the price rise has to be curtailed and the two digits inflation has gone, but this does not correspond to the daily experiences of the people since what applies to the whole sale price index does not apply to the consumer price index in urban and rural areas. People do not see why they have to pay high price for food grains when 30 million tones are in the granaries, some of which is rotting because of improper storage facilities and preservation.

While in the name of fiscal discipline people have been made to pay more for railway, power supply and banking services, there is a steep deterioration in the quality of these services. On the other hand, the people in power have not shown the slightest consideration for the people suffering from sustained inflation by cutting down their extravagance expenditure. They have not abandoned conspicuous standard of living and enormous expenditure incurred on the maintenance of these public functionaries including the expenditure on their security. There has been no detailed and comprehensive exercise for curbing public expenditure of the sort undertaken by Raja Chelliah for reforming the tax structure. No wonder people feel the same way as the Roman did when Nero fiddled while Rome burnt or the French fest when Marie Antoinette asked people to eat cakes when they complained that bread was not available!

Deregulation

In the command and control economy, which emerged in the wake of planning, deregulation was no doubt long over due. It was stifled by a jungle of permits and licences. Rajaji had asked for long back for the end of the licence –permit but Nehru gave short shrift to his call. While in the wake of the new economic policy, Centre has taken bold initiative in removing licencing for most of the industries, there are still all sorts of serious hassles and impendiments at the State and municipal levels as for example, in acquiring land or power supply which are essential pre-requisites for setting up on enterprise. The small industry feels that the era of inspector Raj has not yet ended.

Similarly, while the danger of international bankruptcy has been obviated with foreign exchange reserves spectacularly rising from $1 billion at the time of economic crisis of 1991 to a $ 2 billion now, this has been accompanied by a rise of foreign debt from $ 70 billion to $ 90 billion which is bound to create problems of payment of interest and repayment of debt in the years to come. The fundamental improvement in the shape of sustained and sustainable increase in exports has yet to materialize. That would depend on improvement in productivity and quality which should be a conscious objective of the economic reforms. This cannot just be left to the spur of competition.

Nor have people so far enjoyed the fruits of deregulation and globalisation in shape of conspicuous increase in the rate of growth of industry. The progress of industry has not been such as to provide gainful employment opportunities to the educated unemployed which has left a sense of frustration and insecurity among the educated youth of the country. The Prime Minister and Finance Minister have given figures which show boost given to the flow of foreign investment in the county. But people are yet to get the fruits of the foreign investment. The multinational enterprises have been producing soft drinks like Coca Cola and Pepsi Cola or potato chips. Or if they are in the infrastructure sector like power, the investment is conditional on a government qurantee of an assured return. Domestic industries have complained that they do not have a level playing ground. In the meanwhile, what they have seen and heard of the activities of the foreign banks in the country relating to the enormous scam running into hundred and thousands of crores of rupees has not improved their trust in the benefits of globalisation. The bank scam has left a bad stink. People are disappointed that no responsibilities have been fixed and no heads have rolled. All this has greatly hurt the pride what N.T. Ramarao called, 'Atma gouravam' and a sense of self reliance of the people'.

Nor have the people any particular reason to be enthusiastic about privatization of public enterprises which Nehru asked them to look upon as 'commanding height of the economy'. People feel that they could be a source of strength to the economy and the nation. If they are wele managed and fraud from political interference. Privatisation is not proper just to raise budgetary resources and filling up the fiscal deficit. However, under the pressure of the need for raising resources, private enterprise has been carried out in such a manner that even C.A.G. has castigated the Government for sale of shares at throw away prices causing a loss of crores of rupees to the State exchequer.

The new economic policy seems to have been concentrating only on the private enterprise. The preoccupation of the government with the liberalization policy has led to the neglect of public investment in social sectors and in agriculture and rural development despite steep increase in anti-poverty programmes by way of what the World Bank calls the 'safety net'. Seven successive good monsoons have undoubtedly come as God send and helped the government in cushioning the effects of inflation. But one drought can cause havoc, and the nation will have to pay heavy price for the neglect of agriculture and rural development.

Finally in the wake of marketisation and economic liberlisation, planning has become a thing of the past. Planning has no doubt to change its character. Planning has to be more of indicative planning, planning of the public investment and micro planning in rural areas, but of late in the quest for market, planning of even this nature has taken a back seat.

Time has, therefore, come for the Central Government to get over the euphoria of liberatlisation, understand the implications of the new economic policy in terms of the welfare of the people and introduce necessary corrections. India cannot forget the hardship caused by the World Bank sponsored structural adjustment programmes in Brazil and Mexico. While reforms to make the economy vibrant and efficient should be persued, they should come along with austerity and productivity of public expenditure, curb or luxury expenditure, elimination of corruption and extravagence in public expenditure and attention to the social sectors.

Chapter - 5

Budgeting A Country's Finances

Though the presentation of the budget by the Finance Minister to the Parliament is an annual feature, the event is always awaited with a great deal of anxiery and expectation. It generates both hopes and fears, hopes for relief in tax rates or generous welfare measures and fears of higher taxes, withdrawal of tax concessions or cut in subsidies, leading to increase in prices of comoditites whether essential for daily life or luxury durable goods. These hopes and fears influences the behaviour of consumers as well as producers. They tend to hold on to the commodities whose prices are expected to rise.

Formally speaking, the budget is only a statement of public expenditure and public revenue i.e. the various sources from which money will be raised for the public exchequer to incur the public expenditure. But is more than that. It is a barometer of country's economic health. Or to change the metaphor, it provides medicine to cure the country's economic ills and tonic and nutrition to boost the national economy.

When the role of the State was limited to maintenance of law and order and defence, the size of budget was comparatively small. Some major sources of revenue like corporate tax, income tax, etc. were considered adequate to meet the need of the public expenditure. The budget was also governed by the orthodox principles of finance that revenue and expenditure should balance – that is the principle of 'a balanced budget'. If your income is hundred rupees then your expenditure should not exceed ninety nine rupees ninety nine paise. If it is true for an individual, it is also true for the nation – that is principle which governed the orthodox principle of balanced budgeting.

In the wake of the 'welfare state' and the 'development state', this approach have undergone a great deal of transformation. The welfare State was expected to look after the citizen from 'the cradle to the grave' or 'from the womb to tomb'. In Post World War II Britain, the following recommendations of the

Breveridge Report, a scheme of social insurance was introduced to provide comprehensive insurgence against accident, health or unemployment. The resources for the support of the needy were raised by a scheme of progressive taxation which meant a redistribution of income from the 'haves to the have nots'. This was the old 'rob Peter to pay Paul' principle.

In the second half of the twentieth century, the concept of the 'development state' was adopted by the newly liberatred countries emerging to freedom. They were underdeveloped countries embarking on a process of development with active state intervention and public investment. India was the leading country which adopted this approach. The budget became, therefore, an instrument of development and integrally linked with the plans of development. Gore was the old approach of laissez faire and balanced budgeting. The State took the responsibility for promotion of industries, modernization of agriculture, building up of infrastructure, establishment of major public enterprises in the field of basic and strategic industries and amelioration of poverty. Vast amount of budgetary resources had to be raised for all these projects and programmes which were a part of the development plans. A distinction was therefore introduced between plan and non-plan expenditure, and revenue and capital budget.

In the wake of welfare State and development, the size of budget increased several fold. In India the Central Budget used to be of the order of a few hundred of thousand crores. Now it runs into a few lakhs crores. Mobilisation of resources for mounting expendiature therefore, became a challenge to the Finance Minister.

Apart from steeply rising the level of taxation, a number of surchages were levied and a number of new charges were raised like the wealth tax and the expenditure tax. Also the principle of balanced budgeting was given a gob. It was argued that keeping the expenditaure within the limit of resources, was a static principle not relevant to a dynamic situation where an unbalanced budget was justified on the ground that deficit was financing public investment. Such deficit finance would no doubt create the inflationary potential but it would be mopped up when the investment would yield returns.

This always did not happen and deficit financing soon became an addiction to such an extent that soon deficits went out of control and a time came when capital surpluses were utilized for meeting revenue deficits! The revenue deficits went on increasing thanks to the relentless increase in administrative expenditure, defence expenditure, subsidies and interest on accumulated public debts. This was indeed a danger signal.

The realization of the dangers of chronic deficit financing has brought about a return to the old fiscal orthodoxy. Fiscal discipline has once again become the hall mark of sound budgeting.

The compulsions of the new policy of reduction of budgetary deficit and fiscal discipline has meant that all kinds of subsidies such as food and fertilizer will have to be progressively reduced as also administrative expenditure and there would have to be even a cut-in public investment and strict application of the 'value for money' principle. Public enterprises are asked to raise their own revenues and not to depend on the public exchequer.

However, such has been the growth of commitment of the modern state that it is doubtful whether even after the adoption of the new policies, the size of the budget, any deficit will go down substantially. The United States which is the champion of the philosophy of limited role for Government, has budget with deficits of enormous size running into trillions of dollars.

It is, therefore, important that whatever be the size of the budget, the optimum development of resources for attainment of pre-determined goals should be applied with strict commitment to economy in expenditure. It is with this end in view that the technique of 'performance budgeting' was introduced some two decades ago. This technique demands that allocation of funds should be made with reference to definite physical objectives – may be the completion of projects or the provision of education and health facilities. This would avoid careless allocation of resources without timely completion of projects and programmes or for those which do not yield adequate returns. Performance budgeting should also be the basis for periodic performance reviews in course of the fiscal year.

A more recent technique is called the 'Zero based budgeting'. The concept of this new technique is to put an end to the old system in which a budget was burdened by automatic accumulation of past liabilities from year to year besides the additional commitments for new items of expenditure. While new items are added, old obsolete items are not deleted. Time bared and outdated programmes continue to saddle the public exchequer. Zero based budgeting requires de novo look at the entire past expenditure so that it comes under a fresh scrutiny and is not passed automatically or mechanically. Is the continuation of past items justified? Is spending money on them justified? Zero based budgeting would thus help in eliminating outdated and in fructuous expenditure, while at the same time providing for new items which have become relevant.

Thus in idealistic concept of a budget today would be an exercise based on a comprehensive scrutiny of all sources of revenue and all items of expenditure. It will aim at optimum allocation of resources on priority needs with strict eye on economy. It would place the burden of resources on those who most benefit from the economy and have the ability to bear the burden and it would be a plan of a long term perspective for the development of a heathy, dynamic and a vibrant national economy.

Chapter - 6

Satyam Episode and Indian Corporate Image

The Satyam scandal has shaken not only the corporate world but the entire governmental system at the state and the central level. The Prime Minister was himself deeply worried. He described the scandal as a blot on the corporate image of India and expressed his determination to go at the root of the scandal. He should have rather realized that the scandal was a scar on the neo-liberal policy which he initiated in 1991 and time has come to get at the root of the policy and the government and the economic system which has come into existence as a consequence of that policy.

Satyam has been India's Enron. Satyam was preceded by several other scandals like the securities scandal and the financial adventures of desperadoes like Harshad Mehta, Ketan Parekh and Bhansali who played ducks and drakes with the Stock Market with the use of bank money. Enron in US was followed by many other scandals like the world.com and since September last, the collapse of one major financial institution after another like the Lehman Brothers, Fannie Mac and Freddi Mack, AIG, Merril Lynch, Goldman Sachs, Stanley Morgan Investment and Washington Mutual Bank. These are not fortuitous events. There is a clear link between the policy of neo-liberalism, unbridled capitalism and financial scandals. There should be a searching analysis and exposure of these and re-appraisal of the policy of neo-liberalism, however agonizing it may be.

Philosophy of neo-liberalism

Policy of neo-liberalism is a modern incarnation of the nineteenth century policy of lazier faire which laid down that "that government is the best which governs the least" Modern policy of Neo-liberalism goes much beyond this and is based on the stipulations that there should be more business in government and less government in business" and indeed "the business of government is business". This was based on a number of "mythologies" created in the name of sound economics propounded by the Chicago School led by Milton Friedman and zealously adopted by conservative radical leaders like Ronald Reagan in US and Margaret Thatcher in Britain. The first was that the free market economy (a non ideological term for unbridled capitalism) alone can lead to economic efficiency based on rational allocation of resources and distribution of income in proportion to "productivity". Second, free market economy is a self correcting system. If any problem like inflation or unemployment arises, the system would automatically bring into operation its corrective mechanism and cure the problem in due course. Thirdly, any government intervention to solve the problem could only lead to aggravation of the situation. Indeed these should be complete deregulation, minimal government, vacation of traditional state sector in favour of private enterprise, reduced public expenditure and minimum taxation. Government has no business to claim a large chunk of tax payer's money as it could only lead to extravagance and waste at the hands of public agencies. The role of government agencies is only to promote private agencies and enterprise. There is no such thing as "public purpose" which government has to promote. Public purpose can only be the result of private enterprise governed by the signals of profit and loss in the market.

Nor should the heavy hand of public agencies control and regulate private enterprise. The "command and control economy" known in India as "licence permit Raj" must be dismantled. Laws and rules there under, to control private business (like Industrial Development and Regulation Act, Monopoly and Restricted Pracices Act, Export-Import Control Rules, Foreign Exchange Regulation etc.) should best be abolished or at least drastically modified in the direction of liberalization.

In framing budgets and economic policies it become de-rigueur for the Government to take advice of management of private business. It become obligatory for the Heads of Government to address annual conferences of Chambers of Commerce and Industry and Confederation of Indian Industries. Ministers of Finance and Industries started attending shows of private newspapers and T.V. Channels and started distributing awards and even accepting them. US setup a tradition of looking at executives of big business corporations and financial world for appointment as Treasury Secretary. Big business delegations started accompanying heads of government in their visits to important developed countries. Government and business delegations together started attending World Economic Summit at Davos.

Changing climate of public administration

The transformation of government in favour of big business inevitably influenced the climate in government agencies especially the economic ministries. The higher civil servants become "business friendly". Their mindset changed or had to change since instead of being controllers or regulators as in the bad old days of "socialism" they started playing second fiddle to the business magnates. They developed with them bonhomie as members of prestigious social clubs and started attending lavish business parties or even accepting hospitality. A theory was propounded that Civil servants should spend sometime in careers in business to gain useful managerial experience and wash away the obstructive bureaucratic tendencies of the past. Civil servants should, therefore be given permission liberally to move to private business for a tenure or even on long term appointment to be eventually absorbed permanently. The friendly civil servants could confidently look forward to lucrative assignments in private business on retirement. On the other hand, executive from private business could be invited to hold crucial positions in government agencies on a tenure basis. The "conflict of interest" that may inevitably arise with this free to way traffic between government and business was conveniently overlooked.

The corporate would with high earnings became more prestigious than government departments with low salaries. The prestige was calculated on the basis of pecuniary affluence rather than "public service". The business executives started lecturing the public servants on efficient performance. "Corporate Governance" become the role model for governance in Government. Construction and management of Airports, Electricity and water supply projects, high ways and metros, was assigned to private agencies, since public agencies were no good. Special economic zones were carved out where there would be no civil agency of government. They would be managed by the private business contractors and builder to whom they were assigned. They became "foreign territory" where normal rules of taxation, labour etc. would not apply. Lands for the SEZ could be acquired under the emergency clauses of the Land Acquisition Act. Lest the land acquisition should be delayed by the lethargic revenue administrative agencies, the agents of private business started sitting in government offices and directing acquisition proceedings.

Economics of Innocent Fraud

But to what extent were the encomiums showered on the capitalistic economic system and the corporate world justified? Did they correspond with reality? In his "Economics of Innocent Fraud", the late Prof. Galbraith exposed he reality hiding behind the myths of capitalism and the corporate world. The myth is that the business world caters to the consumer because in the market "consumer sovereignty" prevails. In reality the big corporations and business interests manipulate consumer demand through misleading salesmanship and advertisement on TV channels for which they incur heavy expenditure ultimately borne by the consumer. The myth is that corporations are governed by the decisions of shareholders and representative Board of Directors. The reality is that corporators are managed by a small coterie of promoters and executives who award munificent compensations to themselves at the cost of the shareholders and investors. The myth is that high standards of corporate finance are ensured by professional accountants and auditors. The reality is that they themselves are a party to corporate scandals. The myth is that corporate scandals can be avoided by appropriate regulations. The reality is that corporate influence extends to regulators and public officials in the regulatory agencies can be unduly compliant. The myth is that with the dismantling of government controls over business, the scope for corruption by ministers and high official will be substantially reduced. The reality is that corruption takes a new form, more sophisticated and of greater dimension. Ministers and civil servants join hands with corporate management in appropriating for themselves huge gains by loot of public resources.

Satyam Scam

It is in the context of the above analysis of the capitalist economic system and corporate business that the huge Satyam scandal can be understood. The scandal of the order of more than Rs. 7000 crores would not have come to light but for the confession by the Chief Promoter Shri. Ramalinga Raju. The scandal was in the form of larger scale defrauding of accounts. False profits and cash resources were exhibited in the financial Statements to create an allusion of a highly profitable business which duped gullible small investors. The financial manipulation has been going for seven long years but neither the so called "independent directors" nor the professional auditors discovered it. The independent directors were acknowledged management experts. They collected huge fees without discharging their duty to safeguard investors' interest because they were puppets in the hands of the promoter Raju. What the accounting firm Arthur Anderson did in Enron case falsifying accounts Price Water house Copper, the celebrated auditor firm did failing to uncover fraud in "Satyam accounts"

This showed how hallow is the grandiose concept which goes by the name of "corporate governance" Raju was showered awards after awards for corporate leadership by prestigious award conferring Institutions in India and abroad on the "sound advice" of acknowledged experts and consultants. Now they are pleading that they did not know ! Another example of innocent fraud".

Over seven years what is disturbing is that the businessman who systematically committed fraud was supported by politicians in power in Andhra Pradesh Government – former Chief Minister Chandrababu Naidu and later his successor Y.R.S. Reddy. Association with the top leaders meant that Raju got huge chunks of prime land at throw away prices for technology park and other purposes and many other facilities which enabled Satyam to expand and grow rapidly. Banks and financial institutions allowed Raju to open thousands of accounts without questioning. They provided statements about company's finance as Raju requested. Raju was allowed inside knowledge of government policies, development plans and projects even before the blue prints were prepared. This enabled him and his consortium Maytas Infra to bid for projects on favourable terms. The whole governmental system was harnessed to sub-serve Raju's interests. Now the bubble has burst and it is obvious how rotten to the core the whole system has become. The new President of US, Barrack Obama has vowed to end "greed and irresponsibility" on the Wall Street which led the prestigious financial institutions of US to collapse, one after another, like nine pins. He has taken to task the greedy business executives who appropriated bonuses of the order of $ 18 billion while the companies they were managing were facing financial ruin. Our government should also take a leaf out of Obama's book and break the racket of business government collaboration which has slowly developed after the policy of neo-liberalism was initiated in the year 1991. That should be main issue of the forthcoming general elections.

Chapter - 7

Recession – Diagnosis and Remedies

I – The new face of financial capitalism

Business cycles i.e. upswings and downswings in the economy, booms and busts, have been a characteristic of the capitalist economy. Many economists have analysed the phenomenon and have come out with empirical findings as well as theories regarding causes and nature of these occurrences and remedies either for moderating the impact or for preventing their occurrence. Gottfeied Haberler's classic treatise "Prosperity and Depression' brought together several theories regarding business cycles – monetary, structural and even those related to psychological waves of optimistic and pessimistic expectations in the business world. In the heyday of neo-classical economies and policies of laissez failure, it was believed that the equilibrating forces of demand and supply in the market, and the balancing of costs and prices would automatically provide the remedy. Thus, during the downswings and recessions, demand and prices fall and the producer will perforce be required to reduce costs. Wages and returns to other factors of production will fall. Reduced costs will reduce prices and demand will consequently pickup. However, it was found that this only exacerbated the situation, converting recession into deep depression. It was in the aftermath of depression in 1929-30, the worst setback to the capitalistic economy that it was realized that there was something wrong in assuming that there would an automatic cure through the equilibrating mechanism. It was at this time that Keynes came out with his theory of macro economic. Briefly, it stated that the level of the economy depends on the aggregate demand. Consumption and investment are the two main components of the aggregate demand. In times of depression when both fall, it is the state which should take initiative in boosting both these components through public investment and welfare programme. The validity of this approach of public intervention to supplement the market was demonstrated by the New Deal programme of President Roosvelt. Keynesian theory brought back the formulations of pre-classical and pre-neo-classical economists regarding under consumption and under production.

The current recession which is so severe in nature as to bring back the memories of the great depression of 1929-30, is however, the aftermath of "over consumption' rather than under consumption'; hence it requires different kind of analysis and theory. However, economists have not come out with it so far.

For the last several years, the successful working of the market (capitalistic) economy was taken for granted. This created a sense of complacency. Keynesian economies itself was thrown aside and superseded by the Chicago School under the leadership of Milton Friedman and his associates which celebrated the triumph and infallibility of the capitalist market economy.

This despite the fact that there were clear signs of new systemic defects creeping into the capitalistic economy of the affluent countries especially the USA. First was the tendency to live beyond means – both at the individual and national level. The families in USA Government became used to living on credit for fulfilling their extravagant life styles. The credit card revolution supported such a life style. Every family would boast of possessing several credit cards which would be operated without discrimination. Also, the sustained policy of low interest rate promoted by former head of the Federal Reserve Allen Greensparn, encouraged financial institutions to lend extravagantly at low interest rates. The leading example was 'sub-prime lending' by the mortgage banks – they lent without insisting or down payment and proof of ability to repay the loan, simply depending on the assumption that the loan was covered by an appreciating asset like a house. Securitisation of these loans provided the basis for further rounds of 'financial products' floated by the investment banks and hedge funds. Soon this gave rise to tremendous facade of 'financial capatalism' in which financial products and their transactions themselves became the core business of investment banks and financial institution like hedge funds without any regard to 'real' transactions. Finance ceased to be the support for the production in the real economy but became a product in itself.

The same tendency seeped in the world of 'real production'. Chief Executives of companies in the production business started aiming at increasing share values in the stock market rather than attending the technological upgradation, human resource development, organizational improvement, and rationalization of production process to raise productivity. Soon the degenerated into corporation scams in the forms of falsification of balance sheets just to improve the image of the company in the stock market in order to attract investors. This had disastrous consequences as illustrated by the Enron scandal in USA and Satyam scandal in India.

The CEO's of corporations started transforming Adom Smith's concept of 'pursuit of self interest' into unscrupulous, greed using their positions to appropriate for themselves disproportionate salaries, bonuses, and corporate facilities like aeroplanes, helicopters and holiday resorts. Neither the accountants and auditors, nor the Board members could stop this naked pursuit of self interest.

This philosophy of insatiable greed became characteristic of the ruling classes and the policy makers as well. After all it was money power which placed them positions of political power. Their policies made America the largest debtor country in the world with internal and external deficit running into trillions of dollars. Yet the dollar could maintain its value because countries like China with higher balance of payment surplus, chose to keep their surpluses in US Treasury bills.'

II – Recession – causes and strategies

This is the background of the US capitalistic economy against which the present recession which had it origin in USA can be understood. The reckless (sub-prime) lending by mortgage banks led to their inevitable bankruptcy. The banking and financial institutions like Fanny Mac and Fredic Mac, Lehman Brothers, AIG, Merill Lynch, Goldman Sachs, Stanley Morgan, Washington Bank etc. which had their financial empires built by securitarisation and leveraging of these loans collapsed like pack of cards. The disastrous failure of banking institutions, led to collapse of confidence in the market choking the credit system. What started as a Wall Street crisis soon became a Main street crisis.

The financial crisis rapidly spread to Europe with similar pattern of collapse of financial institutions followed by collapse of business confidence, both leading to the outset of recession. There was not only fall in growth but also contraction of the G.N.P. and rising unemployment.

President Bush had to face the crisis in the sunset years of his administration. His treasury Secretary Henry Paulson and Federal Reserve Chairman Ben Bernanke worked out a $ 700 billion bail out plan to resurrect the financial institutions. The plan was quite out of tune with he economic philosophy of the Republican Party which for several years had forcefully advocated and pursued the policy of free market economy of the Chicago School. According to them the state should keep away from meddling in the market economy. And now here was a huge plan to bail out big financial institutions on the Wall Street – all in the private sector – at the cost of the tax payer. No wonder the plan was severally criticized as 'Socialism for the rich' reserving capitalism for the poor !

However, Bush administration justified it by saying that the common people themselves would suffer if the credit line for consumption, education and housing would be clogged. The credit institutions had to be revived in the interest of the ordinary people. The road to Main street was from the Wall Street.

Obama who followed Bush had however a different view. He severely chastised the Wall Street barons for their 'greed and irresponsibility' which led to the bankruptcy of the financial institutions. He instead had an alternate plan of $ 899- for surge in public expenditure on upgrading infrastructure, health and welfare measures. He however persisted with the bail out plan. The person whom he selected to succeed Henry Paulson for the post of Treasury Secretary Timothy Geitmer was himself, a head of New York Federal Reserve Bank, closely connected with the business world and has become a leading architect of the bail out plans and justifies them in the name of helping business and consumers and making credit flow again. Obama had however the discomfiture of seeing the bailout funds used for making hefty bonus payment to those very CEO's whose malfeasance had led the financial institutions to bankruptcy. The extravaganza of buying corporate jets and helicopters and holiday resorts did not stop. The Citi Bank at its annual meeting of shareholders did not serve coffee and doughnuts but spent high sums for hiring 50 security guards.

USA and Britain took initiative for convening G20 meeting at London on April 2. There was clear difference of approach in tackling recession. While the US plan was to boost public expenditure to stimulate the economy, the France-German approach was to tighten regulations since it was lax regulation which led to financial mismanagement and consequent collapse of financial institutions. Britain wanted severe action against 'tax havens' which drew away funds from productive investment in business. The meeting agreed to provide a booster dose of $ 1.1 trillion through IMF and other multilateral institutions particularly to the poorer countries.

While admitting that it was the financial mismanagement in USA which led to loss of confidence in the credit system and consequent onset of recession, US Treasury Secretary felt that US needs to be supported by other nations especially the emerging economies like China, India and Brazil in dealing with the recession and protecting the poorer economies from the impact of recession.

The reaction of Indian policy makers to recession was in the beginning, one of denial. Indian banking system, they argued, was strong thanks to sound regulatory mechanism. India economy would be insulated from the recession that as hit USA and Europe. India would stand 'decoupled'. However, as months passed the impact of world recession was apparent. The stock market plunged.

Export sector enterprises like Surat based Gem and Jewellery industry, Kanpur based leather industry and textile industry in different parts of the country felt the impact of recession as cash rich markets of US and Europe dried up, lakhs of skilled workers lost jobs. The flourishing IT Software industry too lost business as outsourcing by banking and other companies in US and Europe substantially went down. Consequently fresh recruitment was halted and compensations of existing staff were reduced in one way or another Building industry too slowed down and real estate prices plunged. A further set back to the economy was withdrawal of $ 15 Billion by the foreign investors.

Government had to come out with a series of monetary measures to improve liquidity such as successive reduction of CRR by RBI and extension of credit line to Mutual Funds. This was supplemented by reduction in Repo and reverse Repo rates to facilitate cheap credit to industry by the banks. But the banks were reluctant to reduce interest and give loans liberally. The recession atrophied the repaying capacity of business establishments and banks feared rise in NPA's. Government supplemented monetary measures by fiscal stimulus. There was across the board cuts in excise duties to reduce costs and prices and stimulate demand. All these measures had, only limited success. Prime Minister Manmohan Singh has promised fresh packages of measures were the voters to bring Congress back to power.

The recession does not seem to have been handled with a sure touch in USA, European Union and elsewhere. As the Economist has pointed out in a recent article, through the rate of decline is slowing, glimmers of hope cannot be interpreted as the beginning of strong and sustained recovery. The worst global slump is far from over. Central banks have pumped in trillions of dollars, policy interest rates are approaching zero and government have provided fiscal stimulus, but the banks have not been purged off toxic assets', and European Banks face $ 1.1 trillion in losses. Budget deficit of the order of 9% of GDP have created serious dangers of inflationary spiral. World Economic Outlook expects global output to sink by 1.3% this year – first fall in 60 years. Big automobile companies like General Motors and Chrysler are facing bankruptcy. If they fold up, there would be cumulative fall in the economy.

Though several months have elapsed after the onset of recession, there is still no clarity of understanding amongst the policy makers and economic thinkers as to how exactly it should be tackled and how long will it last. While some are already seeing signs of recovery, other fear that there will be further waves of recession. The confidence in the selfcorrecting capacity of the free market has been severely shaken and the concept of minimalist state has already been abandoned in favour of the interventionist state. The brash and arrogant claims on behalf of unbridled capitalism have given way to a grudging concessions in favour of mending the defects of capitalism. While the shortcomings of the capitalist system have been exposed, there is yet no clear formulation, no comprehensive theory such as that of Keynes after 1929-30 depression which could provide an alternative reformed model of capitalism. Economists needs to do fresh thinking regarding economic theories and economic policies.

III – Alternative models of capitalism

A realization has dawned that government measures are at best palliatives and efforts have to be made to remove the systemic defects which have crept in the capitalist economic system in recent years. Shri. Narayan Murthy, the founder of Infosys who has become an icon, has came out with his concept of 'compassionate capitalism'. Obliviously he has been disturbed by the ravages of 'rapacious capatalism' as exemplified by Enron and Satyam. A company like Infosys he said, will not, in the face of recession, resort to indiscriminate hiring and firing. Rather it will use the slow down as an opportunity to upgrade the skills of workers through extended programme of training. Well Narayan Murthy's zeal to 'reform' capitalism is commendable, the limits of the concept of compassionate capitalism' are quite apparent. With all its best intentions, Infosys in the face of falling profits, has been compelled to stop fresh recruitment. Even Infosys, for all its success in the boom time, will not be able to ward off the consequences of recession.

What is required is an alternative model of the economic system and fresh set of policy measures to bring it into existence. The neo-liberal model followed since 1991 has created economic, legal and administrative systems which have favoured few 'billionaire' at the cost of ordinary urban workers and millions of farmers toiling on land in the country side. Inequalities of the order that exist in India and the world cannot lead to sustainable development. The unconscionable earnings in the luxury sectors like Bollywood and Cricket and ostentatious style of living of a few cannot be allowed co-exist with horrible conditions of slumdogs who have to live without minimum facilities like clean drinking water, sanitation and housing.

Inequalities in the field of education and health are also quite appalling. Private schools and colleges charging unconsciously high fees co-exist with sub-standard municipal schools which even the poor families do not want their children to attend. Public hospitals are in an appalling state while the luxury hospitals provide up-to-date medical treatment and facilities at a cost which only the rich can afford.

Recession is an opportunity to bring about a root and branch change in the economic policy and the economic system with an aim of not only eliminating systemic defects in capitalism and the evils of un-satiable greed and bubbles of prosperity which they gave rise to, but also by deliberately building public systems of education, health, transport, housing etc. free from corruption, entirely handled by professionals and free from interference by self-serving politicians and parties and devising policies to support agriculture and promote agro processing and village industries like handloom which provide employment to masses of people. 'Safety nets' attached to basically iniquitous economic system will not do. The system itself needs to be made more equitable. Unfortunately neither the Congress, nor the BJP nor the left parties have taken the opportunity of the General Elections to place before the people a comprehensive economic philosophy and policy measures and agenda of action to deal with the consequences of recession and other shortcomings of the present economic system.

Chapter - 8

Economic and Social Policies need reappraisal Planning in the mixed economy after independence

In the first decades of independence attempts were initiated through Five Year Plans which provided schemes in all sectors of the economy, aimed at breaking out of the economic stagnation that characterized the British Rule. The plans aimed at a 'Welfare State' to replace the 'Police State' or 'law and order' state of the time when India was under the British Rule.

The concept of 'welfare state' was earlier developed in Lord Beveridge report in post world war II. Britain Lord Beveridge was appointed by the first Labour Government under Prime Minister Clement Attlee. Lord Beveridge report identified poverty, unemployment, disease, squalor and ignorance as five great evils of the laisser faire economy which the welfare state sought to remove through a comprehensive programme of social security.

This was also the objective of Indian Five Year Plans. The first Prime Minister of the free India Pandit Jawaharlal Nehru was believer in planning. He had headed even before independence the National Planning Committee appointed by Subhash Chandra Bose who was then the Congress President. The leader of the last plans of India's political struggle for independence, Mahatma Gandhi wanted to remove tears from the eyes of India's *Daridra Narayana*. Rabindranath Tagore wanted free India to raise 'the poorest, lowliest and lost'. Political freedom had to lead to economic and social independence'.

After independence on August 15, 1947. Nehru, the first Prime Minister decided to go in for a planned economy because he believed, as most of the economists of that time, that the development of the economy cannot be left to the vicissitudes of market fares; there has to be deliberate planning. Nor could it be left only to the private sector. The State had to play a major role. Nehru was impressed by the Plans of the then Soviet Union under the Communist Rule which brought about rapid development of the Soviet Union. But that was under Communist dictatorship. Nehru did not approve of the dictatorship system because it abridged freedom. He believed in democracy. The Indian Constitution ushered in the system of Parliamentary democracy in a federal setup. So he did not want wholesale socialization of all enterprises. India, therefore, went for a mixed economy with public, co-operative and private sectors. The public sector would occupy the commanding heights of the economy. Strategic industries like Defense and Atomic Energy and heavy enterprises like machine, building and electronics will be in the public sector. The co-operative sector will be the main stay of the rural and agricultural economy. The rest of the economy will be in the private sector.

The first five year plan was formulated in 1951. They were followed by several five year plans. They aimed at making the lives of masses of people 'better, richer and fuller' through comprehensive and planned programme and covering agriculture industry and economic overheads like roads and electrification and social overheads like education and health and most important development of science and technology. India was to be set on the path of modernization of agriculture, industrilisation and economic diversification and expansion.

The Indian agriculturist, in the absence of institutional credit, was in the clutches of money lenders who provided credit at exploitative rates of interest. The agriculturist was never able to get out of the clutches of money lenders – traders. He was born in debt, lived in debt and died in debt. The Rural Credit Survey Committee appointed soon after independence recommended a three tier structure of co-operative credit institutions to provide credit.

Village co-operative credit societies federally linked to District Co-operative Banks and State Co-operative Banks would provide rural credit. Reserve Bank's Rural Credit Survey Report recommend a crop loan scheme for annual agriculture operations. Some part of the credit would be given in kind – seeds, fertilizers and pesticides. For investment Credit Committee envisaged co-operative Land Development Banks who would lend credit for investment in agriculture like digging of wells and land levelling or digging of field channels. Crop production is only the first step. It had to be followed by marketing and processing. Market co-operatives will be setup to enable farmers to come together to sell produce without the intermediate trader – middlemen. Also the farmers could be owners of factories for processing the agriculture products. The rural co-operative Dairy was set up at Anand in Gujarat under the managerial leadership of V. Kurian and Pravara Co-operative Sugar Factory initiated by Vikhe Patil under the guidance of economist D. R. Gadgil setup at Pravaranagar. Following the example a large number of co-operative dairies and co-operative sugar factories came up specially in Maharashtra and Gujarat. They greatly helped to better the lot of farmers.

Indian agriculture was a gamble in rain. To get over this, it was necessary to provide irrigation. Major irrigation projects like Bhakra Nangal, Hirakud Dam, Damodar Valley project and Tungabhagdra Dam provided irrigation for lakhs of hectors. They were supplemented by medium and minor irrigation projects.

But substantial increase in agricultural production came only after the introduction of hybrid and high yielding varieties of seeds. Dr. Norman Borlough and Dr. Swaminathan introduced Mexican varieties of seed of wheat like Sonali, Sonalika and nerma rojo and rice varieties like Taichung and Talinan. All these varieties required substantial input of chemical fertilizers. Hybrid seeds ushered in the Green Revolution in 1966 and later which substantially increased grain production freed India from dependence on imported wheat under PL480 programme of USA.

But the benefit of the Green Revolution mainly accrued to large farmers and irrigated areas. Special programmes were therefore introduced for small and marginal farmers known as Small Farmer and marginal farmer development agencies. For areas prone to periodical draft DPAP – Drought Prone Areas Programme was introduced.

However, the problem of landless workers in rural areas remained. For them anti-poverty programme known as National Employment Guarantee Programme. Such a programme was first envisaged in the study of poverty by V.M. Dandekar and Neelkanth Rath. They recommended public works programme in rural areas, rural roads and embankments to store rain water to provide employment to the landless poor.

While the approach of planned development and mixed economy did break the economic stagnation and set the economy on road to development, it was soon riddled by controls and licence permit raj which stifled for economic growth. While the growth rate of India was well below five percent, the growth rate in East Asian countries particularly in Singapore, Hongkong and Japan was much more spectacular. The economy had to be got rid of the shackles of a controlled economy.

Liberalisation of the economy

The credit of breaking through the shackles goes to Prime Minister Narsimha Rao, who appointed as well known economist Dr. Manmohan Singh as Finance Minister. In his very first budget in 1991, he removed a number of controls and permits to free the forces of economic growth. India became a dynamic economy. The growth rate rose to seven per cent per year.

Unemployment and poverty

However, as years passed by, it was seen that the growth was a jobless growth Development was knowledge and capital intensive and not labour intensive. The arrival of the new computer age further accelerated the process. This created serious problem of unemployment and underemployment.

Growth was also iniquitous with rich growing richer while poor were left behind. In the Mahatma Gandhi National Employment Guarantee Schemes, wages given to workers are less than the minimum wage prescribed, in as many as fifteen states. The workers are barely able to eke out their livelihood. Lack of adequate agricultural land led to sub-division and fragmentation of land and uneconomic holdings. In the new policy approach co-operatives got a back seat. The politicization of the co-operative and the dominance of politician got co-operative a bad name. Co-operative Marketing and processing were not developed except to some extent in Maharashtra and Gujarat.

Neglet of agriculture lead to agrarian distress. Farmers were forced to commit suicide under the stress of mounting indebtedness not only to co-operative credit society and commercial banks but also to private money lenders paying exorbitant rates of interest. Even when agriculture season was good, farmers did not get adequate returns because agriculture prices collapses after demonetisation. Farmers raised in revolt.

Demonetisation seriously hit the cash dependent agricultural economy. The purchasing power of traders-buyers diminished. Agricultural product prices dropped and despite bumper crop such as that of Tur, the prices crashed. Government of Maharashtra was perforce required to make purchase of Tur as market would not lift it.

There was migration of rural population to live in urban areas. Cities and towns grew in population but rapid urbanization has created serious problems of housing. While the leading affluent family of Mumbai has for itself a magnificent mansion of twenty seven floors, the large majority lives in slums and shanties where living conditions are abominable.

Manual scavenging has ended but even now when vast congregation of pilgrims gather at Pandharpur on Ashadhi Ekadashi, conservancy workers have to lift vast quantum of human refuge in hazardous conditions with fitful wages.

Labour intensive industries like textiles and leather have suffered. Textile is the second largest employment industry employing over 3.5 crore people. Workers in textile industry stare at uncertain future. GST will make life difficult for master wester who will have to pay 18% on man-made fibre yarn and 5% on cotton yarn. There is no yarn available amid all the chaos created. Five lakh powerlooms had to be shut down. Various technicians and daily waged workers have been hit hard.

The new rules regarding the sale of cattle have made it difficult for leather industry to get leather. Leather industry is one of the largest industry in India which is labour intensive. The attack on Dalits in Una in Gujarat taking out hide from dead animals have made them to stay away from their traditional work. Now the non-Dalits would themselves have to do the not very agreeable job of taking away the hide.

Agricultural Distress

The agricultural economy is in bad shape. Half the country's workforce and two-thirds of the country's poor are in agriculture but it accounts for only 15% of GDP reflecting low earnings in agriculture. Faced with growing indebtedness to co-operative banks, nationalized banks and even private money lender at exorbitant rates of interest, young farmers are driven to commit suicide. That this should happen seventy years after independence is a sad commentary on our performance. The neglect of the co-operative sector in the wake of the policy of privatization has weakened the entire co-operative credit structure. Demonetizations gave another blow to District Co-operative Banks. The Reserve Bank refused to accept demoneitised notes from the District co-operative Banks. They accumulated with the District co-operative Banks on which they had to pay interest to those who had deposited the notes. It is only after the Chief Minister of Maharashtra represented the problem to the Union Finance Minister and after long last the RBI relented. In the meanwhile the Banks suffered losses and their financial position worsened. Farmers who were committing suicide gathering outrage at long last and went on strike. In Madhya Pradesh farmers demonstrated. Police fired bullets to disperse the demonstrators. Eight farmers lost their lives. The farmer friendly Chief Minister went on fast unto death which he soon ended after sitting for a day.

Distress of the farmers needs to be properly dealt with. When farmers went on strike The Chief Minister of Maharashtra had to pumph in 34000 crores of rupees to write off farmers debt under certain conditions. He rightly said that this was not the solution. Agriculture he to be made more secure by substantially increasing area under irrigation.

Health and Education

In social sectors like health and education, the disadvantaged people are suffering. Public health facilities are limited. The number of public hospitals is inadequate and wards are overcrowded. There is shortage of doctors and paramedical staff and essential articles like syringes and medicine in public hospitals. The people have to go to private doctors who charge fees which the poor can hardly afford.

The Right to Education Act was to provide access to the children of the poor to educational facilities 25% of seats in private schools had to be free.

The private schools had to be compensated by Government for their free seats. So far the Government had paid nothing throwing the entire financial burden on the private schools. While Right to Education Act has removed barriers to entry and there is no detention, students of the poor dropout because the parents want them to work and earn. It is a peculiar irony of our educational system that there is craze for English medium schools even from the pre-primary stages. The Municipal schools where the medium of education is the mother tongue, seats are lying empty. In countries like Japan and Korea, Sweden and Finland education is in their mother tongue This indeed is the irony of our educational system. Mahatma Gandhi and Gurudev Rabindranath Tagore had said that the mother tongue should be the medium of institutions for primary and early secondary education. English could be introduced later as it was even during the days of the British rule. Free India has seen the distortion of the use of English even from pre-primary stage. Out entire system of social and economic policy needs a complete reappraisal for the benefits of the poor and the disadvantaged.

Chapter - 9

Agonising Reappraisal of Liberalisation and Globalisation

1991 marked a water-shed, almost a U-turn, in Indian economic policy pursued over forty years from 1951 to 1991, often described as a Nehruvian model of economic policy. The major features of that model included what came to be known as the 'socialist pattern' of society, a planned economy, emphasis on public sector enterprises and heavy industries which were expected to gain the commanding heights of the economy, *autarky*, import substitution and self-reliance. The new economic policy introduced in 1991 by the Narsimharao minority government was a shift from planning to marketization, from public sector and co-operative sectors to private enterprise, from command and control economy to de-regulation, from autarky to inter-dependence of an open economy, and from progressive taxation to moderate taxation on the high income groups and corporates.

Genesis of liberalisation and globalisation

The genesis of this policy has to be traced to the economic and political crisis with which the country was confronted and which was a big challenge faced by the Narsimharao Government. He appointed as finance minister in his cabinet Dr. Manmohan Singh, an erstwhile civil servant, who had held high positions in economic administration. On his appointment, he immediately entered into discussion with the World Bank and International Monetary Fund who agreed to provide a standby loan and further assistance, subject to the conditionality of India's acceptance of Structural Adjustment Program. The policy of liberalization and globalization initiated by Dr. Manmohan Singh reflected all the elements in the structural adjustment programme which included fiscal discipline requiring heavy cut in public expenditure, incurred in the name of the welfare of the common people. It also reflected the theory of 'the minimal state' i.e. a state which has no direct role in economic activities and gives free scope to the private enterprise.

The new policy was always described as a policy of economic reforms. But the Government did not shown courage to state that it has consciously and deliberately rejected the Nehruvian model. It's approach was somewhat timid and cautious so as not to invite criticism. Those who did not quite agree with the so called economic reforms raised larger issues relating to the pattern of growth to which the economic reforms gave birth namely unequal distribution of the fruits of the liberalization, growing disparities between the rich and the poor, rise of consumerism, and the growing influence of the multi-nationals in the economy and the erosion of national sovereignty.

As the five year term of Narsimharao government was coming to an end, it decided to slow down the new policy lest it should alienate the common people. Despite this the Congress lost power in 1996 general elections. But the non-Congress governments from 1996 to 2004 of which six years were of the BJP Government led by Atal Behari Vajpayee continued the policy of liberalization. The rate of economic development accelerated and BJP made 'Shining India' as its election slogan. But the BJP was in for a shock. In 2004 general elections the Congress emerged as the largest party and formed government with outside support of the leftist parties on the basis of the 'common minimum programme'. This put constraint on the reformist agenda of the Prime Minister Manmohan Singh, the chosen candidate of Sonia Gandhi and P. Chidambaram, as Finance Minister, who could not undertake large scale disinvestments of the public enterprises and opening up of retail, Banking and Insurance to the multi-nationals. Nor could the 'UPA Government, in its second term take the decisions for the so called, "second generation of economic reforms' i.e. Liberalisation and globalisation of the three sectors mentioned above. This attracted criticism of the big business and industry tycoons who made a setting criticism of the government for its 'paralysis in policy making.' Touched to the quick Government suddenly announced the opening of retail business to foreign direct investment raising its share to 51 per cent. This decision was opposed by the opposition parties including the leftist parties as well as the BJP. What was worse for government the two supporting parties the SP and BSP – the regional parties in Uttar Pradesh set for Assembly elections as well the two allies viz. Trinmul Congress and the DMK also opposed the decision. In the face of imminent assembly elections, even two Congress MPs expressed their opposition. Newspaper reports stated that the Cabinet decision on the issue was not unanimous and some ministers, including two Congress members had expressed the reservations. In the beginning government. took a trough stone. The Prime Minister categorically stated that the government cannot roll back the decision and would stand by it. It ignored the nationwide one day strike of the retail traders. But they had to reckon with the adamant stand on the issue of Mamata Banerjee, the TMC head. Government tried to convince her and other about rationale of this 'reforms'. Anand Sharma, the Minister for Trade and Industry held a press conference to explain the rationale. According to him the opening of the retail trade to multi-national, like Walmart (American) and Tesco (British) would provide much needed modernisation of the retail sector. It would benefit both the farmers (better prices for farm produce) and the consumers (lower commodity prices by elimination of the exploitative middle men there by reducing widen gap between producers' prices and consumer prices. Foreign investors would substantially build up the back end infrastructure like cold storages, refrigerated transport and roads, reduce wastes and improve the marketing system as a whole and create ten million more employment opportunities. Name of these arguments carried conviction. On the other hand, what was feared was that crores of small retailers in urban and rural areas, all self employed, and their families would be thrown on the streets creating economic and social crisis. The multi-nationals work for profit and as soon as they got hold of retail market, they would use their monopolistic or oligobolistic strength to hold the farmers and the consumers alike to ransom. Mamata Banerjee, Chief of TMC was not convinced by Anand Sharma's arguments. Pranab Mukherjee the Finance Minister spoke twice to her on phone (she refused to see him) but she insisted that the decision must be put on hold. When Mukherjee said that he would speak on the issue only in Parliament (earlier he had insisted that it was an executive decision and government does not have to take Parliamentary approval forgetting that the executive decision was announced when the Parliament was in session and sound Parliamentary convention required it. But Mamata did not stop for Mukherjee to announce in Parliament. She publicly announced that government will put the decision on hold indefinitely Mukherjee meekly announced that this decision will be indefinitely suspended till there would be unanimity amongst the 'stake holders'. Mukherjee added by way of explanation that if government had pushed through the decision. The nation would have had to face mid-term elections! The bluff of a party with minority of seats in Parliament was called. This was a blow to the introduction of the so called second generation of reforms.

Another aspect needs that mentioned. An officials of US embassy publicly declared support to the decision giving rise to the accusation that the decision was taken under the pressure of US government and the multi-nationals government denied this, but suspicion persisted.

'Reforms can't afford to ignore the common man'. No attempt has been made to explain the policy of liberalization to the people nor has the new policy improved the lot of the common people. Rather it let to the neglect of public investment in social sectors and agricultural and rural development.

Liberalisation and the welfare of the common man

The Central Government should get over the euphoria of liberalization and pay attention to the implications of the new economic policies in term of the welfare of the people and introduce necessary corrections.

The policy of liberalization has led to rural-urban divide. The economic reforms has overlooked the need for spatial planning, industrial dispersal and provision of public services in rural areas. Rural and agriculture economy suffered comparative neglect.

Its extreme manifestation was the tragic phenomenon of nearly two lakh farmers committing suicide in the era of liberalization. The farmers were forced to commit suicide when they fell in a debt trap. While the cost of agriculture inputs increased, the prices of the agriculture produced fluctuated widely. The agricultural extension services got weakened and failed to provide necessary guidelines to the farmers. Institutional credit both by co-operatives and commercial banks failed to meet the credit requirements of the farmers who were forced to go to the money lender, despite the usurious rates of interest. What was required was a comprehensive policy including large public investment in irrigation and rural infrastructure, rejuvenation of co-operative credit, marketing and processing system, strengthening the agricultural extension services and sympathetic administration closely working with the farming community. Unfortunately, no such policy was formulated either by the Congress led government or the BJP led government. The larger aspect of the policy should have been strengthening the natures' life supporting system by widely dispersed projects of soil and water conservation which would have provided ample employment opportunities if they had been taken up under the 'Right to employment program'.

The policy of liberalization as also led to continuous inflationary pressure with the result the prices of essential commodities have gone up from time to time putting them beyond the reach of the common people. The public distribution system went into disrepair. The chief economist of the Finance Ministry Kaushik Bosu has recently admitted that the Government has been left without any instrument to control inflation.

The policy of liberalization and globalization has also led to exclusive emphasis on profits by the private enterprise at the cost of public interest. The tendencies of grabbing and acquisitive mentality has filtered down throughout the society. Instead of liberalization leading to reduced corruption because of the end of "licence permit raj", it has instead led to new opportunities of corruption in misuse of public resources by the private entrepreneurs like builders and unscrupulous businessmen who joined hands with unscrupulous politicians in power. The fall in ethical standards has gone hand in hand with liberalization in other countries as well like China, Russia, Italy and even

Japan. No wonder era of liberalization in India has witnessed financial scams and scandals of huge proportions. The high traditions of public life laid down by the leaders of India's freedom movement have all been forgotten. The corporate sector which talked of high standards of 'Corporate governance' has also been thoroughly exposed by the Satyam episode. The Cancer of Corruption has spread throughout the economic and social system and needs drastic measures to curb it.

India's economic growth is often compared with that of China. China has progressed much faster but it has an authoritarian government. On the other hand India has a democratic system and therefore, Indian economic growth, it is said, would be enduring and democracy would provide a mechanism for preventing corruption and financial crisis. Unfortunately this has not happened. Indian democracy is flawed and the mechanism of automatic correction of abuse of power leading to misuse of resources does not function.

Swadeshi which was the watchword of great leaders like Lokmanya Tilak and Mahatma Gahdhi has often been decried by the advocates of neo-liberalism. Swadeshi needs to be dynamically interpreted in the present context. Inter dependence which is implied in globalization should not degenerate into dependence on dominant countries, nor should the state go down under the pressure of mighty multi-national companies. It should not give up its role to give a sense of direction to the economy in public interest.

Liberalization means that we have accepted the free market economy. But free market economy should not mean complete abandonment of planning. The market is not always rational, and needs to be corrected, it works under the pressure of those who command more resources at the cost of the common man. We should rather follow the example of countries like Japan which plans on the basis of macro economic forecasting and France which has system of indicative planning. The planning commission should concentrate on the formulation of the long-term policies. Planning has to be multi-level and decentralized.

Globalisation

The imperial powers had created a global system under which the economies of the colonized countries were tied to the appron strings of the economies of the imperial powers over a period of five hundred years of imperialism from 1498 onwards. The ample raw materials in those colonized countries were fully exploited by the colonial powers. The colonized countries emerged to freedom after the world war–II. The erstwhile colonial powers took a lead in creating a new international order through establishment of the global institutions like the UNO and its subsidiary bodies, the World Bank, the IMF and more recently in 1995 the World Trade Organization.

After the collapse of socialism and disintegration of the Soviet Union, USA remained the-unchallenged super power which has been trying to shape the world system according to its own design and for promoting its own interest. The present system of globalization is a product of the efforts of the super power. The US Secretary of States Madelaine Albright had once boasted that US is the only indispensable country in the world, it, therefore, does not hesitate to make a disproportionate claim on the available natural resources and disproportionate use of energy without any regard for pollution and global warming. The so-called inter-dependent economy based on free flow of goods and services capital and finance entrepreneurship and management and technology in fact works in the interest of the US and other dominant economies. The World Bank, The International Monetary Fund and WTO work under the dominance of the USA and follow countries which have come to be known as Washington consensus. This distorted system of globalization has often led to instability and has also led to growing in-equalities. The structural adjustment policies imposed by the World Bank on countries in Latin America and Africa have led to disastrous consequences as in Argentina and Brazil. The one sided approach of the World Bank and the IMF was also seen in course of what came to be known as east Asia Crisis of 1997-98. No wonder that peoples' movement against global capitalism have emerged for mobilization against globalization to create a more humane and equitable economic and social order.

Economic Theory of Neo Liberalism

The Chicago School under Milton Friedemen asserted that the capitalist market economy is self correcting. But the collapse of giant American financial institutions in 2009 gave a serious setback to the claims of unbridled capitalism. The collapse of American institutions had a cascading impact on Britain and other European countries as well as Japan. President Bush had to introduce a huge plan to bail out the American financial institutions. He was criticized for preaching capitalism to the ordinary people while promoting socialism to protect the huge financial institutions. America has not yet come out the recession. It will not do so unless the systemic defects which have crept in to the capitalist economy are overcome. On assuming the post of President of USA Barak Obama attributed the financial crisis to insatiable greed of the CEO's of American companies but he has not yet not been able to overcome the systemic defects of the American Capitalism.

The US recession and economic crisis in the European Market countries persists. The European leaders are at wit's and as to how to deal with the crisis. The nightmares of the Great Depression of 1929-30 have come back. India which had boasted in 2008 that the banking crisis of 2008 has not affected India because Indian banks are 'regulated, has also started feeling the consequences of the crisis on US and Europe. The rate of economic growth has slowed down. Fiscal deficit have not diminished. Inflation persists. Prices of essential commodities are continuously rising. Export figures inflated by wrong computer entries are found to be falling. The Finance Minister has admitted that the economic situation is deteriorating-Government and their vaunted set of economists have no clues for dealing with the problems. Their predictions regarding tall in inflation have been found to be no better than the predictions of astrologers! All that is done is the RBI repeatedly increase cash revenue ratio and interest rates. These measures have not been effective in controlling inflation. Clearly the problems are structural and not monetary in nature.

The theoretical foundations of neo-liberalism are not sound. After World War the II Keynesian economics drew attention to the factors behind unemployment in the capitalist countries and emphasized the importance of public investment and redistribution of income to overcome the same. Also a new body of economics known as "development economics" was formed which emphasized the importance of 'big push' to be given by the State to enable the people of the developing countries to get out of the poverty. However, the ascendancy of the Chicago School banished both these new schools of thoughts and restored the primacy of the neo-classical economics and its backing of a totally free market economy with no role for the State. This thinking is at the core of what has come to be known as Washington Consensus which is at the back of today's liberalization and globalization. But a critical examination of the propositions of the neo-classical economics shows that its foundations are not sound. The market is never perfect and human beings are not rational economic entities. There are different motivations behind the economic transactions. A number of economists including those who have been Nobel prize winners have shown the need for re-examination of the basic propositions of free market economy and liberalization and globalization based on it. The reality of capitalism is far different from the myths of capitalism propagated by the Chicago School. If socialism has failed, capitalism has not succeeded in solving the problems of the humanity. There is need for the search of alternatives. One alternatives is 'participative economics' as propounded by Michael Albert. The other is the Gandhian philosophy which has emphasized that the blind pursuit of material achievements is not the be all and end all of life. It is at the root of conflict and violence which we witnessed in the world in our competitive pursuit of economic interests. The essential propositions of Gandhian ideology are of great relevance today in the era of liberalization and globalization.

Chapter - 10

Coping with Seasonalty and Drought

After three successive years of good monsoon, large parts of the country are once again under the shadow of a severe drought. It is reported that 29000 out of 40000 villages in Maharashtra are in the grip of drought. Gujarat, Rajasthan and Madhya Pradesh are also very badly affected.

The occurrence of drought is of course only to be expected. Two Third's of the cultivated area in India is subject to periodic droughts. After three years of complacency once again attention is reverted on the strategy of dealing with drought. This is what makes the book under review of immediate relevance. It is a study of strategies adopted by different types of households in a village in the semi-arid and chronically drought prone region of Gujarat State to cope with drought. The study is based on research carried out during 1987 which was third year of severe drought in the region.

The drought of 1985-87 was real drought since it was spread over a succession of years. Many parts of Gujarat suffered shortfall during these years. In all the villages of the area where the study was conducted, the 1985-87 drought was considered the worst in living memory.

Over the past three decades, Gujarat experienced wide spread drought over 8 years and localized drought every year. Maatisar village, located in Dholka taluka of Ahmedabad district a drought-prone region, is severely affected by droughts every five years. Although the area under irrigation has expanded, monsoon crops are still grown under rain fed conditions and remain highly sensitive to rainfall. Ground water aquifers need to be regularly recharged and are sensitive to shortfall in rainfall. Even though close to Ahmedabad city, the District remains relatively underdeveloped.

The village had a feudal set up till recently. The situation changed after the introduction of Land Reforms during 1950 and 1960 and the institution of

Gram Panchayats in 1963. The political power shifted from the socially higher caste and the numerically dominant castes.

The traditional economy of the village was organised on caste lines. Among the important caste are the Bhrahmins who cultivate lands, Thakkars are engaged in trade, shop keeping and money lending, Bharwads are engaged in animal husbandry, Prajapatis are engaged in potmaking, Vaghris are engaged in cultivation as wage labourers and hunting, Vinkars are engaged in weaving, and Koli Patels work as farm workers. The village has also service castes like carpenters (Sutars), Barbers (Navi), Geneologist (Barub) and Priests (Pujaris)

Under the old jajmani system various caste groups rendered servers to the feudal lords but in 50s these wee abolished. In the early, 80s many household derived secured livelihood from the hereditary caste occupations but with increased population density and division of property, the hereditary occupation did not provide adequate sustenance. Thus, many caste were forced to enter into the wage labour market.

The different households belonging to different caste and engaged in their traditional occupations have evolved their own strategies to cope with risks and uncertainity arising out of seasonal changes. They have tried to build flexibility in their basic livelihood system in order to make mid-season and cross-season adjustments. One way of building flexibility was diversification of occupations and resort to various subsistence activities such as gathering of fuel, fodder and water which are carried on by women. Reduction of the consumption, drawing-down of inventories, entering into labour market, entering into and sharing group arrangement, drawing on social relationships, drawing on community resources like trees and grazing lands, pawning assts like jewellery and household utensils are the normal ways of coping with risks and uncertainty associated with seasonality and drought.

During 1987 drought, most landholding and occupational groups reduced their consumption of food grains, milk and vegetables as the drought advanced. Festivals were celebrated with less expenditure. The bride price was lowered and the marriage cost were reduced. However, the number of marriages increases dramatically!

In adoption of various strategies, villagers depend on economic and social institutions. The traditional patron client relationship, jajmani system and kinship and caste provide the traditional social security system which has been considerably eroded in modern times and consequently their ability to minimize the impact of drought on their economy. In the traditional system patrons were required to underwrite substantial consumption needs of the client and provide protection in return for services, and respect and loyalty of their clients. With the introduction of cash transactions, the economic basis of the patron-client and jajmani system has gradually eroded. Market forces have replaced traditional modes of transactions in tenancy, labour and credit market which do not guarantee subsistence during the slack season for the period of uncertainty particularly in drought areas.

In the earlier years of drought, peasants were able to draw on the water supply to sustain wheat and barley cultivation. When rains failed, farmers resorted to usual strategies of replanting, defering planting, substitute planting and growing fodder crops. However, when the drought was prolonged there was a short-fall of grains production and people had to seek employment opportunities on non-farm occupations. As the economy weakened because of the drought, the local labour market collapsed. The co-operative sugar factories were forces to close because most of the sugarcane crop had been sold as fodder. The demand for labour in brickfield and rice mills also dropped.

In normal areas the labour from 50 households in the village would migrate. Because of the collapse of the labour market there was a drop in demand for migrant labour.

The 1987 was the worst year for weavers. They could not sell their shawls as the market had collapsed. The demand for the traditional services of barbers, genealogists and priests also dropped as their patrons adjusted to the drought conditions. The potter household suffered a decline in demand for pots. Surprisingly, trader and money lenders who normally prosper in drought years also suffered a decrease in volume of trade.

In these conditions, the scarcity relief work played a crucial role in averting large scale starvation. Landless labourers and artisan caste actively participated in the relief work. As the drought became more severe, peasants household from all categories also joined the relief work. Even those castes like shepherd who did not engage in wage labour also joined the relief work. 70% of the small farm household, 80% of the Vankar weaver household and other half of the labour household participated in the relief work. Even the land-rich household joined the relief work. More women than men participated in them. No doubt there were weaknesses in the relief work like corruption in the actual operation of the scheme, but it benefits providing social security to large number of people outweighed, abuses or leakages of the system.

Due to the effective presence of relief work there was no aimless wandering in search of employment opportunities. There was little evidence of family disintegration during the 1985-87 drought, because of the employment offered by the Government relief system. Labour households did not suffer significant trade entitlement failure despite the collapse of the local migrant labour. In fact labour household were able to exchange their labour for more days in 1985-87 drought than in the normal years. The peasant cultivators and tenant farm household suffered both direct and trade entitlement failure because of the prolonged nature of drought. They depleted their stocks and their capital reserves, and many cultivators were in debt. Shepherds suffered both from direct entitlement and trade entitlement failures and were forces to migrate to South Gujarat and during their forced migration they lost their animals, their major engowment. The venkar were forced to close their weaving operations. The Thakakrs did not suffer significant failure. The Brahmins suffered significant entitlement failure.

The Maatisar drought of 1985-87 turned out to be primarily a fodder drought. As a result farmers no longer allowed other villages to collect grass and weeds from their cultivated fields, or to graze animals on their fields and women began to quarrel over rights to collect cow dung from public places. The Jains as a matter of charity ran camps for sick and dying animals.

The voluntarily organization SEWA played a significant part in lobbying for relief work and in transportation and sale of fodder from south Gujarat to the drought areas, in constructing a cattle through and in providing subsidized seeds, fertilizers and fuel. There was a significant demand for production loans from institutions. Because of the active help of the relief work only 40% of the total loans taken were for consumption needs.

The suffering people in 1985-87 drought was much less than that 1899-1900. This was because in 1985-87 while there was a sharp decline in production, there was no sharp decline in consumption because of the effective presence of relief work and public distribution system through which food was made available. As a result food prices did not escalate drastically.

The study has drawn attention to several weaknesses in the relief work undertaken. First, the quantum of relief work is not always adequate to meet the demands during severe droughts. Government funds are limited and finances are not adequate to meet the working capital requirements. Second, the productive component in relief works is not upto the mark. Thirdly, even before the crisis hits, there is always the demand for seasonal public works on a regular basis.

The significant long-term effect of the drought is the adverse impact on ability of the individual households and traditionally social security system to recover after the drought. The most significant conclusion of the study is that public drought management is isolated from regular development strategies. Both seasonality and drought should be considered as key variables in development policy. Long term approach to drought must replace the crisis management approach.

There should be more emphasis on development in drought management. Rural development programmes must be resource specific in relation to arid or semi-arid areas. Development has so far focused on high potential areas and have neglected dry areas. The drought management approach has been developed in isolation from ongoing development strategies or chronic subsistence needs. Village economy remains vulnerable to drought despite growth and development. Drought needs to be analyzed not only as short-term isolated phenomenon but as long-term repetitive phenomenon which together with seasonal fluctuations affect rural livelihood options.

Chapter - 11

Abolition of Planning Commission

Modi government has abolished the Planning Commission – *Yojanaa Aayog* and replaced it by the National Institution for Transforming India – NITI *Aayog.* What does the decision imply? Does it mean mere not only abolition of planning commission or the concept of planning itself? And the system of formulation of five years plans and annual plans for the country as a whole and for states or does it mean abolition of the concept of planning itself?

It may be argued that the abolition of planning was inevitable in the wake of policy of liberalization introduced by Narsimha Rao and Dr. Manmohan Singh way back in the year 1992. In fact it was long over due. The logic of planning is in sharp destination with the logic of liberlisation.

The logic of planning was that the development of the country cannot be left to the vicissitudes of the market forces. It has to be planned by deliberate action of the state.

The logic of luberalisation was that the development was the outcome of the functioning of market. Free working of the market economy would lead to 'rational' allocation of resources and give optimum results. Basic decisions as what to produce, where to produce, when to produce and for whom to produce should be taken by the free operation of the market of course market is not always 'free' and to that extent state intervention may be necessary to remove imperfections in the market economy such as lack of information and influence of monopolies and oligo politic forces on the functioning of the market or behavioural aberrations which make decisions irrational. But the scope of such market intervention by the state is limited.

But planning does not imply just method of management of the economy planning is 'purposive arrangement of the future' and in this sense is universal.

Every individual, institutions and the society as a whole ahs to 'plan' its future. In this universal sense planning cannot be abolished.

While the concept of planning in clear, the concept of 'transformation' is vague unless we give .... meaning to it. It is a grandiose term convening the entire gamut of political, economic and social institutions and the altitudes of the people as always their work ethic and extent of mutual trust prevailing in the society.

Can such 'transformation' be brought about by a single institution, however grandiose its nomenclature? It requires the combined efforts of not only the state but also the entire gamut of economic and social institutions and indeed by every individual. It requires changes in the attitudes of the people.

ADMINISTRATION -V

Chapter - 1

Whither Indian Bureaucracy?

When India became independent, it decided to setup a democratic state and not a bureaucratic state. Bureaucracy was to be the instrument of democracy for the fulfillment of the national purpose viz. rapid economic development and abolition of poverty. Nehru believed that a reformed bureaucracy could be the agent of socio-economic change and instrument of transformation of the police state into a welfare state.

To be sure, it was a conscious departure from the role of the bureaucracy in the colonial era – the role of maintenance of law and order and collection of revenue. But it was felt that there was no other organised force except that of bureaucracy to undertake the myriad tasks of development – rural and agricultureal development, industrial promotion and building up social and economic infrastructure. Whether it was designing of new scheme and programmes, setting up new organizations or even mobilizing the people to participate in the programmes, it was bureaucracy that came into the picture. This opened vastly new fields of action to the bureaucracy and gave its members a heightened and much nobler role which could give them a sense of fulfillment. The glow of this euphoria lasted for several years after independence under the leadership of the stalwarts who were at the helm of affairs.

Soon, however, this new atmosphere of the post-independence era started losing its élan. The idealistic glow of the administration of the early years began to fade. And the limits of bureaucratic action started becoming apparent.

For example, rural development and poverty alleviation turned out to be tasks far too complex to be fully tackled in the bureaucratic mould or through stereotype schemes. As Gandhiji noted long back sustained and dedicated work over years was needed to bring about a transformation even in a single village community. It was unrealistic for a transferable official to accomplish this task. The administrative effort was too dilute to make an indepth impact or to bring about a lasting change.

Bureaucratic limitation was also seen in the management of public enterprises – another new task for bureaucracy. The management of economic enterprises needed flexibility and fast decision making which was not possible within the framework of financial rules and regulations of government. The imperatives of public audit which insisted on strict conformity to these rules further tightened the straight jacket on these enterprises making them too rigid to respond to changing economic environment. Moreover, as a result of the ethos of the sociolist pattern of society imposed on these enterprises on one hand and the burden of social responsibility and welfare on the other Multiplicity of objectives amongst which profit making appeared to assume a position of low priority, no wonder that there survival started depending on an increasing measure on the support of the public exchequer.

Planning and control mechanism also brought out the short-comings of bureaucracy. Centralised planning led to centralized administrative attitudes which inhibited impulses and initiatives at state and local levels. Central mechanism made private enterprise concentrate on manipulating levers of administration rather than on promoting economic efficiency and productivity which are components of real economic performance. With big public spending and powers of control, the lobbies of big business and contractors increasingly attracted the bureaucracy even at higher levels to the lures of easy money.

Degeneration set in another way also. One of the essential attributes of bureaucracy is political neutrality As Dr. Rajendra Prasad the first President of free India observes, "it is the business of democracy to represent al interests but it is the business of bureaucracy to eliminate all interests." The doctrine of political neutrality was intended to enable bureaucracy to work under governments of different political parties with a sense of neutrality, objectivity and impartiality. But with the same party in power for several years after independence both at the Centre and in the states this was forgotten and bureaucratic autonomy in its own sphere was increasingly eroded – autonomy to give frank and free advice rather than a convenient advice on policy matters and to apply law and implement policies and programmes without fear or favour. I remember even Jawaharlal Nehru presiding over an annual general meeting of the IIPA taking objection to the concept of neutrality which was the title of the lead articles in the Indian Journal of Public Administration released on the occasion. His contention was that bureaucratic neutrality was all right during the colonial era but was not appropriate in free India where bureaucracy cannot be neutral to the welfare of the people. From this it was logical to proceed to the next step – the concept of neutral bureaucracy giving way to the new concept of 'committed bureaucracy'. And this is what Indira Gandhi did and with disastrous consequences to the objective and impartial working of the bureaucracy. When politician used to long enjoyment of seats of power started confusing public assets with private property, and public purpose with party and partisan interests, the doctrine of 'committed bureaucracy' handy to unscrupulous politicians to twist the bureaucrats at will to achieve their objectives. The essential vulnerability of bureaucracy ensured that a large majority of its members would crawl when asked to bend. Those who appeared to be reluctant to compromise could easily be marginalized if not actually penalized. Rightful claimants could be reduced to abject suppliants and thus made pliable. No wonder objectivity and impartiality became a casuality. Also clever politicians, in such situations, could rind easy scape goats in bureaucracy for actions for which they themselves were responsible. It is notable that in post-independence India while a few members of bureaucracy have been penalized, not a single politician has met the fate of some venal politicians in a state like Singapore!

Bureaucracy lacking in objectivity and impartiality and expertise and indepth knowledge (which frequent transfers at will without any career planning cannot allow to develop) increasingly lost its capabilities to do the tasks which it was expected to discharge viz. at higher levels contributing to policy making and at the field level competent policy and programme implementation. Bureaucracy's role was squeezed out between experts of various sorts giving convenient advice to politicians on policy matters and plticians themselves deciding who would be the beneficiaries – witness loan melas and now public funds being allotted to Members of Parliament and Members of State legislatures for distribution at will. No wonder a young IAS officer working as private secretary to a Union Minister told me sometime back that in Delhi there is a feeling that IAS is no longer needed! In the states officers of the State Civil Services have started questioning the supremacy of the IAS and attacking it with increasing ferocity. In this they have the ready support of some State Politicians who find the 'independence' of the IAS an inconvenient obstruction in rendering 'public service'.

A question arises whether in the wake of privatization and politisation, bureaucracy – neutral and development – oriented, has any role to play. True privatization would mean vacation by the State of the 'commanding heights' of the economy and increasing reduction of its role in direct management of the economy. But even the 'vacation' has to be an orderly process as seen in UK, whose Prime Minister, Mr. Major has offered to our government his coutry's expertise in the divesting the state of as involvement in public enterprises. Even for orderly arrangement of disinvestments, efficient bureaucratic action is necessary. Furthermore, the need for the state setting up a proper legal, financial social framework a strong infrastructure for the operation of the private enterprise would continue. Years ago, Gunnar Myrdal characterized India as a 'sort state', a state where laws rules and regulations are not properly enforced. A system cannot work if the rules of the game for the working of the system are not observed by all concerned. It is for the State to see that the rules are observed. A soft state with a weak bureaucracy cannot do so.

While politicization has gone a pace in the country with the broadening of democracy, the ear of monopoly of power by a single political party has come to an end. Bureaucracy need not be bonded servants of a single political party or a political personality. Civil servants can now act as servants of the nation and the government in power – no matter of what political party or headed by what political personalities. The political arrogance emerging out of a continuous engagement of political power need not any longer frighten them so long as they act according to rules, their prescribed duties and code of conduct and in public interest.

In the wake of politicization, elective institutions and non-governmental organizations may have a greater role to play. With the 73rd amendment to the Constitution, Panchayati Raj institutions have become the third tier of the Indian polity and as many as 29 items – most of them related to local development have found a place in the local list. The NGO's have grown in number and variety and could undertake the responsibility for implementing an increasing number of programme of local development. Yet neither Panchayati Raj nor the rise of NGO would spell the euthanasia of bureaucracy at the district level. Panchayati Raj Institutions cannot function without administrative support and a good high level bureaucracy would still be needed at the local level.

The role of bureaucracy as envisaged at the dawn of freedom might have to undergo a change. But the need for a good bureaucracy at all levels continues in the interest of objective administration necessary for an orderly development of the country and its stability.

Chapter - 2

Reflections on an Era – Memoirs of a Civil Servant by S. Bhothalingam

The autobiographies of the officers of the Indian Civil Service who divided their careers between pre-independence and post-Independence era have now started coming out. One of them is a posthumous autobiography of Shri. Bhootlingam. At a late stage of life between 1985-87, he dictated his recollections but alas breathed his last before publishing his autobiography. We are therefore, grateful to Bhootlingam Literary Trust for making his notes available in the form of an autobiography.

The name of Shri. Bhootlingam is taken along with another stalwarts of the civil service, the late Shri. L.K. Jha who took significant part in the economic administration of the country in the early years after Independence.

Bhootlingam joined the ICS in 1931. Unlike other officers of the Indian Civil Service. Shri. Bhootlingam had only a short spell in the districts as Sub-Collector. Settlement Officer and Collector in Madras province before he was transferred to Delhi, where he spent the rest of his Civil Serivce Career till his retirement. He belonged to the 'Central Pool' of the Indian Civil Service officers to which surprisingly enough Shri. Bhootlingam makes no reference. Normally officers of the Indian Civil Service was expected to divide their career between the spells in the states and central government. However, as an officer of the Central pool Shri. Bhootlingam had long spell at the Centre which enabled him to take a significant part in national economic policy making and administration in the Nehruvian era.

What came to be known as Nehruvian model consisted of planning in mixed economy aimed at mobilizing economic resources for economic development with equity and social justice. In the wake of this policy came large public sector which Nehru expected to occupy the commanding heights of the economy, as also legislations like the Industrial Development and Regulation Act and Monopoly and Restrictive Practices Act to ensure that the Private Sector worked in the framework of planning.

It is the context of this policy that Shri. Bhootlingam played his part as Secretary in the Ministry of Steel and Ministry of Finance. As Secretary in the Ministry of Steel, he played a pioneering role in setting up three large steel mills at Durgapur, Bhilai and Rourkela in collaboration with the British, the USSR and the German Governments. As Secretary, Economic Co-ordination during the Chinese war, he recalls how several airports were built just during six months.

While as a civil servant Shri. Bhootli-lngam played his part in the management of a controlled economy, his post-retirement reflections show how critical he was of it. He points out that the controls were hangover of the war economy, when a panoply of controls – sugar control, iron and steel control, food rationing, petrol rationing etc. were introduced, but in post-independence period they acted as fetter to the free forces of economic initiative in the country. To be sure, Shri. Bhootlingam claims that he did try to soften the grip of these controls but obviously he did not act sufficiently vigourously or did not have the authority to dismantle the framework of controls which strangled the economy leading to economic stagnation manifesting in low growth rate. The removal of controls had to await the liberalisation era of the nineties.

Shri. Bhootlingam has discussed the big event of the devaluation of the Indian rupee in 1966. The over valuation of the Indian rupee had created the necessity of a number subsidies for imports or exports and replenishment scheme under which the licences could be sold at profit. The World Bank put pressure on devaluation of Indian rupee so that such subsidies could be abolished. Shri. Bhootlingam explains at length how care was taken to maintain complete secrecy about the proposal. The devaluation of the Indian rupee proved to be politically unpopular and Shri. Bhootlingam had to bear the brunt for the decision. On the top of it, Shri. Bhootlingam had the discomfiture of seeking that devaluation was not allowed to work and Indian had the worst of both the worlds.

In course of his long spell in the central government, Shri. Bhootlingam came in close touch with stalwarts like Rajaji, Sardar Patel, Pandit Jawaharlal Nehru the first Prime Minister of free India for 17 years and the Finance Minister Shri. T.T. Krishnamachari. Bhootlingam's reminisances about these stalwarts and now they worked are extremely interesting and revealing.

Bhootlingam, describes Rajaji as 'philosopher' with clarity of mind and a freshness of outlook and Sardar Vallabhbhai Patel as the architect and builder between whom there was good collaboration and understanding about the pattern of free India.

Pandit Nehru modelled himself as an all round Philosopher king. He acted as truly patriotic Indian concerned for the welfare of the ordinary people of India. Thus, while visiting the public sector steel unit what upset him most was inadequate housing for the workers which he thought should be of higher standard. Nehru also intensely disliked the use of army for dealing with situations of civil strife. Nehru acted as a democratic leader of Government, who could delegate a great deal to the civil services. The author fondly recollects Nehru's informal and gracious ways of dealing with civil servants.

Even in the early years after independence there were times when the civil servants were in placed a delicate situation out of which they could get out only because of the gracious behaviour of the stalwarts who were at the helm of affairs. Shri. Bhootlingam recollects the story of the meeting of the Khadi Board called by the President Dr. Rajendra Prasad. Bhootlingam felt that the President could not call the meeting at all. In doing so President Rajendra Prasad was behaving as though Prime Minister was dealing with Secretary to Government. When Bhootlingam brought this to the notice of the Prime Mnister Jawaharlal Nehru, he adviced him not to create a crisis and assured to sort out the matter. Next time when Shri. Bhootlingam met Shri. Rajendra Prasad he explained to the President that how the matter had to dealt with through the administrative process and would take sometime. Dr. Prasad agreed to leave the matter to the Secretary and the crisis was solved through good grace.

T.T. Krishammachari made a significant contribution to economic development of India next to Nehru. He was highly intelligent, well versed in Vedas and Upanishads but also had successful practical business experience. However, he had rough edges of his temper. He was an excellent economist and was ambitious to become the Finance Minister, and was disappointed when Shri. Deshmukh was appointed. However, he accepted the post of Minister for Commerce and Industry. He was an efficient and dynamic Minister, quick and vigonous in action.

Shri. Bhootlingam narrates an incidence. T.T. Krishammachari paid a surprise visit to the office of the Chief Controller when he found an officer having tea with his feet on the table. He didn't bother to get up or to greet T.T. Krishammachari, for the simple reason that he did not recognize him. T.T. Krishammachari suspended him on the spot. Later on, after the Bhootlingam briefed him about the ways of bureaucracy. T.T. Krishammachari called him back and said "Put that fellow out of his misery, but tick him off well and proper. How you do it and fix your files is your bloody business." Swaran Singh was a perfect example of an ordinary man. He was always calm, covered freely but without saying anything in particular. Shri. Bhootlingam recounts the amusing experience of his addressing the Queen of England, using Majesty almost like comas, to the great embarrassment of the queen!

Shri. Bhootlingam recollects pugnacious nature of Shri. Krishna Menon and his relationship with his Secretary Shri. Pulla Reddy. He disparagingly said that he had neither pull nor was he ready! Shri. Bhootlingam visited the High Commission when Menon was the High Commissioner to make an assessment of the Indian Stores Department. Menon deliberately gave very early appointment to call on him at half past eight, and made a rude remark about the late rising habits of the officers of the Indian Civil Servants Officers forgetting that as district officers they were used to getting up quite early.

Moraraji Desai gave appointments to ambassadors and other dignitaries during lunch hours having himself arrived at the office at 11 hours after a brunch. After Shri. Bhootlingam suggested, with considerable hesitation, that it was not right to give appointment to foreign ambassadors during lunch hour and would be construed as a discourtesy, no appointment was given during this period. Moraraji claimed that he was an 'ashtawadhani' doing many things at the same time. When Bhootlingam told him that he could do only one thing at a time, Morarji observed, "It is not everybody who has my gift." On most files he wrote 'please speak', and would give orders before giving a chance to the Secretary to speak about the matter. Bhootlingam, therefore, developed a style of handing him over a note before he could speak. Morarji went along with the proposal in the note!

Even a distinguished civil servants sometimes suffers at the end of an illustrious career! What came to be known as 'steel scandal' broke out at a time he was engaged in pushing through the major decision of devaluation of the Indian rupee. It caused him great mental strain. Six months looked like six years! He also had to pay the price of foregoing appointment as ambassador to EEC at the Brussels. However, at the end of the enquiry, he came out without any blemish.

After his retirement Shri. Bhootlingam was appointed as Chairman of the Committee for direct taxes. Instead of indulging in elaborate process of collecting evidence, Shri. Bhootlingam availed of information from the books and gave a report in a language which every one could understand. He suggested the scheme for introducing for Public Provident Fund and abolition of the Expenditure Tax. Both proved to be sound recommendations.

Altogether a successful career, although eclipsed at the end by an undeserved calumny! Book review article on 'Reflections on an Era – Memoirs of a civil servant by S. Bhothalingam.

Chapter - 3

Dealing Effectively with Law and Order Situations

Recent years have seen the State resorting the greater and more frequent use of its coercive agencies to deal with law and order situations and at the same time, an increasingly greater inability of these coercive agencies to deal effectively with the problems of law and order.

The normal coercive agency of the State for dealing with the internal disturbances is the police. It has not only been augmented but reinforces by special types of police forces of diversified nature like the armed reserve police force, the Railways and industrial establishments protection force, the Border Security force, the Assam rifles, black cat commando etc. It has been noted that with unease that all this coercive power of the police has fallen short or requirements and the army had to be called in frequently, but even this has also proved to be counter productive.

Thus, it has been reported that in Manipur the army has been ineffective in dealing with the insurgency situation there. "The insurgents can kill many people at a time but we cannot get any one of them. They snatch away arms but we cannot get them back. They loot cash but we recover nothing." And yet the army is accused of 'excessive use of force.' To prevent the army from getting involved in civilian operations, the late General B.C. Joshi conceived of a new agency viz. the National Rifles as the Army outfit for dealing with internal disorders. The situation of the police is even more unenviable. Thus, recently in Goa, the violent agitation against the Nylon 6, 6 project led to firing by the police and a young agitator died in police firing. Such was the mob fury against the police that when the curfew was imposed, it was the police which was conspicuous by the absence since the agitationists warned the police that if they ventured to come out in the city of Ponda, they would be met with dire consequences at the hands of the activists.

The increasingly effectiveness of the coercive agencies of the State is a matter of great concern. If these coercive instruments are blunted through frequent by ineffective use, the State will be left with nothing to rely upon in containing the increasingly turbulent agitations disturbing the law and order situation in the country holding the common man to ransom.

It is necessary to go into the causes of the phenomenon of increasing ineffective of the coercive agencies rather than going in for the old approach of the more of the same that is sending more platoons and putting greater reliance on ever increasing augmentation of the coercive force. Unfortunately, the Home Ministry at the Centre and Home Departments in the States have been prone to resort the coercive action rather than to understand what gives rise to frequent breakdown itself could be prevented and furthermore by not using coercive forces far too frequently, the potential threat of bringing the coercive forces into action could have its salutary effect.

It is a matter of astonishment that inspite of the existence of democratic parliamentary institutions and democratic government in our country, the politicians either as legislators or as members of Government, scarcely have any understanding of the situation, do not recognise early warning signals and are unable to act on time before the situation gets out of hand. In a democratic polity politicians would be expected to feel the pulse of the people with the feedback received from them, anticipate dangers inherent in a situation before it erupts into violence and to avoid its occurrence by taking preventive actions through discussions and negotiations with the people concerned.

Unfortunately, the politicians have been unable to play this role, the reason for this is that politicians have become more interested in enjoying the fruits of power rather than acting as representatives of the people. As the legislators and other politicians seem to be busy feathering their own nest when the unrest occurs, rather than facing the agitating public, they are more anxious to approach the police forces to save their own skin.

Since the politicians are unable to feel the pulse of the people and play as the buffer between the people and Government, The Government seems to rely more and more on the intelligence reports. The politicians have developed a pathetic dependence on these reports since they have no independent sources of information directly through the media of the people. The reliability of the intelligence agencies is always very doubtful, since the intelligence agencies at the field level often depend for their material on sources of doubtful authencity. If the primary sources themselves are unreliable, depending on them the government may easily be led to take wrong action in dealing with law and order situations.

If the administration is alert, it can play the role which in a democratic polity should be played by the political representatives. However, increasingly the bureaucracy has become office oriented or guided by the dictate of the political VIPs. Touring has become less intensive. The direct contacts with the people have diminished despite the proliferation of programmes. As a result, even field level administrators are out of touch with reality. On the top of it, they are not free to make their own judgements as in the past. The weakening of the field agencies has weakened the law and order situation.

It is therefore, obvious that unless basic thinking is done by those in power about causes of the breakdown of the law and order situation and the way in which it should be dealt with the frequency of the situations of breakdown of law and order and their severity and gravity will only increase. The Home Ministry must give up looking at law and order with the eyes of the police and solely depending on police management of the situation. A wider approach based on deeper understanding of the socio-economic scene and some anticipatory action and alert responses by the representatives of the people and administrators can alone save the situation from getting out of hand in the years to come.

Chapter - 4

Decline of the District Magistrate

The gruesome lynching and brutal murder of the District Magistrate of Gopalgunj Shri. A. Krishnaiyya has send shockwaves throughout the country. Bihar Chief Mnister Laloo Prasad Yadav hurriedly announced monetary support to the bereaved family, setting up of a special investigation team and a special court for speedy trial of the assailants. But this is hardly an adequate response. For what happened is not just commitment of an isolated crime; it is the agonizing culmination of a creping phenomenon which is emerging for long in the working of the District administration in our country – the phenomenon of the growing debility of district administration and the decline of the authority of the institution of the District Magistrate.

The institution of the District Magistrate also known as Deputy Commissioner or Collector was set-up by the British rulers who considered the District as the pivot of the Indian administration. The District Magistrate was looked upon as the local representative of the Government. He was not only the head of the revenue and law and order administration, but general administration of the District as a whole. Whether it was a natural calamity like flood or disaster like wild fire, outbreak of an epidemic or depredations of a wild animals, it was the District Magistrate who was expected to take initiative and co-ordinate and mobilize the district administration as a whole. He was primus inter pares amongst the District officers of all departments including the police and this gave his position a great deal of authority which made for effective administration. Very often a local crisis could be resolved with a word from the District Magistrate without the actual use of force.

After the attainment of independence, in the wake of state sponsored process of planned development and the transformation of the 'police state' into a 'welfare state', the position of the district officer became all the more important. The District Magistrate also became District Development

Commissioner. He was saddled with multifarious responsibilities for the implementation of a variety of laws and programmes in fields like land reforms, community development and extension, co-operation, public distribution, poverty alleviation and removal of social disabilities. In Hindi speaking states, he came to be known as zilladhish thus underlining the importance of his position. But while in the wake of the 'development state', his responsibilities increased, in the wake of the 'democratic state' his authority declined.

A decade or two after independence, the equation between district administration and the local politicians started radically shifting in favour of the latter. The local MLA started looking upon himself not only a representative of the people in the legislative assembly but as a super local administrator who had the authority to direct the local officers not excluding the District magistrate not only by ventilating the grievances of the people or articulating their felt needs but also by asking for a particular decision in a particular case, even in quasi-judicial cases or for posting a particular officer at a particular place. All this came to be known as the phenomenon of political interference in administration which became increasingly pervasive making a mockery of the rule of law and objective administration. People started feeling that work would not be done in the normal course without the use of political influence.

In the years that followed, a new and a more frightening phenomenon appeared on the district scene viz. criminilisation of politics. First politicians supported by criminals and later criminals themselves turning politicians. Political interference meant interference by criminals.

A third phenomenon was the use by the politicians of the police force to settle their political scores. This had bizarre effect on the police administration. While the senior police officers like the DIG and S.P. started questioning the authority of the District Magistrate in law and order matters, the subordinate police on the pay roll of the criminal-politician nexus started ingnoring the authority of their own superiors!

A total rot set in the district administration. The murder of the hapless District Magistrate (only in name) in broad day light by rowdy elements led by the local MLA and his politician wife herself an MP, without police coming to his rescue is a sad commentary on the state of district administration in our country.

It is time we realize the validity even today of the doctrine of the British administration that District is the pivot of the Indian administration and if that pivot breaks, the whole administrative façade would collapse – as seems to be already happening in Bihar. The revival of authority of the district administration should be our prime national concern and we can ignore it only at the peril of civilized and orderly administration in the countryside, throughout the length and breadth of our country.

Chapter - 5

Dealing with Maoist Challenge

The Dantewada massacre of 75 jawans of CRPF ambushed by the Maoists followed in the next week by blowing off a bus carrying civilians in which some Jawans of CRPF were also travelling taking a heavy toll of 50 lives has forced agonising reappraisal of the strategy adopted so far by the Union Home Ministry in dealing with the Maoist challenge. A senior member of the Congress and Ex. Chief Minister of MP Shri. Digvijay Singh openly criticized the Home Minister for his wrong headed approach of dealing with Maoist by the use of armed forces rather than through programmes of development. Shri. Chidambaram, the Home Minister himself admitted that a major blunder was committed by the senior officers of CRPF in conducting the operation. The precautions expressly mentioned in the standard offending procedure were ignored leading to the Jawans being exposed to the Maoist ambush. Obviously the authorities had not reckoned with and underestimated the superior intelligence, weapons, guerilla tactics and capacity of carry out operations with pinpointed accuracy of the Maoist. A retired head of CRPF Shri. Rammohan was appointed to investigate what happened and give a quick report which he did. But what was notable was that apart from pointing out the mistakes made in carrying out the operations, he emphasized the importance of development and good governance which was lacking in tribal areas.

Shri. Chidambaram who became a target of attack, open and insidious, by his own party people, let alone the unremitting criticisms of the intellectuals and the human rights activists, was put on the defencive. Apart from rendering apology to the nation, he went ahead and submitted his resignation to the Prime Minister which he declined to accept. In a TV Interviews, Chidambaram spoke of his 'limited mandate' to explain away the failure to effectively deal with the Maoists who had extended their sway to some 250 distress in the forest areas extending from West Bengal and Orissa, to Jharkhand to

Chattisgarh to Andhra Pradesh and to Maharashtra. When this gave cause to the opposition BJP to attack the UPA Government for tying the hands of Chidambaram in dealing with the Maoists, Chidambaram tried to wriggle but by saying that by "limited mandate" he meant the inevitable limitations of the Central Government since Law and orders is according to the constitutional provisions a state subject. This was like the singing the favourite tune of the previous incumbent of the Home Ministry, Shri. Shivraj Patil, the then Union Government who had been constantly shirnking its responsibility in dealing with the large scale violence let loose by the Maoists by harping on the constitutional position. This came as a disappointment after his apparently pro-active role. Chidambaram too was falling back to the same position as that of his predecessor.

A state subject or responsibility of Union Government?

As recently pointed out by the doyen among security analysis, Shri. K. Subrahmanyam (dealing with Maoism IE, June 9) the Indian Union cannot abdicate its responsibility and seek refuge behind the plea that law and order is the responsibility of the states, "Ultimately all people of India" would look to the Indian Republic/ Union for exercising the fundamental right of peaceful living. The objective of the Maoists is not merely to subvert law and order in tribal areas in various states but wage war against the Indian Republic and the Indian Constitution. Under these circumstances, the Union Government will have to consider invoking article 355 of the Constitution which states, "It shall be the duty of the Union Government to protect every State against external aggression and internal disturbance and to ensure that the governance of every state is carried out in accordance with provisions of the Constitution'. The Union Government will have to work out a co-ordinated plan of operations by all the States carried out in an integrated manner."

Role of the State Police, CRPF and the Army and Airforce

Apart from the Central-State issue, another important aspect is the relative roles of the state police, the Central Armed reserved forces and Army and the Airforce. The position taken was that it is basically the responsibility of the State Police, the Centre only supplement the State Police Force by providing troops of the Central armed reserve police force. After the recent ghastly massacre. the Home Minister felt that this approach may not be adequate and the help of the Army and the Airforce will have to be invoked. This thinking is a sharp departure from the heither-to held position that Army is meant to and equipped for dealing with external aggression by forces of the hostile country and not with the people of the country. This principle has already been sacrificed in dealing with disturbances caused by insurgency in North East States like Manipur as well as in Jammu and Kashmir which has for long been the victim of externally induced terrorism. The Disturbed Area Act and Armed Forces Special Powers Act have been designed to facilitate the active role of the Army in these border states. Now the same approach, it was suggested, had to be extended to the tribal area to introduce the army to deal with the Maoist challenge. The Army and the Air force were reluctant to get embroiled in this problem. Heads of both the organizations gave open expression to their views and had to be cautioned by the Prime Minister not to give public expression to their views. Ministry of Home Affairs, considering the reluctance of the Army and Airforce, have been trying to work out a compromise. The army is prepared to send Officers of the Army on deputation to the States to give guidance for carrying out effective operations. This could also provide training to the State police force. The Army has been openly criticizing of the standard of work and training of CRPF which is not to the liking of the senior officers of CRPF who try to rebut the army criticism. As for the Airforce, they are prepared to provide helicopters for surveillance and transport. All these and other matters formed part of the proposals in the paper submitted by the Home Ministry to the Cabinet Committee on Security presided over by the Prime Minister himself. Having regard to the opposition of the Defence Ministry to any kind of involvement of the Army and the Air Force, the Committee adviced the Home Ministry to recruit on contract basis the ex-service men to help in the operations against the Maoists.

Basic Approach

But even more important than the two issues viz. respective role of the Centre and State and the roles of State Police, the CRPF and the Army and the Airforce are matters relating to the basic approach itself. Everybody including Chidambaram would agree that the basic approach should be two pronged or three pronged first using coercive powers of the state to combat and defeat the guerrilla war of the Maoists challenging the authority of the Indian Republic and the Indian political system of Parliamentary democracy, second promoting ' development' to improve the living of the tribals and third providing 'good governance' to win the confidence of the tribals. But the problem of this approach is like "what comes first – chicken or the egg?" There cannot be development and good governance without law and order and there can not be law and order without development and good governance. How can the state machinery of administration function and development schemes be executed successfully if the 'Maoist Army' attacks the police chowkies taking away weapons from the armory and tehsil and block officers, schools and panchayat officers and abduct officers to be displayed as prisoners of war? Normal administration cannot function and development programmes executed in an atmosphere of fear. At the same time Maoist forces cannot be defeated without gaining confidence of the ordinary tribals and getting intelligence from them about the movements and strategies of the Maoists leaders, who seem to function according to a definite plan. Such is the terror let loose by the Maoists, that either out of fear or of loyalty, they seem to support the Maoist leaders and their henchmen rather than the functionaries of the State. It is not easy to resolve these contradictions. It is all right for people like Digvijay Singh to advice Chidambaram that development should come first and use of coercive power later but how can development take place at all with constant sniping by the Maoists? Chidambaram whose ministry is incharge of law and order and internal security therefore feels that "let us first end the Maoist challenge by the use of force, and create conducive atmosphere for development.

The human activists pooh pooh the approach., They pose this as the issue between Moists terror and 'state terror' through the use of coercive power. They equate Maoist violence and State Violence and adopt a neutral approach, condemning both them as responsible for the present dangerous situation. They even extend moral justification to Maoists and term as legitimate their terrorist tactics as an answer to the brutal use of force of the State and violence let loose by it. The severity and brutal violence of the recent events does not to make these intellectuals who include such well known personalities as Mahashwetadevi, Arundhati Roy and Promilla Thaper to come out and openly condemn the violence of the Maoists despite the appeal to do so by the Union Home Minister and Union Home Secretary. They seem to use their moral authority in favour of Maoists rather than the state. So far the state has not taken any action against them.

What kind of development?

There are more basic questions relating to the three pronged approach. It is not enough to talk glibly of development and good governance. The question is what constitutes 'development' and 'good governance'. Often it seems that what is done in the name of development viz. exploitation of forest and mineral resources has, far from improving the lot of the tribals, deprived the tribals their traditional means of living and destroyed their 'way of life'. In the name of 'development', forest and mining contractors have ruthlessly exploited national resources and displaced the tribals from theirs national habitats which were their for thousands of years. The so-called benefit of development has enriched the contractors and their owners and impoverished the tribals. And the State machinery of government has supported the contractors and the exploiters rather than the tribals when conflicts inevitably arose in the name of development. This process of disparate development has been accelerated in the era of marketisation, liberalization, privatization and globalization which started in the name of economic reforms in 1991 with the blessings of IMF and the World Bank. The multi-nationals became the main actors in this vast process of development. Governments signed agreements with Indian and foreign companies in complete disregard of environmental and social consequences. Tribals were compulsorily deprived of their land and natural resources by the wrong application of the provisions of the Land Acquisition Act. When there were confrontations between the tribals and the contractors of the multi-nationals, the State machinery of Police and civil administration was mobilized in favour of the contractors and against the tribals. Incidents of firing on the protesting tribals as at Kashipur and Kalinganagar in Orissa brought before them the brutal face of governance. What happened in Orissa happened in other states as well. Collection of minor forest produce like tendu leaves, honey and wood for fuel was for the tribals both a life support system and means of meager earning. The hills and caves were the objects of worship of tribals for centuries When the 'market' supported by the State machinery destroyed the life supporting system of the tribal community, there was bound to be wide spread disenchantment and anger in the tribal communities. They look upon their exploiters and the government officers who join hands with them as their enemies whom they cannot trust.

The District administration in tandem with the police and the politicians have acted almost like the advance guard of companies. (Quotation by Ramchandra Guhas in India after Gandhi. Ramchandra Guha in his magnumopus "India after Gandhi". (page. 708, 709) As pointed out by Guha in March 1999 a group of social scientists visited Rayagada (in Orissa) and issued a report warning the Orissa Government that 'unless the popular discontent among local tribals over the acquisition of land was properly addressed the peaceful district may turn into a hot bed Naxlinte (Maoist) activity'. Similar predictions were made by the environmental journalist Daryl Demonte.

The present situation in the so-called Naxal affected districts is the outcome of accumulated larger built over years. This kind of 'development' has accelerated in the years of the policy of liberalization and in the wake of open invitation to multi-nationals to setup huge steel plants and other mining projects. The consequences of this type of development were clearly foreseen.

Stereotype schemes like 'NAREGA' are no answer to deal with this kind of situation. The centrally designed scheme based on the idea of 'one size fits all' are hardly the answer. The tribal areas have special problems and schemes of development should be designed and tailor made to meet the special needs of the tribal communities and their way of life. In earlier days after independence there were schemes like special tribal development blocks and tribal co-operative societies helping the tribals for the collection and sale of minor forest produce so that the benefit of price paid for the produce in the market would go to the tribal members of the co-operatives. Such schemes are no longer talked of. Instead of using the market for the benefit of the tribal community through a sympathetic machinery of administration of tribal community development blocks and tribal co-operations, the tribal are thrown to the wolves in the shape of the contractors and multi-nationals who ruthlessly exploit them and have no sympathy for their welfare. In the early days after independence, Jawaharlal Nehru had consulted Verier Elvin who dedicated himself to the welfare of tribals and who lived with the tribals after marrying a tribal woman. Thakkar Beppa a Gandhian worker, spent a lifetime serving the tribals in Dangs so did the communist leader Godavari Parulekar in Jawhar area in Maharashtra. Dedicated selfless people like Baba Amte and his sons Vikas and Prakash who spent years in tribal areas, providing them medical service. So do the couple Abhay Bang and Rani Bang. They are respected by the tribal society but the government does not feel it necessary to consult them and take their guidance. Instead selfish leaders from the tribal communities rule the roost and instead of helping their own community they promote their own interest and those of their families. Indians democracy has thrown up tribal leaders like Madhu Koda and Shiboo Soren who have ruthlessly exploited their positions in government as Chief Ministers and Ministers for indulging in corruption and making fortune for themselves.

The Maoists leaders, most of them from Andhra Pradesh's old Telangana movement have exploited the opportunity provided by the accumulated anger of the tribals to steadily build up their network and trough inducement and fear, gathered tribal support for their rebellion against the duly elected democratic governments of Indian republic. They describe the present day of democracy as sham which is not for from truth, considering the hideous acts of corruption and misuse of power by those in authority.

A new approach

The answer to Maoism or Naxalist blind use of force is not the power of regular police, armed reserve forces, or the army but root and branch changes in our democratic system so as to make it an institution for serving the people with honesty and selflessness. This is what our long suffering people – not just the tribals expected from one democratic governments. Unless policies make quick amendments to correct themselves, the anger will spread to non-tribals as well, engulfing the nation in violence outbursts all over the country which may sweep away our façade of democracy.

As a beginning, time has come immediately to put a moratorium on what goes on in the name of development, starting with mega projects of steel and mining and compulsory acquisition of land for the irrigation projects submerging tribal communities and ruthless deforestation by forest contractors. This would leave the tribal free to carry on their traditional occupations of collection and sale of minor forest produce. This may appear to be a setback to 'development' but policy announcement to this effect may assuage anger and create a climate for winning over the tribal communities. In the hurry to become a superpower we cannot alienate our own people. If we do so, we will dig our own grave.

We will have to refashion our administration of tribal areas. A large number of young people with dedication and idealism, conversant with tribal language, culture and way of life would have to be put in service in administrative positions in tribal areas. Sooner such new approach is adopted, the better.

Chapter - 6

Independence of CBI and of Police and Administration

Taking exception to CBI sharing its progress report on 'Colgate scam' with Law Minister and joint secretaries in Prime Ministers Office and the Department of Coal, the Supreme Court characterized CBI as "a caged parrot speaking its masters voice" – "one parrot with many masters". The Court further observed that CBI should have stoodup to pulls and pressures. The Court did not directly mention who it was that put the agency in the cage. The court, in course of hearing, had observed that the action of the CBI of sharing the report led to an 'erosion of trust' reposed in the agency by the Supreme Court which expected that the report would be kept confidential before submission to the Court. Earlier the Law Minister Ashwani Kumar had tried to play down his action by saying that as Law Minister he was entitled to vet the draft and what he had done was only to correct 'grammatical mistakes' and no substantive changes were made. Supreme Court noticed that vetting amounted to changing "the heart of the report". Significant portions stating that no guidelines or objective criteria were laid down for allocation of blocks nor any record maintained of the proceedings of the screening committee which took decisions regarding sanctioning of the coal blocks allocations to the agencies concerned were omitted. As it turned out, many of the selected agencies did not have experience nor technical competence needed. As a result several blocks remained unused. The whole scandal was exposed by the CAG's report on the process of allocation which resulted a huge financial loss to the exchequer running into thousands of crores of rupees. It was when the case came before the Court in a public interest litigation, that the Court asked the CBI to investigate into the matter and submit a report. The Court trusted the CBI to make an 'independent' investigation and submit the report but the agency failed to come up to the expectations of the Court and betrayed the trust reposed in it by the Supreme Court. It showed the draft report to Union Law Minister Shri Ashwani Kumar who had summoned the CBI Chief to his office where the top law officers, Attorney General Shri. Vahanvati and Additional Solicitor General Shri. Raval were present. Both the law officers had told the Court that they had not seen the report but later Raval, with his conscience pricked, wrote a long letter to his Senior AG Shri. Vahanavati accusing him of pressurizing for making knowingly a false submission to the Supreme Court and submitted his resignation in protest. His resignation was accepted. Vahanavati himself invited the wrath of several members of Supreme Court Bar Association for his un-professional behaviour and contemplated action against him which has not been withnessed so far. When the case came for hearing on 8th before the Supreme Court, it asked Vahanavati to take necessary legal steps to insulate the CBI from executive interference.

The action of Joint Secretaries in Prime Ministers Office and in Coal Ministry who went to CBI and met officers in CBI were also faulted by the Supreme Court. It was obvious that these officers could not have gone to CBI Office on there own without directions and instructions of their superiors viz. the Secretary to Prime Minister and Secretary Department of Coal and ultimately the Prime Minister himself.

It may be noted that Supreme Court found fault with CBI for sharing the report but not with the Law Minister in express terms. It called CBI's act a mistake. The CBI admitted the mistake but explained that the Director met the Minister as 'desired by the Minister' and not on his own. CBI explained that it is an agency of government under its control and had to abide by the directions of the higher authorities. Though this may generally true, in this case Supreme Court had given specific instructions to submit the report confidentially to the court.

This however, leaves open the question of the status of the CBI as the investigating agency especially when the investigation is into allegations against ministers for malfeasance and political interference. If impartial investigation to be expected, high traditions should be laid down and followed by the highest agencies including Minister and even by Prime Minister. Unfortunately in recent years standard of rectitude in governance have woefully fallen first in states and later at centre as well. This make it necessary that things are not left to tradition and convention but necessary charges in law are made to insulate CBI investigation from interference of Government.

Media reports earlier stated that the Government had decided to 'brazen out' the uncomfortable situation but late in the evening President of the Congress party Smt. Sonia Gandhi called on the Prime Minister and conveyed her decision that the Law Minister should resign and late in the evening Minister Ashwani Kumar submitted his resignation., Such was the adverse public opinion and pressure built up in the media that President Congress Party felt it necessary to ask the Prime Minister to ask for Ashwani Kumar's resignation.

Minister Ashwani Kumar in his statement after resignation showed no remorse at what was perceived as a clear attempt to tamper with the report to be submitted by CBI to the Supreme Court by way of a cover up of the coal scam. He said 'his conscience was clear, he had done no wrong and the Supreme Court, itself had not said anything by way of his indictment. His resignation was only for political reason, to avoid unnecessary controversy. The Minister did not realize that though the Supreme Court did not directly indict the Minister, it did question interference in the investigation report of CBI by the superiors. But if a Minister takes a stand as taken by Ashwani Kumar, the Supreme Court could well be compelled to indict a Minister. After all in neighbouring Pakistan Supreme Court of that Country summoned the Prime Minister to Court who refused to take action against the President Zardari for keeping illegal accounts in Swiss Bank. The Supreme Court could not have been unaware that whatever CBI had done was at the behest of the Law Minister, Prime Minister Office and the Department of Coal. CBI candidly admitted that it was but a part of the executive and did not have independence of action especially while investigating a case where those in the dock are governmental authorities – both political and executive.

This is not the first time that the Supreme Court had insisted upon the independence of CBI in investigating cases especially when persons holding high position in Government are themselves involved in malfeasance or criminal acts. Fifteen years ago in a landmark judgement in 1993 in a case, a public interest lititation filed by Vineet Narayan for honest probe in hawala case the Supreme Court bench headed by the late Chief Justice J.S. Verma laid down a system under which CBI would be supervised by the Chief Vigilance Commissioner (CVC). The Government contemplated appointing an officer of questionable integrity to the post of CVC despite the opposition of the leader of opposition and as a consequence had the discomfiture of seeing the appointment quashed by the Supreme court.

While implicitly disapproving Law Minister Ashwani Kumar's interference with coal scam investigations, the Supreme Court pointed out that the Prime Minister who had administrative jurisdiction over the CBI did not have the power to interfere in CBI investigations. This is not the question of power but of the propriety in the use of power. Power of a position in government should be used in public interest and not in partisan or private interest.

There is no law at present to ensure independence in investigation by CBI. At present CBI derives its powers from Delhi Special Police Establishment Act under which it is only an investigating arm of the Central Government.

The political class wants investigating agents to be under its control – whether in centre or in the states. Chief Ministers want to control police and to curtail police independence.

It is only after being nudged by the Supreme Court the Government moved to make changes in CBI Investigation Act to ensure independent investigation by CBI. The observations of the Supreme Court in Vineet Narayan and Prakash Singh cases, have been gathering dust for a long time. According to Chief Justice Vermas's observations, the CVC and Lokpal would have supervisory role over CBI. This would make it more autonomous. The act should be well thought out and lay down mechanism for selection of CBI Director and its internal structure which will make it professional and independent.

In order to make CBI an independent agency, CBI director should be appointed by a collegiums which should include Chief Justice of the Supreme Court, Prime Minister and the Leader of opposition. CBI should have a stationary status similar to Election Commission and CAG.

With the Supreme Court setting July 10 as the deadline for the Centre to come out with a law to insulate CBI from external influence, the Government has constituted a Group of Ministers headed by Shri. P. Chidambaram to draft a new legislation for the agency within three weeks. The legislation is expected to provide for extension of powers and jurisdiction of CBI a separate cadre of its officials, and an independent directorate of prosecution as also a Committee for the appointment of CBI director.

II. Independence of Police

It is not as if the case of CBI is sui generis. All administrative institutions and authorities have to function independently within their jurisdiction to discharge their duties and functions within the frame of law, rules and general instructions as laid down from time to time. Any arbitrary intervention in the discharge of duties as laid down by law is illegitimate and should be eschewed. This is the basic condition of good governance.

These conditions are often violated. Years ago the Police Commission made recommendations for police reform to facilitate independent and professional functioning of the police. Among other recommendations was the constitution of an independent board to make appointments. But the recommendations of the police commission have remained on paper. Recently it is reported that R.R. Patil, Home Minister of Government of Maharashtra has taken charge of transfers and promotions of the police functionaries, reducing the DGP, the head of police to non-entity. How can the police chief make the police machinery accountable to him, when all transfers and promotions are in the hands of Home Minister? It is reported that the Minister directly speaks to officers in police stations and gives instructions. Under such conditions police can not be expected to act impartially while discharging duties for maintenance of law and order.

Shri. Prakash Singh former D.G. of Central Security Force has been fighting for Police reforms which included preventing political interference in police work. The recommendations of the Police Commission in this respect have been put in cold storage both by the Centre and States. Prakash Singh filed public interest litigation in 2006 in Supreme Court which ordered reforms to preventive political interference in police work. But there has not been much progress.

III. Independence of Administration

What is true of independent and professional functioning of the police is true in the case of all the administrative agencies. Independence and autonomy is required not only for CBI but also for police, and for all administrative authorities at all levels and in all sectors in the interest of good impartial, fair and transparent administration. It is wrong to state as is often stated that the police and civil servants have to work under their 'political masters'. In a democracy there are no masters. There are only public servants – whether elected or selected for various public services on the basis of professional criteria and by independent public service recruitment board. The duties of public servants are prescribed and have to be carried out according to provisions of relevant law and rules and circulars etc. thereunder. They have also to be in public interest and not in private, partisan or personal interest. Any public servant who acts in infringement of law and guidelines there under or in partisan private or personal interest causing loss or damage to public interest, should be liable for penal action through after his guilt is established through a departmental inquiry.

If these stipulations are rigorously followed, governance and administration would work well in the interest of people. Unfortunately these stipulations have gone by the board because of arbitrary actions of politicians in power and their interference in administration. Those honest civil servants who do not fall line end corporate with the misdeeds of politicians in power are often sidelined or even penalized by frequent transfers and punishment postings, denied promotion or even suspended. The case of Khemka, an IAS officer of Haryana Cadre who had 44 transfers in a service period of 22 years is an eloquent example of what happens when a civil servant discharges his duties as per law. For doing his duty a civil servant, needs protection under law and as per conditions of service. To protect a civil servant from unfair and arbitrary penal action, Article 311 of the Constitution lays down that 'no member of Civil service in Union or All India Service or a Civil service shall be dismissed or removed or reduced in rank except after enquiry in which he has been informed of the charges against him and given a reasonable opportunity of being heard in respect if charges". While this is the constitutional shield for an honest servant doing his duties, it is not enough because it does not give protection from arbitrary and frequent transfers causing grave inconvenience to his family and even humiliation. The politicians in power often play with civil servants favouring pliable civil servants and penalizing the 'difficult' once who refuse to bend law and rules to suit the wishes of politicians in power. If a civil servant works in Secretariat, he is entitled to place his views clearly on the file and not write down a note convenient to a Minister or at his behest. If he is working in the field – whether as a Divisional Commissioner, Collector, Tehsildar, he has to act strictly as per law and duties prescribed and not at the dictates of politicians in power.

Unfortunately in recent years, more and more civil servants even at higher level are seen to be compromising and going down under political pressure. This has led to lack of efficiency, impartially, fairness, honesty and transparency in governance and administration.

Time has now come to bring about a basic structural change in our system of governance and administration. The politicians in power should confine themselves to formulation of laws and policies in which public servants can provide assistance. But the actual implementation of laws should be entirely left to administrator without political interference. Of course this does not mean of freedom to civil servant to do what they want. Any civil servant found guilty of acting against law and rules or anything contrary to public interest should be severely punished through effective disciplinary action. Independence of administration is as important as independence of power of judiciary. If this is done there will be no 'parrots' or 'chickens' in administration nor any animals praying on ordinary citizens.

That given independence of action, civil servants can deliver is shown by the two agencies which enjoy constitutional independence viz. CEO and CAG. The CEO's performance in successfully conducting successive elections in free and fair manner has been exemplary Shri. Seshan who used to be subservient to political superiors, while in service, showed striking independence as CEO and put the fear of God in politicians resorting to questionable methods to gather votes. The CEO has no separate machinery of administration to performs election duties. The same civil servants who work in the normal administrative system, work for running elections. But when they work under independent Election Commissioner they work fairly and impartially. The same holds good in the case of CAG. Vinod Rai had not shown his combative colours when in Government. But when he came to occupy the constitutionally independent position of CAG, he did not hesitate to confront government and exposed scams after major scams which brought out the ugly face of corruption in our administration and governance. Conferring the same kind of independence on the entire machinery of administration, would bring about dramatic improvement in our administrative performance and make it efficient and impartial. Political neutrality has to be a feature of civil service in our system of parliamentary democracy. Different political parties may come in power, and political complexion of the government may change. But the civil service has to work with the same sense of commitment. Unfortunately, in our democracy there is tendency for the governments to change the officers in positions like the Chief Secretary and Director General of Police in the States and Secretaries and other positions in the centre with every change of Government. This kind of approach demoralizes the civil servants and compromises their integrity. The system of separation of administration machinery and political authority does exist in a country like Sweden known for good governance. We should follow their example.

Chapter - 7

Yet Another Mega Scam

Political impact of CAG report

The nation was reeling under the impact of two mega scams – the Commonwealth Game Scam and 2G Scam when it was struck by yet another scam now known as 'coal-gate' scam relating to the allocation of coal mines. It burst open, when a prominent newspaper carried a headline about a ten lakh crore scam in allocation of coal mines – several times bigger than the notorious 2G scam. This was when the relevant CAG report was yet to reach government. A draft report was about to be submitted by the CAG to Government for comments. The final report was submitted at the time when in the previous Parliamentary session was about to close. The Government did not place it immediately on the floor of Parliament. It did so only at the beginning of the monsoon session. Though the final report considerably watered down the magnitude of the sum involved in the scam, to a sum of Rs. one lakh eighty six thousand crores, it was still bigger than the sum involved in 2G scam. The CAG observed that there were windfall games made by some private companies. What added for the seriousness of the scam was this fact, that during many of the years to which the scam related, the Minister concerned was the Prime Minister himself! The Opposition BJP, therefore started targeting the Prime Minister calling on him to resign. They argued that in 2G scam the Minister concerned A Raja of DMK had to resign and now since the Minister concerned was Prime Minister himself he should also resign.

As soon as the monsoon session opened on Monday August 21, the members of the principal opposition party, the BJP got up and started shouting with one voice that the Prime Minister should resign, not allowing the house to function. The speakers of both Lok Sabha and Rajya Sabha were perforce required to adjourn the house till the next day. The same story was repeated on succeeding days of the session. The whole session was wasted. The government hoped that the first day of second week would have a better beginning. But that was not to be. The BJP members persisted with their shouting not allowing both the houses to function. The other parties in NDA including Shiv Sena did not join the BJP in their protest and shouting. Nor did other parties like BJD which had to face similar behaviour of the opposition in Orrisa Assembly, in their case the Congress party.

The Congress leaders started using the media to articulate their reply to BJP. Finance Minister Chidambaram accompanied by his colleagues Kapil Sibbal and Salman Khurshid told in a press conference that there was no loss, since coal deposits were safe in 'mother earth' and therefore there was no corruption! He did not use the term 'zero corruption' used by his colleague Kapil Sibbal in 2G scam case which turned out to be wrong as subsequent events showed. Obivously, there was hardly any difference between Sibbal's term 'zero corruption' and Chidambaram's 'no corruption', both of which turned out to be false.

The Prime Minister on his part observed that 'policy issues' are not within the ambit of the CAG who had no business to comment on them in its Audit Report. Policy issues, he insisted are the exclusive preserve of government. Shri. Manish Tiwari the spokesman of the Congress Party in his article in Indian Express, Aug 28, argued that CAG had no constitutional mandate to make policy prescriptions and then utilise them to compute 'notional' loss. He drew attention to Articel 149 of the Constitution which lays down that 'the Controller and Auditor General shall perform such duties and exercise such powers in relation to the accounts of the Union and the States and of any other authority or body as may be prescribed by or under any law made by Parliament. In 1971 Parliament enacted the Comtroller and Account General's (Duties, Powers and conditions of Service Act 1971. Under the provisions of the Act the statutory mandate of CAG was to audit all money paid into and expended from the consolidated fund of the Union and the states, as well as contingency fund, subsidiary funds of Government companies and statutory corporations and all bodies financed by government. Tiwari also referred to OM dated June 13, 2006 saying that CAG's performances audit is concerned with audit relating to the economy, efficiency and effectiveness of the receipt and application of public funds.' Tiwari argued that in all this, formulation, there was no reference to policy. But by the same token it could be argued that policy issues are not specifically excluded from the ambit of the audit reports of CAG. If they impinge on the 'economy, effecienty and effectiveness of the receipt and application of public funds.' CAG is well within his rights to comment on them.

Minister Salman Khurshid in his article (Times of India, Aug 28) made out a case for the business firms which got the allocations. 'Business firms and profits are no longer bad words in our public vocabulary'. He was obviously referencing to the policy of liberalisation and privatisation initiated by Dr. Manmohan Singh, a Finance Minister in Narsimha Rao Government in 1991. He found fault with CAG's 'simple exercise' in arriving at a figure of 1.86 lakh crore loss instead of doing a sophisticated 'cost benefit analysis'. The Minister further wrote that to judge the honesty of a bargain in proportion to the benefit to a private party is stupid". The minister should have known that there is a concept of 'social cost benefit analysis'; which is different from 'private cost benefit analysis'. As a public servant the Minister should have a concern for the former rather that act as an advocate of private business. The CAG took exception to that part of the financial gain which accrued to business which could have been tapped by government by taking timely decision on 'competitive bidding' for the allocation of the coal blocks." The Minister argued that delay in adopting the policy of competitive bidding was mainly because of categorical resistance by the coal producing states, mostly ruled by opposition'. He also said that legislative amendment required for introducing competitive bidding would have taken time and would have denied coal required for power, steel and cement production neatly overlooking the fact that the same Ministry of Law changed its opinion later and said that it could have been done by administrative notifications.

Apart from the articles critical of CAG written by the two ministers, many Congress politicians made personal attacks on CAG Shri. Vinod Rai. For example, Digvijay Singh, General Secretary of the Congress party alleged that the CAG had political ambitions, which motivated the report, citing the precedent of Shri. T.N. Chaturvedi, who as CAG made a report on Bofors case, later using the publicity to join the BJP and using his membership as a platform to become a member of Rajya Sabha and Governor of Karnataka.

What really caused alarm annoyed the politicians whether in power or not is the drastic change in the nature and scope of the audit reports in the last two, three years. Audit reports in the past drew attention to minor financial irregularities such as excessive TA Bills, or expenditure without requisite budgetory provisions. These were to be handled by the officers of the departments concerned who had to appear before the PAC where the CAG was present to 'assist' the PAC calling the department to account for failure to take suitable action on audit objections. The scope of the recent reports whether relating to 2G case, GWG case, the Delhi International Airport case or Coal mine allocation case was much broader and the politicians in power like A Raja, Suresh Kalmadi and Praful Patel had to take responsibility. The former two had even to go to jail on the orders of the courts where CBI filed cases against them. In the coal mine allocation case the Prime Minister himself was involved as Coal Minister over the years where the allocations were made.

PM's statement

Having waited for a week, the Prime Minister who was to leave for Iran the next day for attending NAM Conference in Teheran, read out a statement on the floor of the Lok Sabha and Rajya Sabha on the coal allocation on the Aug 27, the first day of the second week (after the first week of the Parliament sessions were washed away). He had to read the statement amidst disruption in the House. It was drowned in loud shouting from the members of the BJP. But the statement was still laid on the floor of the house.

Prime Minister in his statement said, "I take full responsibility for allotments by the Coal Ministry" He found fault with the findings of CAG on 'multiple grounds'. He asserted that there were no 'impropriety or irregularity'. The so-called benefits to private firms were clearly notional.

Coal mines, the Prime Minister said were allocated to 142 private parties to meet the energy needs of the country. But the fact that all the mines save one remained un-exploited even after allocation showed that the objective for which the allocations were made remained unfulfilled. This made a mockery of the case for urgency in allocating the mines.

The coal Minister Jaiswal argued that the auction procedure would have increased the price of power leading to increase in the form of electricity for the consumers – a strange argument by government which has accepted the market mechanism as the best for allocation of resources !

The BJP leader Arun Jaitley made fun of Chidambaram's 'no loss' doctrine similar to Sibbal's zero loss statement in 2G case. 'If I give corruption money to a public official who simply put it in his pocket but does not spend it, could it be construed that there was no corruption?" Zero loss theory proved to be a zero sum gain of the UPA.

Prime Ministers assertion that there was no impropriety' was soon falsified by investigations of CBI who unearthed ten cases where companies fudged facts and gave wrong information to qualify for coal blocks. Due diligence was not exercised by to prevent such companies from getting mines. Such cases had led to prosecution of these companies as in 2G cases. Amongst these mentioned by CBI in FIRs were Vijay Darda, a Congress MP and Manoj Jaiswal whose name was linked to Minister to Shri. Prakash Jaiswal.

The proceedings of the screening committee which made the allocations were not transparent and gave no cogent reasons for allocations leading to the suspicion that the allocations were made in an arbitrary manner and perhaps under the influence of private parties and political pressure both in 2G case and coalgate case.

IMG and CBI investigations

Having made his statement of 'nounpriety' the Prime Minister asked an Inter Ministerial Group (IMG) under the Chairmanship of Additional Secretary Department of Coal, to go into allocations made. The IMG recommended cancellations of allocations in those cases where companies had given false information or undertaken no work or had sold their licenses soon after allocations and made windfall profits. In several cases the Group recommended confiscation of guarantee amount. Obviously Prime Minister was in too much of hurry in asserting "no impriority' in his statement in Parliament.

Both 2G and coal gate scams, big companies had made an entry in public administration in the wake of the policy of privatisation, liberalisation and public private partnership which has given rise to 'crony capitalism' and influence of big corporations on public policy. A striking example of politician-business nexus was the SKS case in which minister Subodhkant Sahay wrote to Prime Minister recommending one firm called SKS in which his brother Sachin was a director who had represented the firm in the meeting of the screening committee. Instead of finding fault with the Minister for misuse of public office, the Prime Minister himself marked that as 'most important' and sent it to Coal Department. SKS was one firm which the IMG has now recommended for de-allocation.

Danger to constitutional institutions

Public institutions like CAG, not to talk of integrity and will power of civil service, are being sacrificed under the influence of politicians and big business. Public Account Committee through presided over by a Chairman who is a senior member of the BJP sees the spectacle of the Congress members putting the CAG himself in the dock! Objectivity and independence of even a constitutional authority are sacrificed at the alter of greed and avarice let loose by the policy of liberalisation.

The greatest tragedy was that Parliament the supreme democratic institution where debate on 'public issues is expected, was made non-functional. The BJP justified their obstructive action by saying that such debate serves no purpose (as was seen in 2G case) since government gets round the opposition by manipulating vote to get majority and giving short shrift to the cogent points made by the opposition. This may be so, but making parliament non-functional can never be justified.

Need for policy framework – the example of South Africa

The 'coal-gate' scam took place because there was no policy framework to guide individual allocations. The Government of India should well take a lesson from South Africa, where are located mines with very valuable minerals like diamonds. As, De Clerk, the last white Prime Minister said in course of an interview on a TV channel in India, there were no scam, no irregularities, no corruption, no political interference because there were clear cut guidelines and procedure prescribed which gave no scope for such malfunctioning. We should do well to follow their example.

Post Script : The DMK Minister A Raja who was sent to jail was acquitted by the CBI Court on the ground that CBI had utterly failed to provide any available evidence. A Raja was out of Jail.

Chapter - 8

Good Governance

Recently a small group of citizens including big people like businessmen Azim Premji, Jamshed Godrej, Deepak Parekh and Anu Aga and former Governor Bimal Jalan and former Judge of the Supreme Court Shri krishna wrote to Government expressing their concerns at the state of the nation and suggesting some specific actions and recommendations.

They are worried that if the present state of affairs continues, India's growth potential would be adversely affected. They have mentioned corruption as the biggest issue corroding the nation. But the suggestion they have made viz. appointment of the *Lok Ayukta* and *Lokpal* was made long back by the Administrative Reforms Commission in 1970.

They have also reiterated the recommendations made way back by the Police Commission headed by the late Dharmavira that the 'Police' (Law enforcing agency) should be made independent of the executive and elected legislatures. They have pleaded that leaders must respect the integrity of the national institutions and repose confidence in them.

It is necessary to realize that behind the suggestions are some basic principles of good politics and good administration. The first principle was the one enunciated long back by the sociologist Max Waber viz. that no one own's any public positions and holds it only for specific period of time for which he is either elected or appointed. The person holds the position only to discharge duties attached to that position. He is entitled for compensation in monetary or non-monetary terms, only as allowed under specific rules, Secondly, through civil servant are accountable ultimately to an elected in political executive democracy. They are not a personal servants of politicians. Every civil servant holds a position to which duties are attended, he is recruited to the post if he fulfilled the prescribed qualifications and hold the position only for the prescribe to that tenure. He is recruited by authority duly constituted recruiting as per the prescribed provisions pursuit of public interest to the exclusion of personal, private and partisan interest.

It follows that no politician, though elected and holding a position of minister in government, can ask the civil servants to commit an act which is either illegal or inconsistent with the public interest. The rule of law and the rules thereunder are as much binding on the elected politician in power as an appointed civil servants. There is clear line of difference between politics and public administration. Though politics represent all interest public administration has to eliminate all interest. It is the business of politician in a democracy to work in parliamentary institution and get its approval for laws and policies. The civil servants do contribute to the formulation of laws and policies but they are ultimately approved by the civil and elected executive and but subject to law and rules thereunder. Thirdly, public interest is paramount and it is expected that both the administrative and political executive discharged their duties in pursuit of public interest.

The civil servants are bound to carryout their prescribed duties under the law and the rules. No elected politician should be allowed to tell the civil servant what should be done in individual cases. If a civil servant does any act which is against the law and procedure, he is liable for punishment after due inquiry.

Unfortunately Indian politicians have chosen to ignore all these sound principles of good governance and good administration in democracy. The group of citizens mentioned above and all those making well meaning suggestion should realize that improvement in Governmental system should be reform within. It can not be remedied only by the appointment of external agencies like Lok Ayukta, or even by passing the Right to Information act.

Sound administration in democracy should be open and accessible and the scope for secrecy should minimal in a democracy. Nothing should be hidden from the citizens who have a right to know all information regarding the working of the administration. Unless these basic principles govern Indian administration system, it is bound to deteriorate to the detriment of the people.

EDUCATION - VI

Chapter - 1

Rethinking the University Setup – Take Care of the Fundamentals

There is a feeling in our country that all is not well with the University set-up. Suggestions are made from time to time for its reform. However, these suggestions for reforms do not often go to the root of the problem and deal only with some of the external aspects without touching the inner core. The inner core consists of attitudes and outlook, the spirit and atmosphere, rather than mere organizational or procedural aspects. When the atmosphere is spoilt, even the best of organizational and procedural reforms are likely to fail.

An institution or organization will succeed if its mission and goals are clearly defined and all those working in that organization and institution understand them and are committ to their fulfillment. What is the concept of the University and in terms of the concept how could its mission and goals be defined?

Concept and Mission of the University

The University is essentially an association of teachers and students in pursuit of scholarship. The primary goal of the University is to promote knowledge and to disseminate it, and prepare the young people to enter in life to assume higher positions in various fields like science, technology, education, administration, business management and entrepreneurship. A University is rightly described as a temple of learning. Nehru expected the University to be an institution constantly engaged in search of the truth, adventures of ideas and the quest of knowledge. The frontiers of knowledge in all field are continuously expanding. We see veritably an explosion of knowledge and technology in all fields. Every University has not only to keep pace with the fast progress all over the world, but also to make its own contribution. These indeed are the lofty goals of a University.

From sublime to the ridiculous

Unfortunately, in practice the goals are not understood and there is fall from the sublime to the ridiculous. The Universities are treated as no more than mere teaching shops or factories for the award of degrees. Even these degrees are slighted, and are described as nothing better than toilet paper by some newspapers who should know better. This calumny is a consequence of the fact that very often the young people coming out of the University do not find ready employment. The phenomenon of educated unemployment is growing year after year adding to the frustration of young people and leading to the questioning of the very basic purpose of the University and its raison de'etre. This accusation persists despite the clarification often given that it is not the responsibility of the University to create jobs. Jobs emanate out of the functioning of the economic system and University is not incharge of this system.

Human Resource Development – the goal of the University

Nevertheless, the fact remains that knowledge is not only the end in itself, but also a means to the end – the end being the welfare and progress of the society, the development of the economy and creation of a richer, better and fuller life for the people. It is, therefore, necessary that the knowledge produced and provided by the University is relevant. This creates a dilemma because the practical relevance of fundamental knowledge is not always apparent. Its relevance unfolds itself, tangibly or intangibly, over many years.

Nevertheless, the fact remains that the goal of the University, at a less sublime level, could be legitimately defined as one of the human resource development – of producing qualified and educated personnel to hold higher positions in social and economic life of the country. That is why it is necessary to continuously modify and diversity courses of higher education in the University to make them relevant to the needs of the society.

Delinking job from degree

Surprisingly, despite the validity of the formulations made above, a point has been that job must be delinked from the degree, and this point has even found its place in the new education policy. It is difficult to understand the rationale of this proposition. Jobs cannot be held by people who are not qualified and a degree, if it is worth anything, has to be given in recognition to the fact that the possessor of the degree is qualified and holds the necessary knowledge of the subject in which he is qualified. A person is offered a job if he has a degree which is found relevant to the job to be discharged. It is true that very often the knowledge given in the University would not be enough for the job and additional training has to be given but that training is super imposed on the foundation of knowledge which the University imparts.

Those who ask for the delinking the job from the degree would like the students to be recruited to their jobs immediately after the XII year of education. Only those who want to pursue higher knowledge would then come to the University thereby reducing the load on the University system. Thus, would be applied even to those who would desire to join the higher Civil Services of the country like the Indian Administrative service, in the manner of recruitment to the military services. The protagonist of such a view do not seem to understand that the products so exclusively trained in the Civil Service School after XII year are likely to lack the breadth and flexibility of mind which the University would provide rather than an exclusive school of administration. The narrow single track mindedness generated in the Civil Services School for school leavers is likely to be detrimental in the long run both to the quality of the civil services and the quality of the University education. This does not mean that for every job in government, a degree should be insisted upon. For lower and even middle level jobs, a degree may not be necessary. But for higher jobs requiring width of knowledge, everything has to be said in favour of University degree as a qualification. The relevance of a University degree has diminished not because there is no relevance but because of the deterioration in the quality of knowledge imparted in the University academic programmes. It is said that the products of the University are unemployable. In that case the need is for improvement in the quality of the academic programmes of the University

Commitment to goal

This would only be possible if amongst all the constituents in the University, there is a single minded commitment to the primary goal of the University namely, acquisition of knowledge and education of young people in various disciplines.

An organization or an institution achieves its goals if there is congruence of outlook amongst all those who participate in the institution. If there is a discordance and working at cross purposes, then the goal is not accomplished.

Are all the components and participants in the University united in fulfilling the goals of the University? This is the basic question to which all concerned with University affairs should address themselves.

University as a system

The University is a system which consists of many components. These components consist of post-graduate departments and under-graduate colleges either directly run by the University or affiliated to it. There is a view that the entire system of affiliation should be done away with, and all the colleges should be run by the University. The other view is, that since the colleges are far too many, they cannot be run by the University and the colleges should be treated as autonomous bodies. Whatever be the merits or demerits of the organizational reforms suggested above, it has to be understood that these by themselves would not lead to the attainment of objectives. Autonomous colleges would not serve any purpose unless there are autonomous participants who are committed to promotion and dissemination of knowledge. Otherwise autonomous colleges would only lead to greater discordance and working at cross purposes. They would prove counter productive and lead to lowering of standards. On the other hand, in the system of affiliated colleges what is required is a closer interaction between the faculty of the post-graduate departments and the teachers in the affiliated colleges. This is quite feasible in small universities, but difficult or even impossible in larger and unwieldy universities with hundreds of affiliated colleges. Gajendra Gadkar Committee had recommended that a University should have about 30 affiliated colleges. With a bigger size diseconomies of scale set in. Gajendra Gadkar Committee norms regarding the size of the University should, therefore, be implemented in a phased manner.

Discordance amongst participants

Whatever be the organizational setup of the University, it is important that the system should work in a harmonious and mutually supportive manner. The participants in the University system namely, teachers, students and staff should all be aware of the primacy of the goals of the University and single minded dedication to the cause for which the University stands. Universities fail to achieve their goals and indeed often become goalless because the three groups participants perceive their goals as contrary to those of the University and place their goals above the basic aims and objectives of the University. This puts the three groups of participants in antagonistic relationship with the University and with each other. It is often said that if students do not study, the teachers do not teach, and the karmacharies do not work even though all of them are dependent on the University and are duty bound to promote the cause of the University. However, the fact remains that they do not see their role in this manner and go about setting their own goals which are contrary to the goals of the University. This is the tragedy of many Universities and of many organizations in our country.

Deterioration of teachers and students

The teachers often run after their own privileges., forgetting that a University teacher today is a very privileged person with fairly satisfactory UGC scales, security of tenure, freedom of working and little load of work as compared to persons in other walks of life. A profession in which pursuit of knowledge and teaching is a goal in itself, is a most enjoyable profession where work is its own reward and yet it is sad spectacle to see some teachers wanting to do everything else except engaging themselves in their main occupation, indulging in University politics and politics outside, running parallel coaching classes and making a fast buck, or all the time running after greener pastures elsewhere neglecting the work in University. It is this which gives a death blow to the very basic purpose of the University. The neglect teaching and scholarship by the teachers affects the students. If the students find teaches neglecting their teaching studies and scholarship, the students who lives teachers are expected to mould turn cynical and the bonds between the teachers and students are snapped. Students left to themselves then lose all sense of values and indulge in all kinds of anti-social activities.

In this they are often encouraged by the foul atmosphere around. The students often see themselves in the role of successful but unscrupulous people in the society who include power hungry politicians, black money businessmen and corrupt civil servants. The cinema and mass media depicting unruly and unsocial behaviour create in the young mind a high degree of perversion and even recklessness. It is one of the objectives of the University to create a sense of values. But when these values are subverted in the society at large, University students get misled and assume that the University is also a place of perverted value system.

In this, the students are held to ransom by some unscrupulous elements. These are the professional students leaders. These latter do not take their studies seriously and consider the students leadership as a stepping stone to politics. Sometimes even teachers encourage these elements by resorting to the shortcut such as getting the students on their side by all manner of non-academic behaviour including questionable evaluation of the performance of the students.

When such wrong attitudes develop, they make mockery of all academic procedures for establishing standards. The rules insist on minimum attendance and yet students do not often attend lectures. And yet in the prevailing permissive atmosphere, no action is taken against them.Even minimum amount of reading is not instated upon. The students miss the University classes and resort to coaching classes outside. New methods of teaching and evaluation are stoutly resisted. Methods such as assignments, self studies, tutorial work, etc. require a more intensive interaction between teachers and students in academic work. But all this is avoided. Reforms in teaching and evaluation are not possible without proper attitudes on the part of teachers and students.

University administration

The role of administration and the administrative staff is to support the academic activities. Often this is forgotten and the administration gets the better of academic requirements. The University bureaucracy is sometimes even worse than the bureaucracy in the government. Often the University is loaded with a set of statutes and ordinances which rigidify the functioning of the University. It is forgotten that statutes and ordinances are only a means of promoting academic work, and not an end in themselves.

Actually, much of the University work can be done on the basis of proper understanding of the goals of University by all concerned and the objectivity of a high degree in perceiving the goals and working for realizing them. If teachers lack objectivity, then the evaluation process losses its credibility and mere statutes and ordinances cannot restore the credibility.

The karmacharis or the staff instigated by outside political element often go on strike on the slightest pretext obstructing the working of the University. On the other hand, the academicians always do not understand the importance of admnistration and tend to neglect it. Without smooth co-ordination between administrative work and the academic programmes, the University cannot work smoothly. The University ought to evolve its own administrative procedures for speedy and efficient discharge for the various functions of the University and the staff needs to be trained in such administrative work. The academic and administrative wings of the University should not produce a dichotomy but a unity.

University bodies

The work of the University take place through the University bodies such as Syndicate (Executive Council), Senate (Court), the Academic Council, Boards of Studies, Planning Board, Finance Committee, etc. The functions of these bodies are laid down in the University statutes and ordinances. Unfortunately, some of the older University Acts and even some of the new University Acts are full of anomalies. It is these which breed academic politics. The University bodies constituted under the older acts try to behave in the role model of political institutions. If there is a disorder in the Legislative Assembly, why not have it in the Senate? If there is lobbying in the Assembly, why not in the University bodies? It is forgotten that democracy is not the only method and in any case it does not apply to institution whether civil service, military and University where other principles are more relevant and appropriate. In any case the core of democracy is reason. Participation and discussion and not disorder, log rolling and intrigue. If appointments to the University bodies through a process of elections leads to politics and disharmony which impedes the working of the University, it is high time that the scope for elections is reduced if not altogether eliminated. This applies to student bodies also. If the elected students bodies indulge in mere politics rather then promoting healthy co-curricular activities for all round development of the student community, then it is as well that the method of elections is replaced by nomination of merited students.

Discipline

The upshot of all this is that without a modicum of discipline and dedication on the part of all concerned viz. students, teachers and staff, the University cannot achieve its purpose. The discipline in a University cannot be imposed through use of force. It has to be a self-discipline and self-discipline can only be the product of a healthy atmosphere.

A University is an academocracy and not just a democracy. It is self-governing institution in which all elements viz. the Vice-Chancellor, the Registrar, the administrative staff, the; academicians have to play their role in an objective and impartial manner. The University should be wholly free from interference of the government and politicians, and should have the dignity of an autonomous self-governing institution.

Financing

This financing of higher education has become a serious problem in the context of the financial crunch experienced by the State and Central Government alike. Higher education, all along, had been heavily subsidized by the Government. Consequently, a feeling and developed in our country that the higher education should be made available at only a minimal cost, and it was everybody's right to have access to higher education. Persistent criticism about the deteriorating quality of higher education created a perception that there was not much value in higher education. What is not of much value should not also cost more. Thus, whilst students and their parents are prepared to loosen their purse-strings on a widening range of material goods of life, and in recent years more specially on entertainment in all forms, when it comes to paying for higher education, there is a reluctance to pay. Middle class parents put up with heavy fees on convent and public school education for their children, or on coaching classes. But the payment to the Universities or colleges should be only a token amount, never keeping pace with rising tide of inflation reflected in the higher dearness allowance paid to teaching and non-teaching staff engaged in higher education.

This basic perception that higher education can be cheap has to give way to the acceptance by all concerned that it is expensive and has to be paid for. The 'Gurudakshina' has to be sizeable. The fee for higher education must have some relationship to the heavy expense at which it is provided. The Maharashtra State woke up after many years and suddenly raised the fees leading to violent demonstrations by the students and their supporters all over the State which even took an ugly form. But these self-righteous protestors did not wait to find out the cost of higher education as compared with the amount spent by these very students over material goods and possessions.

May be the rise in fees has to be phased over a period of time, but it cannot be token. It has to be substantial. In particular apart from professional education some of the specialized departments of higher education could also charge substantial fees. These would include departments of Management studies, Computer education or Biotechnology whose products are in great demand in the market. If the students have difficulty in paying fees, then loans should be made available to them from the banks on concessional terms, specially to students from the economically weaker sections of the society. The loan could be repaid by the students during his first years of employment, after they leaves the portals of the institution of higher education. This is indeed a good system, and eventually much of the cost of higher education could be paid through this revolving loan able fund made available by the banks to the students for higher education.

Pending the availability of adequate resources, through fees, the State has to bear the bulk of the budget both capital and maintenance budget. The Universities are established under an Act of the Legislature and hence the Government has to take up the responsibility of supporting them and yet this commitment is often forgotten. Government takes sometimes a niggardly attitude in supporting the institution of higher education. They try to evolve some 'pattern' of grant-in-aid assistance to the universities. However, the grant-in-aid formula applied to a charitable or welfare institution has no relationship to the grants to be given to the Universities which have to be treated as mandatory in character. The grants should fully support the maintenance of the University. Having set up the University, the Government cannot escape its financial responsibility. Often the release of grants is unconscionably delayed, thereby seriously hampering the working of the University. The University officials have the discomfiture and humiliation to repeatedly approaching even minor officials in Government to get the grants released. This is derogatory to the dignity of the University. It is the duty of the Government and the departments concerned to ensure timely and orderly release of instalments of budgeted grants.

Thus, while there should be firm financial support from the Government, fees payable by students must be of a adequate quantum. Universities of their own part could generate their own independent resources by developing several 'profit centres'. These would include in library and laboratory services often made available to the outside institutions and individuals. These services should no longer be made available gratis or at nominal rates applied to teachers and students but at a substantially higher level of fees. Secondly, the universities could undertake substantial amount of consultancy work and applied research work for business, industry and commerce. This could earn the University substantial income. Unfortunately, our business and industry is not much interested in R and D and does not have foresight of the gains which it could derive from a long-term collaboration with the University and institution of higher education. Thirdly, the University facilities like Guest House and Conference Hall could be made available to hold conferences and seminars by management and professional bodies which should not hold them at Five Star hotels at heavy cost. Fourthly, business, industry, philanthropist from community at large could given munificent donations to the University. The concept of 'educational foundation' is not very well developed here as in USA where several Universities are supported by private philanthropists. The example of Sir Hari Singh Gaur who gave a munificent donation to establish the Saugar University is perhaps an exception.

Amongst potential donors are the past students of the University. The students do not have the feeling of obligation to their alma mater. That is way the students do not think it fit and proper to make donations to their University after they start working and earning. It is worthwhile establishing alumni associations through which the idea of extending support to the University could be developed.

The finance of the State Government are supplemented by the University Grants Commission under their specialized schemes. But these are only marginally supportive to the finances of the State Universities.

The concept of the University Grants Commission itself deserves to undergo a change. It is today partly a grant giving body and partly a body incharge of setting satisfactory standards of higher education. Both these functions are discharged very inadequately. The constitution and functioning of the University Grant Commission needs a second look. Firstly, it should not be an aloof bureaucratic agency but must be of the nature of confederation of Indian Universities themselves. This would mean some kind of merging of the office of the Association of Indian Universities and the present. University Grants Commission. Secondly, at present there is a proliferation of Councils in various professional disciplines like the Indian Medical Council, Indian Pharmacy Council, Bar Council and All India Council of Technical Education. These councils are independently responsible for setting standards in their respective disciplines but are conversant with the University system. The proposed confederate body of the University should have within it all the councils which have proliferated over time. If the basic concept is accepted, then the constitution and functioning of the confederation could be worked out.

In this exercise, were may draw upon the good points of the Constitution and working of the British University Funding Council- The Council's general aim is the maintenance and development of Universities as high quality and cost-effective institutions providing for the advancement of knowledge, the pursuit of scholarship and the education of students, thereby playing their parts in meeting national needs. Specifically, the Council encourages universities to identify and develop their strengths and opportunities, so that a growing range of choices is provided to students, organizations and others.

To maintain and enhance the quality of teaching and encouraged further flexibility to provision.

To improve access to initial and continuing education for mature and part-time students, and for students from a broader range of social, educational and ethnic backgrounds.

To maintain and enhance high quality research and scholarship, the fruits of which should be increasingly accessible.

To exercise their autonomy, with the minimum of UFC involvement in universities' affairs, while remaining accountable for the use of funds provided by the Council.

To enhance their funding from an increasing range of sources, without prejudice to the level of Government support.

To develop further their management capabilities, ensuring maximum exploitation of new opportunities and the efficient use of resources.

To increase their contribution to industry, public services, the professions and other areas of society through teaching, scholarship and research.

To expand their roles as regional and local resource centres.

To increase collaboration with other educational institutions where this is of mutual benefit or in the national interest.

Conclusion

To conclude, what is required to tone up the University set-up is taking care of the fundamentals.

Firstly, there has to be a all-round appreciation that the goal of the University is pursuit of knowledge and scholarship. Examinations and awards of degrees are only incidental to this main goal. Secondly, the functioning of the University should be based on co-operation and not confrontation between different participants in the University viz. the teachers, students and staff.

Thirdly, a University has to be wholly autonomous in character, without any interference from government or politicians. The Government should realise the need for academic autonomy and at the same time proper funding of the University. Till the University builds its own resources, they should given full financial support to the University should give a guarantee of dedicated performance and satisfy the Government, the Legislative Assembly or Parliament and indeed the Society at large that the University is pursuing its mission with a sense of dedication.

Chapter - 2

Quality of Higher Education

Indian system of higher education is one of the largest in the world. It has undergone rapid development in the post-independent era. When the fisr five year plan was launched in the year 1950-51 there were in India only 28 Universities, 695 college and 174,000 students. Today we have more than 200 universities, more than 7000 colleges and nearly five million students. Inspite of this large size, the system is expanding year after year with about 200 colleges starting every year, though way back in the year 1956 Dr. C.D. Deshmukh, Chairman of the University Grants Commission had clearly advised that the growth should be curbed. However, such has been the revolution of rising expectation about higher education in the country that the phenomenon of opening of new colleges has gone on inexorably and the phenomenon has not yet lost its momentum.

The Undergraduate system

Of this system of higher education, the undergraduate system constitutes the predominant part. This constituted 89% to the higher education system in our country. Most of these undergraduate colleges are of the nature of affiliated colleges. Majority of the undergraduate students study in Arts, Science and Commerce faculties, the percentage of enrollment in medicine, engineering and technology and law is very small being 1.1%, 4.9% and 5.3% respectively.

Quantitative expansion but qualitative deterioration

One great positive outcome of this development is that in respect of higher education in almost all fields and disciplines, the country is not dependent on the institutions in the developed countries. This cannot be said about many other developing countries in the world. Thanks to the institutions of higher education, the country is able to produce all the man-power needed for the country's economic, political and social development.

Despite this, the fact remains that the system has not been able to accomplish the goals of higher education. It has been commented by several educationists and academicians that though the number of higher education institutions have increased by leaps and bounds, the quantitative expansion has been accompanied by qualitative deterioration. Facilities in the institutions of higher education have been limited and stretched to tearing points, standards have declined enormously.

To be sure, a part of the system does fulfill the criteria of standards. But only a small elite group is privileged to have access to the well equipped institutions of higher education. These prestigious colleges and Universities are monopolized by the elite and the rich classes. The weaker classes of the society and the poor have to make do with less prestigious colleges and Universities with inadequate facilities. The disparities have been widening.

Shortcomings in relation to standards.

Baring exceptions as mentioned above, the normal run of institutions of higher education in the country leave much to be desired when looked at from the point of view of the purpose of higher education. The Education Commission (1964-65) said that the goals of undergraduate education of the first degree is to bring students 'to the frontiers of knowledge and threshold of the world of research'. Our first degree colleges of Arts, Science and Commerce do not come up to these standards. Our degrees are not considered to be of international comparability.

Why is this so? As the document 'Challenges of Education 1985' points out, a large majority of these colleges are engaged in mere ritual of teaching. There is very little of self study. The students are expected just to learn text books and not understand the subject. But perhaps they do not even do that. They just rely on dictation of notes and guide books or private coaching classes which have emerged as a parallel system of higher education in the country. No wonder the students lack in communication skills, have only limited knowledge and information, hardly any sense of social or national responsibility or world view.

The root cause of the malaise

What is the root cause of this malaise of undergraduate education in the country? At the recent UGC conference of the Vice Chancellors held in Delhi on December 20, the UGC circulated a paper on the academic structure of undergraduate education in the country. While the paper brings out the shortcomings of the undergraduate education, suggests some remedies, it does not go to the root of the matter or bring out the fundamentals or basics of the problem. In my view, the root cause of the malaise is a purely examination oriented approach which makes a mockery of the basic purpose of higher education. It not only distorts the process of education but introduces several malpractices such as leakages in question papers and copying in order to pass the examination by hook or by crook and obtain degrees. But since the degree holders have little knowledge or skills, they remain unemployable thus adding to the growing mismatch between the educational system and the employment market and exacerbating the phenomenon of educated unemployment.

Goals of Higher Education

Obviously the goals of higher education is not to award degrees only on the basis of indifferent institution and dubious and unreliable system of evaluation. The goal rather is to develop the younger people of the country in such a manner that they not only have a satisfying personel life but can also make a worthy contribution to the progress of the society to which they belong. The institutions of higher education, therefore, have to provide all-round development of the students, intellectual, physical, moral and spiritual; development of the mind, body, heart, personality; disseminate knowledge, promote skills and develop outlook so as to produce young men who are intellectually alert, physically strong, morally upright, esthetically sensitive, socially committed and economically self reliant. Then alone can the institutions of higher education fulfill their purpose. The only way to do this is to ensure that the quality of higher education is such as to fulfill these goals.

Ideas of Tagore and Gandhi

These two greatest Indians of the twentieth century one a poet and another political leader, were also great educationists and though having very different backgrounds, they arrived at the same conclusions regarding the basics of education. Educationist today would do well to remind themselves of the basic ideas of education of these two great stalwarts. I would briefly recapitulate them as follows :-

(1) Education is a preparation of life. It is a lifelong process. Educational institutions only lay down the foundation of the process.

(2) All education is in the ultimate analysis self education. Hence, in a way, none can educate another. Educators are only facilitators. Hence, all education has to be student oriented.

(3) Education is liberation of mind. Each individual has immense potential. Education seeks to bring out this potential. Educational institutions are for intellectual liberation; instead they become intellectual cages.

(4) The purpose of life is to serve the society. Education should build ablities in an individual to contribute fruitfully to society. Education should not promote elitism and social alienation.

(5) Education should promote moral values. They should create in the students the ability to distinguish the right and wrong. This is what is meant by value education.

(6) Education must suit the genius of the people. It should be tailored to the social and economic environment of the people and culture and tradition of the nation.

(7) Education should be in communion with nature. This has been a distinguishing feature of our ancient Gurukul system of education.

(8) Education should be action oriented. Then only it will produce self reliant individuals. Project work and extension should be parts of education. Earning while learning should be encouraged. This should help institutions of higher educatin to reduce their dependence on the State for financial support.

(9) Education through mother tongue should be encouraged. This will help educate people to communicate well with their own people.

It is in the context of these basics of education that we should address ourselves to the reforms of education in general and undergraduate education in particular, so as to remove deficiencies and raise the quality of education.

Quality of Higher Education

The quality of higher education depends first on (1) quality of content and technique of education (2) the quality of teachers (3) the quality of infrastructure and finally (4) on the quality of students.

Content of Education

The quality of education would depend on the content of education. It must fulfill the standards of excellence. The pattern of courses, their curriculae and syllabi, should be well designed. The courses should have relevance to the world in which we live. At the same time they should keep pace with the progress of knowledge in every discipline. There has been a veritable explosion of knowledge in diverse fields and our courses cannot afford to remain stagnant. The students of our institutions of higher education must have access to the new frontiers of knowledge in all fields. Our Boards of studies and Academic Councils are responsible for designing courses and syllabi. They should be ever alert and dynamic. They should introduce new disciplinary and inter-disciplinary courses bearing in mind the twin aspects of expansion of knowledge and the demands of the employment market.

Quality of teachers

Quality of education is however not a mere matter of syllabi and curricula. The teachers must have the competence and the learning which is required for first absorbing the new inputs of knowledge and then passing them on to their students. A good teacher has to be a student all his life. He has to be devoted to scholarship. At the same time, he must also have the capacity to transfer the knowledge. A teacher has to be a good communicator. He should be able to stimulate the minds of the students and invoke in them an abiding interest in the subject. The teacher should be committed to his subject and develop the same commitment in his students. He must be both motivated and committed. The teacher should also adopt techniques of teaching. Far too long has the teachers depended on the traditional class room lecture method. Today, we have a variety of new techniques including the computer technology and electronic media for dissemination of knowledge. These modern methods of teaching should be availed of. Today we have Academic Staff Colleges where teachers are given orientation courses. These courses should introduce the teachers to innovative techniques including assignments to the students, tutorials, problem solving sessions, individual and team studies, practicals, project work, etc.

It is said that the earlier era teachers were less paid but they looked upon their work as a noble mission. They were committed to their students, to their subject and to their profession. Today, in contrast it is said that high UGC salaries are available but the commitment is lacking. The UGC paper referred to by me earlier observers – 'many undergraduate teachers working in the affiliated colleges work for few hours a day, a few days in week, and a few months in a year. Many teachers spend their time in taking private tuitions or teaching in coaching classes.' Of course, there are honourable exceptions.

Quality of students

When the concept of higher education is reduced only to passing of examinations and obtaining a degree, when teachers are not committed and where academic atmosphere condusive to the pursuit of scholarship is not available, the students tend to loose their interest in studies and look upon the colleges years as only a waiting period till they get some job on the attainment of a degree. They tend to indulge in superficial studies, irrelevant activities, indiscipline and even campus violence.

Quality of infrastructure

The lack of atmosphere of knowledge is more made worse by the lack of physical facilities. Compared to the institutions of higher education in the West, ours suffer a great deal in terms of facilities available in the laboratory and the library, both of which need to be strengthened in many ways. The library should provide not only text book but a vast number of books on every subject including the latest. Also unless laboratories are properly equipped, the practicals would be reduced to mere rituals and without practicals, teaching of science subjects cannot be done.

Financial crunch

The hopes of providing needed infrastructure facilities are dashed to the ground by the severe financial crunch faced by higher education in our country. The resources provided for education in terms of the percentage of GNP or Budget of the Government has gone down. Within the broad field of education, Government seems to have decided today to lay more emphasis on primary education rather than on higher education. It would be very wrong to create a dichotomy between lower and higher education and fix the priority in this manner. While education at all levels including primary education has to be promoted, it will be suicidal for our nation to neglect higher education. The country could neglect higher education only at the cost of its future. As Jawaharalal Nehru observed in his address to the Allahabad University, all is well with the nation if the Unversities are all right. In the new era of liberalisation and globalisation, knowledge has assumed the form of intellectual property rights and countries with a high quality of University system can alone emerge as rich repositories of knowledge and get the full benefit of the new GATT agreement.

Better Management – Role of the Principals

It will not, however, do to only to plaintively mourn the inadequacy of resources. It is also necessary for those who are at the helm of affairs to use the available resources in an optimum manner. Also in tune with the spirit of liberalization, the private sector should be motivated to support higher education by way of fulfillment of their social responsibility. Here the role of the Principals of colleges is indeed very crucial. They have to be efficient managers. They have also to play the leadership role. They are the captains of the team; they are the co-ordinators of the activities of all the teachers and staff in the colleges. They have to promote and stimulate both the teachers and students for commitment to scholarship. The leadership role of the principals will go a long way in institution building, in creating a proper atmosphere in order to enable the students and the teachers to give their very best and in developing the infrastructure. As good managers and administrators the Principals can do a great deal for introducing improvements and innovations in the rules of admission, selection of courses, course structure, time-tables, evaluation of students, methods of teaching, purchase procedures, etc.

Principals have to promote both curricular and co-curricular activities. For the latter a number of schemes like the NSS and NCC are available. Often they are reduced to rituals. The Principals must see that these schemes fulfill the purpose for which they are designed. Promotion of sports and cultural activities should be such as to promote the participation of all the studens in one such activity or another.

Goa University' exercise for restructuring undergraduate education

Recently the Goa University has undertaken a detailed a comprehensive exercise of restructuring the undergraduate education based on some of the basic principles mentioned in my address. To mention some of them.

(1) The course have to be upto-date and in tune with the latest development of the subject.

(2) The courses must be relevant, the applicability aspects of the subject must be borne in mind.

(3) They must incorporate certain modern techniques such as use of computers.

(4) They must reflect value for life, concern for environment and promotion of national and international understanding.

(5) Class room teaching should be reinforced by practicals and extension programmes.

(6) Evaluation has to be a continuous process so that there is no cramming at the last moment leading evaluation only of the skill in memorizing. The Goa University is lookoing forward to introducing the restructured programme of undergraduate education with effect from the new academic year 1994-95. Some years ago the University had restructured its post-graduate courses. The complementary restructuring of undergraduate education should go a long way in raising the quality of higher education in Goa. There is a symbiotic relationship between education at various stages and the process of reconstruction has to be taken up at all stages.

Chapter - 3

Accountability in University

A general lack of accountability has been often mentioned as the shortcoming of our administrative system. It is said to be even more pronounced in our University system. In the University system, students are expected to be accountable for their studies, the teaches for their teaching and research and University as a whole, for the quality of education.

However, several well known educationists have stated on more than one occasion that our students do not study and our teachers do not teach. Of course, such a general statement would be doing injustice to many deligent students and devoted teachers. But the criticism cannot be simply brushed aside as totally unfounded. It must have been a painful experience for all those who are working in the system of higher education with a modicum of sincerity to hear in the 'Hello Zindgi' programme of Nalini Singh, students from Indore colleges, both boys and girls, talking without the slightest sense of compuntion or moral remorse about getting degrees without even attending the classes or studying the subject. The students are expected to attend 75% of lectures in the classroom. They are also expected to do assignments as given by the teachers from time to time. They are expected to study the entire syllabus not just a few portions. They have to subject themselves to a continuous process of evaluation.

However, if all these instruments of accountability are set aside by the students, it becomes necessary for the educationist to explore the causes. One is the phenomenal increase in the number of students and institutions. The number of Universities in the country have gone up to 250 – ten times the number soon after independence, the number of colleges has climbed up to 8000 – 12 times that after independence. The number of students have gone up to nearly 5 million – 16 times that after independence. Despite crying halt to the setting up of any additional substand and institution of higher education, a new college is started everyday in the country. The size of the students in a single classroom is some extreme cases has gone up to 300. No wonder, the intimate tie between the teacher and the students, which is the condition of accountability, is snapped. The teachers hardly take attendance and do not bother to ensure the presence of students in the class. Techniques like assignment and project which require a close supervision of the students by the teacher are almost conspicuous by absence.

Even a more important reason for lack of accountability of students than the increase in the number of students is the lack of understanding on the part of the large majority of the students of the basic purpose of higher education or of being a student in an institution of higher education. The overwhelming pre-occupation of the students is with the passing of examinations, and in the case of brighter students, of attaining a high rank or grade. In such perception of students, the purpose of gaining knowledge for the sake of it or mastering the subject is at a discount. Students who do not study, are prepared to go to any extent to get the certificate of passing. They attend coaching classes which supply questions and answers; they resort to unethical practices like smuggling in copying material in the examination hall and now they are even prepared to obtain fake certificates as evidence to having obtained the degree.

The coaching classes charge heavy fees. The students are prepared to pay such fees in the hope that they will be able to pass or get high marks. They are not prepared to tolerate even a moderate increase in fees charged by the colleges and universities, and protest against it. Perhaps they give little value to the education imparted by the colleges and universities.

The behaviour of the teachers adds to the indifference to the students. The teachers are supposed to be constantly pre-occupied with their subject of discipline. They are expected to be interested in their students to ensure that all of them progress – brilliant, middle level and even ordinary students. However, such has been the deterioration in the system of higher education that quite a few teachers have interest neither in their own subject nor in their students.

We have a prescribed system of performance evaluation of teachers, so that they could be held accountable for the academic work in respect of teaching, research, extension, and corporate activities. These were prescribed as a part of the package by the Mehrotra committee. However, if teachers do not feel the need to report meticulously, leaving many entries blank, and if the performance appraisal report are not evaluated, the whole raison detre of the performance appraisal system disappears.

Obviously, a tightening of the performance appraisal procedure and relating it to career advancement would be very necessary. A teacher tends to think that once he is appointed, he is unremovable, and once he is appointed as a Professor, he has reached the academic summit and that is the end of further responsibilities. If such is the situation, then the system of contractual appointments as in USA would well be in order. A teacher would know that his contract would not be renewed if he does not perform.

The traditional system of evaluation of students in our universities is based on the supposition that for objective evaluation, the evaluator has to be other than the teacher. We have recently introduced, as a part of educational reform, the American system of evaluation where the teacher is the evaluator. But the system does not always work here. Some teachers are not prepared to burden their students with too much studies or adopt rigorous standards of evaluation. They want to be popular and pass all students with flying colours. Of course sometimes the same teachers would penalize a student who does not fall in line and demand more knowledge. It has been suggested that just as teachers evaluate the students, the students should evaluate their teachers. Such a system of student evaluation exists in some universities in the Unites states of America.

How can the major distortions in our higher education be overcome? We can suggest changes in the contents of syllabus, methods of teaching and techniques of evaluation. But ultimately, it will depend on the attitudes of the students and the teachers. How can these be changed? It is a matter of creating a proper academic atmosphere, an atmosphere in which the quest of knowledge becomes the sole concern of the students and teachers and becomes a main motivating factor of their performance. To bring this about we have to constantly fight negative forces of cynicism self centredness and the resultant academic politics, and the growing influence of trade unionism amongst teachers and staff to make the institution of higher education what Radhakrishnan called 'the inner sanctuaries' of the nation.

In the ultimate analysis, the University is accountable to the society for a high level academic performance. It should be the endeavour of all universities to win laurels in all fields of knowledge and to provide true knowledge as a source of strength to the entire nation. This requires a total transformation in the scene of higher education.

Through a process of liberalization, we are trying to expand the scope of pecuniary motivation in our national life. However, the University cannot just be a market institution selling knowledge on purely pecuniary considerations. Nor can the University rely on disciplinary proceedings though the conditions of service of teachers should and do provide for disciplinary action and incorporate 'academic ethics'. The disciplinary proceedings however justified, are perceived the academic community as demorlising; at the same time courts which were earlier reluctant to interfere in the internal disciplinary proceedings of an organization particularly like a University which is autonomous in character are now prone to give stays lasting for a indefinite period thereby making a mockery of the disciplinary proceedings. In any case a University cannot be like a military academy nor like a government department where formal authority is the force of ensuring accountability. Universities and institutions of higher education have to go beyond pecuniary or disciplinary process of ensuring compliance and accountability. They have to create a new atmosphere of an inner commitment to knowledge – its generation and dissemination. This is a challenge before all the genuine academicians in India and to all those who are keen to develop universities as centres of excellence.

Chapter - 4

National Accreditation Council – Tasks Ahead

The establishment of the National Accreditation Council has come not a day too soon. For the last several years, several Indian academicians have pointed out that while there has been a quantitative expansion of higher education, it has been accompanied by a qualitative deterioration. In the context of resource crunch, it is all the more important to see that the resources spent on higher education are spent in proper manner to improve the quality of higher education.

The quality of the work of higher education has many facets related to teaching, research, extension work, co-curricular activities on the campus and outside, infrastructural development, student services, etc. The quality depends on the quality of students, teachers and staff as well as the administrative and infrastructural support. There has been a considerable deterioration in all these facets and attributes of a good quality of higher education. A sustained effort is therefore, required to improve the quality of education in University and affiliated colleges. Far too long has there been a sense of drift and even helplessness. But a resolute effort on the part of each of the 250 universities, 8000 colleges, 300,000 teachers and 5 million students could alone go a long way in improving the quality of higher education in India. While for qualitative improvement an internal process of improvement in an institution is essential, external institution like Accreditation can act as a catalytic agent for quality improvement.

The advanced countries like United Kingdom, Canada, Australia and New Zealand have started giving a great deal of thought to the qualitative aspects of education. At the last commonwealth conference of Vice Chancellors held at Swansea in August, 1993, it was seen from the papers submitted at the

Conference and discussion that followed that Universities in these countries have set up quality assessment councils and develop elaborate criteria for assessment of quality and have related financial support to quality improvement. United States has a very long tradition of using the mechanism to Accreditation Council. Higher Accreditation Councils in USA help colleges and Universities in attracting resources and outstanding teachers.

We should draw upon the expertise of United States and Western Countries in developing the work of our own National Accreditation Council. However, we should not go in for a blind imitation. The circumstances in which the accreditation work goes on in United States is very different from those in India. In the United States, a large number of institutions of higher education have come up as private institutions – some of them purely to meet the local requirements. No wonder there is a wide variety of these institutions and the need for some kind of accreditation is a paramount need in that context for establishing standards and norms.

However, the conditions in India are vastly different. The Universities in India are either sponsored or supported by the Central Government or the State Government . They are brought into existence either by the Parliament or the Legislative Assembly. These legislations are based on certain standards and models. Therefore, there is no scope for much of diversification of standards or identity among these at least at conceptual level. However, some universities like Madras, Bombay and Calcutta are very old, while others are comparatively modern. While some function in advanced cities, others are comparatively in backward areas located even in small towns. This leads to a wide variation in the standards of functioning of the Universities and in the quality of teaching, research and infrastructure. The UGC no doubt lays down certain norms and standards which apply to all the institutions of higher education in the country but their follow up depends on each institution.

Thus, while the conceptual or legislature framework has a great deal of similarity, differences in standards take place in course of the actual functioning of the institutions. Different states have different levels of financial support given to the Universities. There are different kinds of relationship between universities and government. There are different traditions of scholarship and student and teacher behaviour. It is the context of these varying standards that the National Accreditation Council would have to evolve its programmes and working so that the Universities and Colleges steadily raise their level of functioning. Some Universities which had very good name and tradition in the past, have steadily deteriorated and shown signs of aging and suffering from accumulated ailments. Some of the new Universities without the baggage of the past can look to the future providing new models and imbibing all the features required in modern institutions of higher education.

The National Council of Accreditation would therefore, have to categorise the Universities and College of higher education according to their environment in which they function, and work out different types of criteria for their assessment. These criteria cannot just be only conceptual or theoretical in nature. They must have relations to the political and other realities of the situations., Standards and criterias, conceptualized in a theoretical manner or brought from the models of universities in United States or Europe, if applied in the Indian conditions may be unworkable and far from improving the quality would only lead to frustration.

Having identified different types of environment in which different universities work, the commission would have to work out a programme for accreditation., The approach of the National Council as envisaged in its constitution is that, the accreditation will be purely voluntary in character. In USA the voluntary character works because it helps to attract resources and talents, that motive does not exist in Indian situation. It is, therefore, wrong to believe that voluntary accreditation approach would be necessary. The Council would have to get actively in touch with the Universities in developing a programme of accreditation.

Accreditation may not be needed for its own sake. There may not necessarily be a relationship between accreditation and State support towards the Universities. A withdrawal to State support to institutions which do not come up to the criteria laid down by the National Council, may create students, teachers and staff unrest and the remedy may prove worst than the disease. The accreditation may have to be accompanied by the detailed suggestions on upgrading the work of an University. Implementation of the recommendations would itself depend upon factors outside the control of the University, such as the financial support from the State, the autonomy granted to that institution, freedom from political and government interference and general respect for education in the society. At present these factors have gone beyond the control of most of the Universities in the country. It will not be easy for the National Accreditation Council to deal with these factors. It will be a big mistake to take a technical approach to its work. It may have to be a more comprehensive approach based on the social, economic and political environment of the country.

Chapter - 5

Why Institutions Fail

Organised society is a cluster of institutions. The strength of a society depends upon the variety and vigour of its institutions in various walks of life. Institutions arise in response to some felt needs. They are set up with certain purpose in view. Often they are the product of the vision and dedication of a person or a band of people moved by some laudable cause. In pre-independence India, with colonial Government limiting its sphere of activity, many of them owed their origin to voluntary effort. After independence, with the State taking upon itself the task of building new India, a number of institutions came up with official support and patronage.

It is a sad spectacle on the contemporary scene that quite a few of these institutions, set up with great fanfare and expectations have today lost their clan; some of them like the Indian Institute of Forest Management established at Bhopal seven years ago are reported to be in doldrums. Some are in state of decay. A letter writer in the Indian Express complained some time back that the Indian Institute of Public Admnistration has become an Institute of mal-administration manipulated by a coterie while its journal contains 'long and verbose' articles of mediocre quality. Some others like the Indian Institute of Advance Study in Simla conceived by no less a person than Dr. Radhakrishnan, are being considered for being wounding up. Another well known institute – the Gokhale Institute of Politics and Economics, Pune, nurtured and developed as his life's mission by the eminent economist the late Prof. D.R. Gadgil is often embroiled in unseemly controversies ventilated in the newspaper from time to time. Another revered institution in Pune viz. Bharat Itihas Sanshodhan Mandal has reached a stage where its members have asked the Government to take it over. The Indian Institutes of Management were set up as centres of excellence for management, education and research. However, many of them developed problems of self-management! The leading Institute of Ahmedabad was headless for two years. When recently Government appointed, at long last, the candidate who had been under consideration all this time, it thought fit to do so by removing its Chairman! And now Government have appointed a high level committee of experts to see how far Indian Institutes of Management have fulfilled the objectives of functioning as centres of excellence.

Why are institutions after institutions falling on evil days? This could well be the subject matter of many a Ph.D. dissertations! But one thing in certain. The phenomenon cannot just be attributed to either lack of infrastructure or lack of resources. Indeed many of them are endowed with on excellent infrastructure as well funded, what seems to be lacking in the spirit of commitment. It seems to be nobody's concern that an institution does fulfills the purpose for which it was set up. After the founders leave the scene, the spirit ebbs and only the structure remains and the structure become counter-productive.

More often than not, such a situation arises out of the infirmities of the very constitution of the institution. In many ways, the position of a an institutions is even worse than that of a Government department. The latter has solid strength deriving from stability and permanence; the institution is in a more vulnerable position. Most institutions today, even though originally established through voluntary efforts, are dependant on Government grants for not only development but also day-to day maintenance. The Government department which handles these grants treats the institutions as no more than 'subordinate offices'. The Minister or the higher officers of the departments have hardly the time to take any interest in the institutions falling in their jurisdiction much less to ensure timely release of adequate grants. The institutions are left to not so tender mercies of junior officers of the department who often ride rough shad over the institutions. This had a demoralizing effect on their functioning.

But the problems arising out of the inner working of the institutions are even more serious. The institutions are often set up as societies under the Registration of Societies Act, 1961. A society had its constitution and rules. Under the constitution, the governance of the society is vented in a body called Board of Management of body having some similar nomenclature. The Board sets up its own committees. The head of the institutions viz. The Director is accountable to the Board. He is the professional/ academic as well as administrative head of the institution. He has a triple responsibility for (a) conducting the societal functions including the meetings of the General Body, the Board of Management and its committees. (b) providing professional/ academic leadership and (c) carrying on day-to-day administration of the institution. While the professional/ academic staff is in charge of the programme of the institution, the administrative staff headed by a Registrar or an officer carrying similar nomenclature has to provide administrative support needed for the conduct of programmes.

The Board may consist of persons elected by the members of the society as well as some nominated by Government in case of institutions where it finances are provided by it. The main function of the Board should be to provide constructive support to the Director in carrying out the work of the institution. But the trouble starts when some members of the Board start feeling that they are holding positions of power and must exercise their clout. They constitute themselves into a cotarie which manipulates elections, provides patronage to staff members on a selective basis and show their clout in the Board meetings by creating difficulties for the Director. Their capacity to help in the work of the institution is very limited. They do not raise the financial resources for which the Director has struggle with the department or the grant sanctioning institution. They have no responsibility for running any of the programme of the institution. And yet they want to exercise authority without responsibility. As a consequence, the societal aspects start operating at cross purpose with the institutional functioning. This vitiates the atmosphere, demoralizes the Director and his colleagues and adversely affects their sense of commitment.

The coteric soon develops the ambition to have a director of their choice. But if the Government have their own nominee, there is a head-on collision in which the Government with control over the purse strings, has it way. Often there is a stalemate and the institution remains without a director for a long time. All this seriously affects the working of the institution. Manipulation gets the better of creative work.

Clever faculty/ professional staff members take full advantage of the situation. They develop links with the coteric and try to undermine the position of the Director, instead of functioning as loyal members of the team. Faculty groupism has disastrous consequences on the output of the institution. Rather than contributing to the work of the institution, faculty members become interested only in what they can get out of it for feathering their own nest – participating in a seminar abroad or getting a lucrative outside assignment. Position in the institution for them is not a place of work. It is only a launching pad. Furthering the work of the institution is none of their responsibility.

When the institution start developing on these lines, the concepts of academic freedom and institutional autonomy get thoroughly missused. Academic freedom becomes another name for non-performance and absence of accountability. In the name of academic freedom every attempt to introduce a scheme for performance appraisal or maintenance of confidential record is stoutly resisted. Institution's time and resources are used for outside projects beneficial only to the individual.

In the name of autonomy, the coteric in the Board of Management resists accountability to governments but autonomy does not prevent it from interfering in the working of the institution, promoting faculty groupism and thereby trampling on the autonomy of the Director.

Caught between the Scylla of the ambitions coteris in the Board of Management and Chair bodies of the self seeking members of the faculty, even a committed Director is hard put it in evenly directing the course of the institution towards its cherished goals. A sense of disgust overwhelms him and compels him to seek a change. This suits the selfseeking members of the faculty. Allied with the coterie, they think of themselves as the permanent core of the institution while the Director is only a bird of passage! But the core is rotten to the core!

In discharging his many aided responsibilities, the Director does not find the 'administration' particularly helpful. It consists mostly of staff on deputation which brings with it the rigidities and routine-mindedness of a government department. The institution is perforce required to follow departmental rules and regulations since funds come from government. These are often not suitable for the work of the institution. Institutional administration must have flexibility and innovativeness. But the departmental straight jacket and hangovers of the deputed staff leave little scope for their introduction. In an academic/ professional institution, the academic/ professional staff should undertake responsibility for devising administrative procedure suitable for the conduct of the programmes. But they have little flair for this with the result that administration becomes a handicap rather than an asset for the dynamic growth of the institution.

Once an institution falls in a rut, it become extremely difficult to give it a fresh impetus. It is much easier to set up a new institution rather than salvage or set right an old institution which has gone on the wrong track.

There can be no uniform formula for ensuring the success of an institution. But one thing is certain. Without discipline and sustained commitment, an institution cannot grow and fulfill its mission. An institutional structure which comes in the way of meeting this basic requirement, will have to be set right at the earliest. A lot of investment goes in the establishment of an institution. Those in authority cannot look the other way, while the institution goes to seeds and then think of winding it up.

Chapter - 6

Positive Parenting and need for Flexibility in Education

Trinity of Education

Students, teachers and parents constitute the trinity of education. It is on the synergic relationship between the three, that the quality of education depends. This is especially true during the formative period of education i.e. pre-primary, primary and secondary stages of education.

The focus of both teachers and parents is on the students – at least that is what is expected. Teachers are parents in the school and parents are teachers at home. Mother is the first teacher of the child and both mother and father are role models for the child. Their personality, behaviour and values leave an indelible imprint on the mind of the child. The parents have to be truthful, diligent and dignified and decent in behaviour if they wish their children to be so. Teachers and parents, therefore, play a complementary role in the process of education. If they work at cross purposes, the process of education gets distorted. On the other hand their combined, complementary efforts enhance the quality of education.

Education - part of upbringing

This is best understood if we comprehend what constitutes 'education'. Education is not just students attending the class rooms, teachers conducting classes in their respective subjects according to prescribed time tables, holding tests and examinations and evaluating the students and promoting them to higher standards on passing of examinations. Now that the new act of Right to education has banned examination, they have become redundant. This is likely to have an adverse impact on the quality of education imparted to and absorbed by the students. A recent survey 'Asar' brought out by 'Pratham', NGO in the field of education shows that even the fifth standards students, do not have elementary abilities in three Rs - reading, writing and (a) rithmetic.

However, education is not just a formal process as described above. Education is a part of upbringing of the child. Up bringing is a wider process of all round development of the child, developing the potentialities and creativity's of the child, developing his or her mind, physique, character, personality, creating in him/ her the abilities to distinguish between right and wrong and building up self confidence. This process is delicate, like a bud developing into a flower.

Negative Parenting

It is in this wider content that we have to consider the concept of 'positive parenthood'. Positive parenthood may be distinguished from "negative parenthood." Parents exemplify "negative parenting" if they feel that their role is over after admitting the child to the school, paying fees and making arrangements for the child being deposited in the school, (these duties are performed now-a-days increasingly by the mothers just as teachers are, in the main, female with only some exceptional male teachers) and collecting the child after the school hours and signing on the 'progress report'. The rest of the responsibility they feel is of the school and the teachers. If the students do not do well, the latter are wholly responsible and must be blamed. They look at education as a 'commodity' which, they have bought at a price viz. Fees. The school which takes fees are the 'sellers of education' and must bear responsibility if the child fails. They do not realize their own responsibility. This is what constitutes 'negative parenting'.

Such parents are so immersed in their pre-occupations whether in the office, business or club, that they have no time to spare for their child. Sometimes such parents claim that they give 'quality time' to their child. It has become fashionable to talk of 'quality time'. The concept of 'quality time' is not clear. Such parents do not realize that sometimes the child faces problems which cannot wait for 'quality time' which the parent can spare. The truth is that the child should feel that parental support is available all time and not just during the so called 'quality time.'

Oppressive Parenting

On the other hand, some parents are obsessed with the desire to see that their child excels in every subject and in every co-curricular activity, whether sports, music, drama and other cultural activities, elocution, essay and quiz competitions. They have high aspirations and ambitions which they expect their child to fulfill. What they themselves could not accomplish in their lives, their child should! In goading the child to accomplish, they have no regard for or understanding of the likes and dislikes, inclinations or proclivities, abilities and capacities of the child. This is "oppressive parenting" and not "positive parenting." It may well lead the child to succumb to such pressure, deform his or her personality and lose the joy of education which should be a joyful activity.

"Indifferent parenting" and "oppressive parenting" are two extremes which are not "positive parenting." Similarly there are two extremes of "excessive indulgence" and excessive discipline both of which are harmful. Fulfilling every single wish of the child, giving in to his or her every demand just became another child has it, is an extreme case of over indulgence. Now-a-days affluent parents tend to tilt towards this kind of over indulgence. On the other hand, are parents who are strict disciplinarian. They keep strict watch on every activity of the child. This saps the springs of freedom and kill his or her creativity and potentiality. No wonder the child rebels against such strict discipline.

Positive Parenting

Positive parenting should steer clear of the both over indulgence and excessive discipline. Positive parenting is a via media, a golden mean between over indulgence and excessive discipline, indifferent parenting and oppressive parenting.

There are no fixed rules of finding a golden mean. It depend on every case. No two human beings are the same, nor do two children. Unless we give scope to the unique individuality of every child, we may commit serious mistakes.

Delinquencies in child

Either of two extremes may lead to a wayward behaviour of the child. It will suffer from hypertension. It rebel against oppression. The more the parents put pressure, the more would the child rebel. It will not listen. It will rebel against everything that the parent asks it to do. It will feel that the parents are hard, do not love or understand its feelings. It will get lost in its own world. It may fall in bad company or habits. It will get addicted to everything other than school studies like watching cartoons on television all the time. More the parent gets concerned about the wayward behaviour of the child, the more wayward they become. What is required in such a situation is a healing touch of the parent.

Flexibility needed in educational system

Unfortunately not only parents but our entire educational system is rigid and does not realise that the personalities and potentialities of children are varied. We impose the same syllabus, the same curriculum, the same lesson, the same tests for evaluation for every child. This may be extremely harmful to quality of the educational system as a whole.

Two examples may be cited which vividly illustrate this incongruity between the inclinations, creativity and potentialities of the child and a rigid uniform educational system. The great poet, Nobel Laureate, Rabindranath Tagore actually ran away from the school and had to be tutored at home. Since he belonged to an aristocratic family, this could be done. Rabindranath Tagore reached great heights with the flowering of all his talents as a poet, a story writer, a novelist, a dance and drama artist, an original musician and an educationist who set up the unique educational institution – "Vishwabharati", which aimed at calling the best in every student, "where 'mind was free' and not bound "by narrow domestic walls."

Another outstanding example was Ramanujan, the great mathematician whose 125th anniversary has recently been celebrated. He failed in the school exam and the first year college examination and could not get a degree and hence did not become even an ordinary graduate. This was because, his entire energy, time and mind was concentrated on one thing viz. Mathematics and numbers – their series divergent and convergent. He produced two notebook full of original theorems and mathematical results beyond the comprehension of even Mathematics professors in Indian Universities. He sent some of his theorems to three leading Mathematicians of Cambridge University, two of whom cold shouldered him. But the third a younger Professor G.H. Herty recognized his genius and his original contributions and arranged to bring him to Cambridge against all odds. Over five years of his stay there, his genius flowered despite his difficulties of adjusting to cold climate and cultural differences. His papers were published in leading Mathematical journals in England and won the appreciation of the academic community. Several years later, Mathematicians in Cambridge and US Universities were still working on Ramanujan's theorems. Ramanujan, who could not get a degree in India, was awarded BA and later honour of being elected as Fellow of the Philosophical society, Fellow of Trinity College, Cambridge and most coveted of all, Fellow of the Royal Society.

Not every child is a potential Ramanujan and Rabindranath. But every child is endowed with divine originalities. The educational system should have enough flexibility to allow for diverse originalities and personal attributes of every child. This is a great challenge before our educational community and educational system.

Chapter - 7

Educational Reforms : Issues of Quality and Equity

'The Right of Children to Free and Compulsory Education Act, 2009' passed by the Parliament and the recommendations of the Bansal Committee appointed by the Government of Maharashtra for the regulation of fees charged by non-aided schools have been the two important measures for the educational reforms which have been discussed in this article.

Fee Fixation by un-aided institutions

Recent measures to introduce educational reforms have put into a sharp focus issues of quality vs. equity.

Taking cognizance of commercialization of education and profiteering by unaided schools, the education department of Maharashtra setup a Committee under the Chairmanship of Smt. Kumud Bansal, former Education Secretary, to suggest norms for fixing fees. The committee was setup as per the interim orders of Bombay High Court in a writ petition in the case of Students Welfare Association vs. Maharashtra Government.

The unaided schools constitute only 10% of the schools in Maharashtra the rest of 90% are either run by local bodies or are aided. In these latter categories of schools, no fees are charged.

The Committee has conceded at the very outset that the unaided schools, many of them affiliated to National Board like CBSE have as their objective excellence in learning. They aim at holistic development of the students through curricular and co-curricular activities. The Committee took the view that the institutions should continue to have autonomy in matters like admission of students, recruitment of teachers and other staff, and determination of fees. However, in the name of autonomy, the schools should not indulge in profiteering for purpose of personal gain or business enterprise. Some guidelines regarding norms for determination of fees have therefore, to be laid down.

In prescribing these norms, the Committee was guided by Supreme Court judgement governing fees of unaided educational institutions viz. TMA. PAI Foundation Vs. State of Karnataka 2002, Islamic Academy of Education vs. State of India (2004) and P.A. Inamdar V.s State of Maharashtra (2005).

The Committee recommended that the fees could be so fixed as to allow generation of reasonable surplus up to 15% of total revenues. Surplus is defined as the difference between total revenue of the institution and total admissible expense. Total revenue include fees and other income if any, while admissible expenses are defined as those contributing to the imparting of quality education to students.

The most important point that arises in the context is that while some parents complain about high fees charged by unaided schools, they nevertheless do not avail of free education offered by Government run or aided school but instead flock to unaided schools because of their perception that while the quality of government run or aided schools is poor, it is high in unaided schools.

I had a recent experience of seeing how desperate the parents are in getting a seat for their child in an unaided school. Bharatiya Vidya Bhavan, Pune Kendra runs two nurseries and two elementary schools and a secondary school. These schools have won a high reputation for quality education. Yet compared to other unaided schools, the fees are much lower. No wonder the 'under pricing' according to the market conditions, invites retribution. For a small number of less than hundred seats, some 1000 parents stood in the queue to seek admission forms. Such was the desperation amongst the parents for getting this much coveted form for admission in the nursery school, that some parents came on the previous evening spending the whole night out sleeping in shivering cold all through the night. Since the forms to be issued had to be limited in view of limited number of seats, hundred of parents had to go disappointed. In their desperation they blamed the school for not issuing the forms and the local Shiva Sena unit even issued a threat. But if forms had been distributed to all, the same people would have blamed the school authorities for profiteering from sale of forms (even here our charge for a form was less than charged by other schools). It is distressing that even parents who cannot afford to pay fees of unaided schools shun the free education offered in government schools and flock to unaided school.

It is high time that the education department of government concentrate on improving the quality of their own schools rather than seeing to regulate non-aided schools and harass them in the name of regulation. The government does not even disburse grants in a timely manner. The proposal to setup an

Apex Committee at the State level to fix fees for each school is palpably impractical and would do more harm than good.

The idea that fixation of fees should have the approval of the Parent Teachers Association cannot also be stretched too far. The idea that each item of expenditure should be open to PTA scrutiny and that the Management should explain and be answerable for each item in the Balance Sheet of Profit and Loss account is not workable. It would throttle the working of the institution and render it non functional. All that can be done is to take parents in confidence through PTA and give reasonable thought to the suggestions made by PTA. After all the PTA is not responsible for running of the school. This is the work of the school authorities and management.

The Bansal Committee has frankly stated that excellence is the key objective of unaided schools (not all should be labelled as 'private' – schools of Bharatiya Vidya Bhavan are run by a public institution of high standards with high ethical and moral values) and has provided an illustrative list of curricular and co-curricular activities and the relevant heads of expenses which contribute to excellence in education.

Universal Primary Education

After the attainment of independence, illiteracy was rightly considered as the first item of educational reform. No country with a high level of illiteracy as in India especially amongst women could hope to develop socially and economically. All countries in Europe, USA and Japan could start the process of development only after universalisation of primary education. India had the largest reservoir of illiterate population in the world. This had to end. Even after two decades of National Policy on Education (1986) and Sarva Shiksha Abhiyan the state has not been able to provide universal elementary education. Universilisatoin of secondary education is a distant dream.

The Constitution adopted on 26th November 1949, enshrined a Directive Principle in article 45 which stated "The state shall endeavour to provide within a period of ten years from the commencement of the Constitution for free and compulsory education for all children until they complete the age of fourteen years." The constitutional directive was categorical and what was required was resolute implementation. But the state failed to live up to the expectation of the Constitution. The objective was not only achieved in ten years but even after fifty years the objective is yet to be reached. As usual, we thought that more legislation would be a substitute for action ! We argued that the goal was not reached because a Directive principle is not justiciable and therefore remained a pious hope ! The remedy was to make it a fundamental right! The N.D.A. Government, therefore got passed the 86th Constitutional Amendment in December 2002 which gave every child between 6 to 14 years right to free and compulsory education. It remained for the UPA Government to get enacted the "Right to Education Bill, 2009". This ensures every child right to education and the obligation of the government to impart it. The Act also provided that the state shall endeavour to provide early childhood care and education for children until they complete the age of six years. The Act prescribed that it shall be the fundamental duty of every citizen of India who is a parent or guardian to provide opportunity for education to his child / ward between age of 6 and 14 years. If a parent/ guardian fail to perform the duty, the State Management Committee may direct him to perform compulsory community service by way of child care.

The Act envisages the concept of 'neighbourhood" school where fee and compulsory education will be provided. Such school will be made available within a period of 3 years from the commencement of the Act. A child suffering from severe disability and cannot attend a a neighbourhood school will be provided alternative appropriate environment.

If for any reason a young person has been unable to complete elementary education by the age of 14 years but is continuing education in a school, he shall continue to be provided with free education in such a school till the person completes elementary education or a until the attainment of 18 years.

Providing free and compulsory education will be the Government responsibility of the Central and appropriate governments. The Central Government will provide (1) Financial assistance to State Government Schools on sharing basis. (2) Educational curriculum framework and standard of qualifications of teachers and training. (3) Appropriate technical support to State Government.

The appropriate Government shall provide financial assistance to Local Authorities for implementation of the Act. It will establish additional schools as required after determining the requirement of schools for providing free and compulsory education and deploy teachers as required. A School Development Council will prepare School Development Plan for provision of free and compulsory education for every local area (i.e. Block, District and Metropolitan region). Duties of teachers are prescribed in the Act. The vacancies in State Schools or full aided schools shall not exceed 10% of total strength. No teacher of a state or fully aided school shall be deployed for non-educational purpose except for decimal population census, election work and disaster relief.

A School Management Committee shall be constituted for every state school and aided school with representation of parents, teachers and representation of local community.

There will be a National Commission for Elementary Education for monitoring for implementation of the Act.

The idea is mooted in the Act that universalisation would be facilitated by making the curriculum less rigorous. There will be no screening procedure for admission to an elementary school. As it is the standard are very low. Research has shown the student even in the fourth standard cannot read and right and make sums. How much more can in the quality be diluted and standard brought down in the name of equity?

The Act be tried to pass on the State responsibility to private (i.e. non-governmental) schools by stipulating that 25% seats in private schools would be allocated to children from disadvantaged groups including differently enabled children in every school. The state would provide needed resources to cover their fees. But state authorities seldom keep their word in fulfilling the obligation in a timely manner. Delay in release of funds would bring the private schools in financial difficulties. Moreover 25% of such students might bring down the general standard of excellence of the school which has been acknowledged by Bansal Committee and other reports.

The schools are prohibited from charging capitation fees. If it is charged, the Management shall be liable to pay a fine which may extend 10 times the capitation fees.

There is a provision for establishing Recognition Authority in every state under which the school will be required to provide needed infrastructure in three years. Here is a case of organisational proliferation which often does more harm than good. Cannot Zilla Parishads and Panchayats take care of this ?

The affluent sections who have prospered in the era of liberalization must be made to provide resources needed for universlisation of primary education through schools with needed infrastructure. A mid-day meal programme is also a way of persuading children of poor families to attend to schools. The constitutional amendment and the enabling Act can hardly be called an improvement over the original Directive Principles of the Constitution. What was required was resolve and a commitment on the part of executives which seems to be lacking. To be sure, a citizen can now go to court if a child is denied the right. But litigation and court pronouncement is no substitute for administrative action. The state of Maharashtra has no full time Minister in charge of education. This is an indication of priority accorded to education. For long we have been hearing that 6% of GDP shared be made available for education. But this has not materialized and remains wall of the wisp. To fulfill its obligation the state has to open more schools and persuade the parents to send children to school. But such is the condition of the poor family specially of the disadvantaged sections that they want their children to work rather than go to school. So here is a dilemma. Development cannot take place without universalisation of education; but universalisation is not possible without improvement of economic conditions.

Chapter - 8

Educational Reforms in Finland and their Relevance to India

Finland, a tiny country of 5.5 million people, in North Europe belonging to the Nordic group of countries, has become a role model for social cohesion and solidarity and rapid economic and technological development Nokia a Finish company has become the leader of mobile all over the world. A remarkable transformation took place in Finland within a short period of twenty years between 1970 to 1990. Reforms in its educational system played a crucial role in bringing about this transformation. It nurtured values of honesty and ethics in dealing with each other leading to mutual trust and confidence which laid the foundation of economic progress and social cohesion.

The importance of education in bringing about economic and social change has been recognised in many advanced countries like USA, UK and Japan which have introduced reforms in their educational system. But Finish approach to educational reforms has been very different from that in other countries. The Finish educational institutions are all in public sector. Education is free for all students. In the place of former grammar schools and civic schools, Finland established comprehensive schools providing basic education for all citizens for a period of 9 years. But more important than the changes in the formal structure are the changes in the philosophy and outlook on education which are very distinct from these in other countries.

For long Japan was applauded for its educational system. Heavy syllabus, long hours, rigorous hard work and pressure on student to excel in tough competition, characterized Japanese system of education. In USA emphasis in educational reforms was on continuous assessment of students through frequent tests. In Britain fixing high standards and inspections of school to ensure conformity to preordained students standard was the way to introduce school reforms. All these above found place in 'Germ' elements i.e. global educational reforms movement.

Finish approach to educational reforms was very different from the centralised reforms imposed by external authority which characterized all these approaches. The Finish reforms are from within. Through there is common framework of curriculum, there is plenty of scope for experimentation by each institution. Creative flexibility rather than blind conformity marks the educational reforms in Finland, 'Less is more' is how the author describes the Finish system of education less pressure on students less frequency testing, less number external inspections but more creativity more originality and more local effort and initiative of teachers)

At the centre of educational reforms are the teachers. In Finland, teachers' profession is considered as 'prestigious' – more prestigious then even the legal and medical profession. In India it is just the opposite. Those who cannot join prestigious professions of medical, engineering, information technology etc., those left out, become teachers. In Finland there is a competition for entering into the teaching profession and only the most promising can enter into the teaching profession. Teachers have post-graduate qualifications. All teachers undertake research. High quality of teachers ensure high quality of education. A special feature of Finish process of education is the career guidance the teachers provide to their students. Also is the emphasis on vocational education. The emphasis is on building the ability to provide solution to practical problems. This type of orientation has made the Finish system of education contribute greatly human resource development. India has much to learn from educational reforms in Finland. The essential features of Finish model deserves to be emulated by us in India for the betterment of our educational system. India is vast country. Its population is 240 times that of Finland. It has great diversity in the composition of its population. The scale of our problems is gargantuan . Yet we should not hesitate to assimilate the lessons of Finish educational reforms. According to PISA (Programme for international students assessment) Finland is at the top and India at the bottom.

Union Ministry for HRD has recently taken some steps for educational reforms one of which is the passing of the Right to Education Act of 2009. The act was passed by Parliament but in the formulation of the Act there were few local inputs though the implementation of the provisions of the Act has to be done by the states. Consequently inconsistencies have arisen between the existing educational situation in the states and the provisions of the Act. Severe problems of implementation have to be tackled. And yet after the judgement of the Supreme Court upholding the constitutional validity of the Act, the local offices of state and educational administrator has started implementing the provisions, specially those relating to reservations, in an authoritarian manner, obviously to save themselves from any possibility of disciplinary action against them by higher authorities. In this authoritarian operation, there is little of any understanding, co-operation or mutual trust. There may be formal conformity to provisions of the Act but the basic objectives not the Act may not be achieved and quality of education may decline.

Finish Lessons – 'What can the World learn from educational change in Finland?' by Pasi Sahlberg published by Teachers College, Columbia University, New York and London, pp. 165, 2011).

Chapter - 9

New Educational Policy- Relevance to elementary Education

Policy Making

Policy is an instrument of transformation of a given environment into a preferred environment. Environment has problems like illiteracy and unemployment which policy identifies. It prioritese these problems and picks up those with the highest urgency and importance. The problems have solutions. Policy chooses those solutions which have highest benefit – cost ratio. Policy is not just declaration of objectives. It has to have a strategy of action. There has to be a policy path from objectives to provisions of financial resources and organization and man-power, allocation of responsibility for implementation, a time-table for implementation, periodic review of implementation, evaluation of policy in the light of implementation and revision of policy or formulation of new policy as needed.

Education and Economic Policy

Education policy is closely linked with economic policy. Education provides human resources with requisite knowledge, skills and values which are a pre-requisite for economic development. Education has to be complementary to economic development. However, very often the products of our educational system are found to be unemployable in a rapidly changing economy. Education must keep pace with economic development. Conversely the economy has to provide financial resources needed for a satisfactory educational system. Kothari Commission (1964-1966) recommended that 6% of national income should be allocated to education. It has not exceeded 3% so far. There is an an urgent need for increased allocation of budgetary provisions for education both by the State and Union Government.

Evolution of Educational Policy

Educational policies have been evolved over many years since independence – policy of 1968, 1986, 1992, Sarva Shiksha Abhiyan Madhyamic Shikshan Abhiyan and the Right to Education Act of 2010 and the latest educational policy. These are based on the recommendations of many committees and commissions like Radhakrishnan Commission (1948) Kothari Commission (1964-1966), Rama Murthi Committee (1990) etc.

Universalisation of Education

The most important goal or objective of educational policy is universalisation of education by giving access to education to all, particularly to children of disadvantaged sections of community, more of them in rural areas. There have to be adequate number of schools with adequate infrastructure and facilities like class rooms, drinking water, toilets, playground etc. Above all there have to be adequate number of qualified teachers.

The fountain head of all educational policies is article 45 of the Constitution which lays down the Directive Principle that the State shall endeavour to provide free and compulsory education to all children up to the age of fourteen.

Universalisation of elementary education was not possible because of barrier or obstacles to access such as interviews at entry points and capitation fees which the children of disadvantaged classes were unable to overcome. These were prohibited under the Right to Education Act. Still the problems for poor children persisted. The families of the poor were unable to provide adequate nourishment to their children. They wanted their children to earn. The Nobel Prize winner Satyarthi drew attention to the wide spread prevalence of child labour. Tamil Nadu State took the lead in introducing a scheme for the provision of food to children. Tamil Nadu's example was followed by many other States.

Even after entry without paying capitation fees, the poor could not afford to pay the annual fees. The Right to Education Act provided for reservation of free seats for students of disadvantaged sections who could not afford fees. The Act envisaged that the State would reimburse the fees of such students, to no grant schools. However, while the State forced the no grant schools to provide 25% of seats to the disadvantaged sections of students, they have failed so far to provide any financial reimbursement, thereby placing the entire financial burden on the no grant schools.

Problem of Drop-outs

Despite universalisation of entry to education, there arose a problem of dropouts. Many children of the disadvantaged sections left schools after the fifth or sixth standard. That was because they could not pass the end of the year examinations and had to be detained. The Right to Education Act prohibited examinations and detention. There would be automatic promotion of all students till the 9th standard.

Quantity v/s. Quality Education

The no examination, no detention policy however, created a situation where according to survey carried on in 2010, the students of fifth standard could not even read and write. Quantitative expansion was at the cost of qualitative deterioration. The new examination policy, therefore, reverses the policy by requiring end of the year examination after the fifth standard.

The Act of 2010 does not pay adequate alternative to qualitative standards. Qualitative standard requires to pay attention to many aspects besides infrastructure like good class rooms, toilets, playground and other facilities. The assessment process must focus on the learning process. There should a 'learning curve' for every student. It should measure how much the student has absorbed, how far their thinking facilities have developed, to what extent, the child can think for himself. There has to be broading of mind and development of critical thinking. There should be a thirst for knowledge. The students should not confine themselves to prescribed text books, (they should of course be studied) but do a lot of outside reading. Education should create a love for reading good books which are the life blood of great minds. The students should be enabled to learn for themselves. They should read stories, essays and novels written by great authors.

E-Learning

The computer age has provided access to students to a vast store house of knowledge on any subject. This has enabled a process of self learning called E-learning. The teachers of today should be able to guide the students in E-learning process.

Role of Teachers

Good teachers play a crucial role in providing good education. Unfortunately there is a great shortage of good teachers. About 2 lakh posts of teachers are vacant.

To attract good talent to the teaching profession, it should be looked upon as a coveted and honoured profession as in Finland which has gained fame for the quality of its elementary education. There has to be provision for in-service training courses for teachers. Unfortunately this aspect is neglected. There is a lack of quality institutions for providing for teacher's training. The performance of teachers should be periodically evaluated.

School – a self governing institution

The schools should be self governed institutions free from outside interference. There should be a system of internal evaluation of every school.

Chapter - 10

Assessment of Students and Quality of Education

Conference Theme

Under the auspices of Bharatiya Vidya Bhavan, Pune Kendra, we have been holding 'Annual Educational Conference' on important issues relating to school education. These conferences have provided a forum for teachers, educationists and education authorities, students, parents and others concerned with education to come together and share experiences, express thoughts and come to conclusions and suggestions for future action by all concerned.

The first conference was held on 'Right to Education Act' soon after the Act was passed by the Parliament; the second was on 'Code of Conduct for Teachers; the third on 'Positive Parenting'. The first conference was focussed on students, the second on teachers and third on parents. Parents, teachers and students constitute the 'trinity' of education who collectively participate in the process of education.

The theme of this fourth conference is 'Assessments of students and quality of education'. It is focussed on all the three and on education as a whole.

Examination as the method of assessment

The two parts of the theme are closely related. The quality of education is judged by the quality of students. If the quality of students is of a high order, then quality of education should be judged high. Conversely if the students turned out are of a poor quality, then the quality of education should correspondingly adjudged to be of low order.

The traditional method of assessing the students are in the examinations. Examinations are held periodically say six monthly and annually. If a student successfully passes the annual examination, he is promoted to the higher standard. If the student fails, he has to continue in the same standard and appear for the next examination which he has to pass before he could be promoted.

The tenth year is the final year of the school studies. The student has to give a public examination which as against the earlier school examinations considered to be the most important by the students, parents and the school.

A school tries its best to see that its students do well in the final examination because the quality of the school is judged by the results of its students in the final school leaving examination. If the results are cent per cent passing, then it is a credit for the school. But that may not be enough. We have a system of giving marks. It the students secure marks above 95% or 90% and if a majority of students pass in first class, it is a feather in the cap for the school. If it shows such performance over successive years it is (as our own school Sulochana Natu Vidya Mandir is doing) surely ranked as a school of high order.

Examination Reforms

In recent years however, the relevance of examination as the sole method of assessing the quality of schools and the examination results as the criterion for adjudging the quality of students are being increasingly called into question. The examination, it is argued, puts a premium on cramming the content of the textbook rather than a real understanding of the subject. Also examinations put excessive burden and anxiety on the students and stifle the real intellectual growth or capacity of understanding. Examinations become such a fetish that they became the 'be all and end all' of education. This excessive pre-occupation with results of examination has given birth to a thriving business of private coaching classes for 9th and 10th years students as also 12th year students, as well as also for competitive examinations to enter into professional colleges and civil services. The private coaching classes charge high fees but parents willy nilly pay the fees of the coaching classes with the sole expectation of good results of their children in examination. In all this, good education, gets a backseat.

In spite of the support of coaching classes, some students carry a fear of examinations which puts them under strain and tension. This can damage the self confidence and personality of the students of weak character leading even to suicides, often reported in the press.

In order to remove the bugbear of final public examinations, suggestions have been made to supplement or even supplant them by alternative methods of assessment like class room work, periodic tests or interactions between teachers and students with a view to developing their understanding of the subject.

The Right to Education Act has gone beyond all this, eliminating examinations altogether for the first eight standards providing for automatic promotion. What does experience of the last three years shows the result of this heroic step? It is often stated by teachers and even parents that as a results of abolition of examinations, students do not take their studies seriously. Automatic promotions makes life easy for them but when they enter into ninth tenth standards, teachers find them unprepared finding it difficult to cope up with their studies leading to final school leaving examination.

Educational process should certainly be all joyful experience but total elimination of all stress of studies may not be desirable. After all, ability to bear stress is a quality which should be developed in school years because when the students enter into world outside the sheltered family life they have face situations of stress. Students who do not develop the ability to bear stress find themselves unprepared in their adult life to face stressful situations which inevitably rise in the life of every adult individual.

Larger Goal of Education

There are also larger issues regarding the goal of education. Surely it is not to put the students thorough the mechanical process of appearing classes, listening to teaching lessons, holding tests, prescribing and covering prescribed syllabus. It is rather the development of potential of every child, call forth the best in every student (to recall the words of Rabindranath Tagore), to bring about all round development of the personality of the child, to promote intellectual, physical and moral development, to develop character, to impart knowledge, develop skills and inculcate values, develop ability to distinguish between right and wrong, to inculcate discipline and ability to participate in team work and commitment to the concepts of liberty, equality, fraternity and social justice prominently mentioned in the preamble of our Constitution. It is by the test of application of these higher objectives that we can assess the quality of our student as well as the quality of our education.

INTERNATIONAL RELATIONS - VII

Chapter - 1

Regional Power – Concept and Implications

American Defence Secretary Carlucci in the press statement at the end of the recent visit to India said that as a "regional power". India has an active role to play in the Afganistan settlement. Indian intervention in Sri Lanka is also justified on the ground that it necessarily arises out of the obligations of a regional power. What is this concept of the regional power and what does it imply in term of the structure of relationships between the regionasl power and other countries of the region? Answer to this question is of crucial importance of India's foreign, security and economic policies if the concept of regional power is to govern them in the years to come. Absence of clarity on the concept of regional power might have repercussions and ramifications which may be unpremeditated and involve India into commitments for which she may not be prepared.

The term 'regional power' implies that the world is divided into regions and in each region there is country which may be considered predominant in the region. Furthermore, such a predominant country is expected to influence the course of events in the countries of the region whether in the interest of those countries, of in it's own interest or in the interest of those countries, or in the interest of the region as a whole.

The term 'regional power' may be said to be in contrast to the term 'global power'. The regional power though predominant in the region may be said to be of no particular consequence for the world as a whole. It may therefore, be content to leave the course of world events to be shaped by the global power.

Let us see the to what extent these formulations are valid.

First, the regions amongst which the world may be said to have been divided. The following regions are often mentioned viz. North America, Latin America, Western Europe, Eastern Europe, South-East Asia, South Asia, West

Asia, the Far East, the Pacific, and Africa-North, East, West and South. Most of these regions have by now some regional formations – some tight, some loose, some strong, some weak. Amongst the strong ones are the European Economic Community (EEC) for Western Europe, Come on for Eastern Europe and ASEAN for South East Asian Countries. Amongst not so strong may be mentioned SARC – South Asian Regional Conference; not so strong because it has recently been formed and yet to develop adequately concerted action on matters of substance.

Not all these regions have a predominant power in them. Thus, members of European Economic community may vary in size measured by area and population, in GNP or in economic power or scientific and technological strength. But these variations are not such as to make any one a predominant power in the region. In the Asia region, Indonesia may be considered much bigger in size in terms of population and area, than other member countries like Thailand, Malaysia or Philippines. Yet it is not perhaps considered a dominant power in the region.

In the Pacific region, Australia may be considered to be a regional power since the rest of the island countries like Fiji, Tonga or Soloman Island are almost tiny in comparison. Yet the Pacific islands have not perhaps taken a concrete shape of a distinct region.

The Far East has two predominantly important countries – China because of its size and economic potential and Japan because of its spectacular economic and technological development. But Hongkong, Taiwan and South Korea though smaller in size, have also shown spectacular economic progress. However, China and Japan are too big to be contained in a specific region like the Far East. While dominating the entire Eastern region, they are not without ambition and influence on the world scene.

The situation in South Asia Region is very different from that in the European Economic Community. While India is a behemoth, Bhutan, Maldives, Sri Lanka and Nepal are tiny in comparison and Pakistan and Bangladesh much smaller. It is this imbalance which readily lends itself to the concept of India as the regional power of South Asia.

But this position of imbalance can hardly be called an unusual or peculiar phenomenon if it is realized that the so-called South Asia region was till recently known as the Indian sub-continent, a term which seems to have gone out of usage and therefore, probably forgotten. The reasons for this are also not far to seek. The perhaps arise out of the allergy of Pakistan and Bangladesh, till recently parts of the Indian sub-continent, to the use of the term which seems to remind them that they are break-away parts of India. Hence, they prefer the term South Asia which geographically seems to be quite inaccurate seeing that the countries like Malaysia and Indonesia are the ones to the south of Asia while Indian sub-continent may be seen to be at the centre of the Asian continent. However, neither the allergy nor the replacement by a new term, can create an illusion that in the place of the Indian sub-continent some kind of a new region has emerged in the world.

However, despite the imbalance in size of the different countries on the Indian sub-continent, and despite the fact that till recent history, they were parts of India, the fact remains that they are now independent countries and members of United Nations each with sovereign rights in managing internal and external affairs. Bhutan may still have the obligation to conduct her external affairs in accordance with the guidance of Government of India but Nepal seems to have given up acting in accordance with the terms of Indo-Napal Treaty which virtually enabled free mobility across the boundary and free convertibility of currency.

People of the region constitute one single sub-continental community, with ties of culture, religion and history and yet this basic truth constituting the hard core of solidarity of the region has been buried under all kinds of external influences and obligations. Thus, at a recent meeting in Delhi on Regional co-operation it was astonishing to hear a Pakistani representative (originally from Madras) talking of Pakistan's 'search for identity' and Pakistan's face towards Arabia, Iran and Turkey in course of such a search. It is then no surprise to find Maldives in the Indian ocean trying to come closer with Malaysia in Asean.

Indeed the very 'imbalance' in 'South Asian region' is driving its smaller members to restore the balance by seeking alliances and support structures outside the region. Pakistan has long and established alliance with USA so recently confirmed by Carlucci and has successfully built up friendship with China only to checkmate India. Even Nepal has persistently sought to balance China with India, claming equal friendship with both (implying no special relationship with India) and in the teeth of India reluctance to endorse, has put forward and solicited the support of all and sundry to her pet idea of 'Nepal as a zone of peace.' Sri Lanka knocked at the door of very other country – USA, UK, Israel before turning to India in putting down the threat of Tamil terrorism only when its effort with others to put its chestnuts out of fire bore no fruit.

On the other hand, does the imbalance in a region necessarily require the preponderant country to play the role of regional power? And if so what is that role? To carve out the region as its 'sphere of influence?' To influence the foreign and domestic policies of the countries of the region? To take charge of internal security and development of these countries? The phrase 'sphere of influence' harks back to the lexicon of the bygone imperial era before the second world war then the colonial countries divided the countries of Asia and Africa into their respective spheres of influence. Any such concept is repugnant to the high principles and noble ideals enshrined in India's policy enunciated before and after the independence – such as those conveyed by the term – Panchsheel viz. respect for sovereignty of other countries, equality, mutual respect, non-interference and non-intervention in each other territory.

While idealistic in purpose, India's foreign policy has always had regard to the practical aspect viz. it should be in India's self-interest, in the interest of peaceful and uninterrupted pursuite of the successful working of her democratic polity and her plans of economic development for raising the level of living of masses of her people. Rising military expenditure, and costly involvement or entanglement in military conflicts or operations or acceptance of unlimited economic burden for development of the countries in the region which must rightly belong to the people and governments of those countries would be quite contrary to India's self-interest in the short run as well as in the long run.

According to report published by US Government Arms Control and Disarmament Agency, South Asia led by Pakistan and India had the highest rate of growth of military expenditure. For 1985 the expenditure on military and defence establishments for South Asian countries was as follows – India $ 7.493 billion, Pakistan $ 2.378 billion, Bangladesh $ 253 million, Sri Lanka $ 167 millions, and Nepal $ 32 millions. The tally of armed forces in India – 1.515 million, Pakistan 644000, Bangladesh 91000, Nepal 25,000, Sri Lanka 21000 as against Soviet Union 4.5 million, China 4.1 million and USA 2.289 million. Military expenditure as percentage of GNP, Pakistan 6.36, India 3.81, Sri Lanka 2.66, Bangladesh 1.69 and Nepal 1.22. Military expenditure per capita – Pakistan $ 23, Sri Lanka $10, India $9, Bangladesh $2, Nepal $2. Armed forces per 100 – Pakistan 6.51, India 1.97, Nepal 1.47, Sri Lanka 1.31 and Bangladesh 0.9. Obviously regional considerations have significantly contributed to the rising military expenditure.

Another dimension of the concept of regional power would be the assertion of 'Monroe doctrine' for the region as a whole. India's involvement in Sri Lanka could interpreted as Indian version of the Monroe doctrine. However, where the superpowers are involved they are unlikely to be deterred by the assertion of the doctrine by what they consider to be mere regional power. Any sustained effort to back up 'Monroe doctrine' by mobilization of sufficient military strength by the regional power against the wishes or interest of a superpower is doomed to be a costly but an unsuccessful effort.

The only deterrence, if any, against the imperialistic behaviour of the world powers is the influence of well meaning people in those countries as well as the mobilization of the world opinion against such a behaviour. This was the grand object of the non-aligned movement established by the triumvirate – Nehru, Nasser and Tito. The movement today though larger in size, has of late lost some of its original moral fervour and commitment.

That needs to be restored and the ideals of the movement continuously reinterpreted and applied to the changing conditions of the world.

Weaning away countries of the region from the hegemony of world powers and persuading them to lend their support and commitment to the ideals of the non-aligned movement, is very much a part of the struggle for the success of such a movement. But such an effort does not need the concept of 'regional power'.

It is not clear who has fathered the concept of 'regional power'. Certainly Jawaharlal Nehru never encouraged such a role for India.

India's role is on the world stage. It cannot and should not be contained to a region. The role is of moral leadership in the pursuit of world peace, disarmament and an international order based on equity and justice. Such a role might be cynically dismissed as idealistic, self-righteous or impractical. But for the humanity at large the alternative to these objective and policies aimed at them is nuclear annihilation.

Good neighbourly relationship with countries of the region is but a part of India's larger perspective and pursuit of non-alignment and world peace. Regional hegemony is no part of this large framework. On the other hand, a confederation of the countries of the sub-continent is a goal which can be accomplished with patience and perseverance, good sense and practical statesmanship, such as the one which inspired Guy Monnet's imaginative leadership in establishing European Economic Community (EEC) which brought together the traditional foes – France and Germany.

What India needs is not some grandiose design stemming from a megalomania but dubious concept of a 'regional power' but the approach of taking decisions on merit in each case in pursuit of her own ideals of peaceful co-existence and sustained pursuit of socio-economic development and with down to earth assessment of her own long term self-interest.

Chapter - 2

Indo-American Relations in Perspective

So, at long last, John Winser's appointment as the American Ambassador to India has been cleared, a post lying vacant for more than twelve months. It was a matter of disappointment for the Indians that the nomination of Solarz to that post went haywire for reasons which even nor remain shrouded in mystery. That disappointment has not been assuaged by the appointment of a seasoned foreign service diplomat who in course of his examination by the Congress had no compunction in saying that India should think twice before releasing the Prithvi missile and that he does not support India's membership of the Security Council. Can he help in improving the status of Indo-American relationships which in recent months reached rock bottom with the gratuitous statement of Ms. Robin Raphel and President Clinton himself on the Kashmir situation? While Raphel in her speech to Asia Society equated the Kashir situation with civil war in Afganistan, Clinton on the occasion of presentation of credentials by Pakistan's ambssador Maleeka Lodhi, shared Pakistan's concerns about human rights abuses in Kashmir. Prime Minister Narasimha Rao's 'working visit' while notable for his address to the American Congress and his interface with American business did not remove the misgivings in the Indian mind about the intentions of the Clinton administration.

Ever since India became independent, there have been up and down relationships between the two countries – major downs than ups! There was every reason to believe that USA would be the best friend of free India. After, all President Roosvelt had taken up the cause of India's independence with Winston Churchill, during World War II. USA stood for liberty and democracy and India, was the first amongst the countries to emerge from colonialism to freedom and to adopt the constitution of a democratic republic. India expected that there would be a special relationship between the largest democracy in the world and the most affluent democracy of the world. Unfortunately this did not happen and India was both intrigued and disappointed. Insult was added to the injury when India found USA actually supporting reactionary and authoritarian regimes round the world - such as the regimes of Shah of Iran and the 'men on horse back' in Pakistan.

USA might have had her own reasons for doing so Nixon found Pakistan a useful go-between for improving relationship with China. Nixon's Secretary of State Mr. Henry Kissinger actually flew from Pakistan on his secret mission to China. Later Pakistan was an ally in pulling down Soviet bolstered regime in Afganistan.

On the other hand, India under Jawaharlal Nehru followed an independent policy both domestically and externally. USA obviously did not relish this assertion of independence. Externally, Nehru's policy of non-alignment, the only policy as Jawaharlal Nehru kept on saying free India could have adopted, was not to the liking of USA. In pursuance of this policy, India developed cordial relationship with USSR and tried to streer clear of the two super powers pitted against each other as leaders of two warring blocs –blocs engaged in a prolonged cold war in which India, in her pursuit for peace did not like to get involved. While India thought that the policy of non-alignment was the expression of India's high moral values, John Foster Dulles described it as immoral! And this froze the relationship between the two countries. John F. Kennedy tried to put American foreign policy on a high idealistic pedestal with his scheme of Peace Corps Volunteeers for developing countries in Asia and Africa. He had a high personal regard for Jawaharlal Nehru and was looking forward to his visit to USA but despite this when they met, Kennedy felt that Nehru was cold and the meeting was not much of a success. Ambassadors like Chester Bowler and John Kenneth Galbraith were friendly to India and made their own contribution to the development of friendly relationship between the two countries but could not reverse the long-term pro-Pakistani tilt of American foreign policy.

As USA under Nixon came closer to China, USA started pitting both the countries against India. In 1962 when China attacked India, USA came to India's rescue but in 1975 when India liberated Bangladesh, Nixon tried to threaten India with gunboat diplomacy which, thanks to Indira Gandhi's courage, did not succeed. But USA saw it as the attempt on the part on India to develop hegemonistic tendencies which it took upon itself to curb. It recognized Chine as a potential superpower but confined India to the status of a regional power. But even as a regional power USA would not allow India to develop hegemony in its own region!

If the policy of non-alignment was one assertion of India's independence, her steadfast refusal to sign the nuclear on proliferation treaty was another. On this also India felt that her position was fully justified on moral grounds.

USA did not take friendly to India's attempt to develop nuclear self-reliance and frowned upon underground Pokharan explosion (implosion). USA has done every arm twisting to curb India's nuclear and satellite technology ambitions, the latest being pressure on Russia to cancel cryogenic engine deal.

Nehru's economic policy was also repugnant to USA – the policy of planning for self-reliance and socialist pattern of society. Socialism in any form has always been an anathema to USA. It could not appreciate India's attempt to find a third way between unbridled capitalism on the side and totalitarian commune on other. Nor did it help India to develop the basic industries in the public sector. While Britain, Germany and USSR helped in setting up steel mills at Durgapur, Rourkela and Bhilai respectively, USA refused to do so. It confined its help agricultural extension service projects and agricultural universities.

In the new world scenario following the disintegration of the Soviet Union, Indian policies both domestically and externally have taken a U turn. India has gone from command-control economy to deregulation and liberalization, from comprehensive planning to marketisation, from public sector occupying the commanding heights of the economy to privatization, from autarky to globalisation. The Western World has started responding positively to these radical changes in India's macro economic policy. Britain and Germany have come closer to India after Major's visit to India and Indian Prime Minister's visit to Germany and his participation in Davos conference. But the same warmth is not shown by the policy makers in USA.

One reason for USA's lackadaisical attitude to India is traced to its perception of India as an overpopulated, poor, illiterate and violent prone country torn asunder by internal dessention. Even a so-called friend of Indian, Patrik Moynihan made the pejorative remark that the only exportable commodity from India was 'communicable diseases'! Thinkers in USA had from time to time written off India too soon. Selig Harroson described sixties as India's dangerous decade and had predicted that Indian democracy would soon dissolve. Paddock brothers applied the 'triage doctrine' to India and predicted that India would soon die of starvation. Both underestimated India's resilence! And now Ruper Murdock the press baron is so much impressed by India that he predicts India to emerge as a leading economic power in the twenty first century!

It was because of the perception that India was weak and insignificant that India, in the USA foreign policy frame work, was consigned to the position of being treated with 'benign neglect'. The latest example of this 'benign neglect' was the manner in which the recent visit of our Prime Minister was virtually ignored by the US media.

Would US policy makers realise that their perception needs to be revised? When they start looking at India as the largest democracy in the world, as a economy whose vast potentials are being liberated through the new economic policy of deregulation, as a country full of rich human resources adept in absorbing new knowledge and technology as seen by Indians occupying leading positions in the diverse professional and technological fields and above all as an ancient civilization with rich treasure of culture, they will realise that the time has come for a total reversal of their recent policy and for putting Indo-USA relationships on the high pedestal of warm friendship based on mutual understanding, respect and confidence.

Chapter - 3

Demise of Soviet Union and its Aftermath

Events have been taking place, in what once was Soviet Unions which is no more, at such breath-taking and mind-boggling speed that the full implications of these changes and their consequences have not yet been fully grasped, much less clearly analysed, even by thinking observers of the scene. What we have witnessed is not just the fall of an outstanding statesman of world stature, not even the disintegration and disappearance of super state, or collapes of an entire economic system or the final and decisive defeat of an ideology but indeed a basic transformation in the very context and structure of our thinking and our outlook on the course of history.

Fall of Gorbachev

That Gorbachev with all his initiative and leardership and his vision of glasnost and perestroika was faultering, because he had no clue for translating his vision into concrete reality had been evident for quite sometime past. Glasnost was running ahead of perestroika and mere invocation of perestroika could not make up for a miserable failure to ensure availability of supplies of essential consumer goods in the shops which became scene of empty shelves and long queues. A Yeltsin, who usurped his place without undue ceremony, observed, Gorbachev tried a half way house between communism and capitalism, the public sector and the private sector, free market and planning, centralization and decentralization and utterly failed in his attempt to harmonise the incompatiables. A country like India has worked precisely with such a system of 'mixed economy' and has been, with all its defects, able to get along with it, because unlike USSR, India never abolished the market or the private enterprise; therefore, the system of mixed economy could function.

Disintegration of a super state

The disintegration of one of the two super states could have been expected to lead to a situation where the sole surviving super state could appear to have the whole world left to itself to dominate and to command, but ironically enough already it would appear that the super state has been left without a role. With the threat of a competitive super state having vanished, it a appearing with all its faults naked and visible to the entire world. The threat of the competitive super state is no longer available as read herring to condone its lapses. It has helplessly to watch the emergence of an alternative power, even sounder and stronger than itself, though not necessarily hostile to it, that is the new United Europe. Nor it can continue to find fault with the emergence of Japan as a super economic power when the fault lies with the lack of competitiveness of its own economy.

Collapse of Communism

Less than three decades ago Kruschev proclaimed from the podium of the United Nations that 'we communists would bury capitalism'. He was articulating the arrogant self assurance and confidence of the communists the world over that the capitalist system was bound to collapse under the weight of its inner contradictions and give way to the superior socialist economic system. This confidence was basesd on the law of dilectic materialism of the so-called 'science of Marxism'. The Marxists confidently asserted that the capitalistic system could not be mended, it had to end. However, the theoretical formulations on which this conclusion was based were suspect from very beginning. Marxian critique of capitalism as an exploitative economic system was derived from the Marxism theory of value which stated that, the value of a good was equivalent to the socially relevant labour embodied in it, whereas the labour itself, the basic factor of production, got no more than what ws necessary to sustain it. The latter was much less then the labour value of goods and services that labour produced. This was the origin of the surplus value which was grabbed by the capitalists. Thus, capitalism flourished on the exploitation of labour. But the capitalism could not indefinitely flourish based as it was on such exploitation because it inevitably led to under consumption, to depression and the collapse of the capitalistic economic system.

All such Marxist prognostications regarding the collapse of capitalism proved to be utterly wrong. John Mayered Keynes was able to provide the theoretical basis for the understanding of the phenomenon of depression and to suggest a set of measures to sustain the capitalistic economy such as a compensatory fiscal policy and a public investment programme. The welfare economists suggested measures for social insurance, for re-distribution of income and regulation and control of monopoly. A capitalistic system need not be ended because it can be very well be mended.

Western capitalistic economies were also able to show that despite their democratic political organization, they could muster and mobilize resources during the war period much better than the totalitarian regimes.

The Marxian formulation of dilectice materialism was based on the economic interpretation of history. While Marxism was quite right in underlining the significance of economic factors in the historical evolution of the human society, it was quite flawed in turning this into sort of inflexible economic determinism which deprived it of proper understanding of human factors and values in human affairs.

On the other hand, economists like Fredrick Von Hayek had shown long back that the socialist system was not workable. The co-ordination of transactions of hundreds of producers and consumers of hundred of goods and services can be done only by the market and not by planners. Any attempt on the part of the planners to assume omniscience and omnicompetence in solving the simultaneous equations relating to hundreds of goods and services was doomed to failure. The plan of decentralized management of the socialist system proposed by Oscer Lange remained only on paper. The innovative management of socialism attempted in socialistic countries like Yugoslavia and Hungary had only a limited success. The predictions of Hayek relating to un-workability of the socialistic system of management of economy have been fully vindicated. In retrospect it is obvious that whatever success the socialistic economy was said to have accomplished in areas of industrialization and high technology was only at the cost of an unacceptable level of oppression. As Hayek had pointed out, concentration of economic power in a planned socialist economy was a road to serfdom. Those who concentrated economic power in their own hands had also the levers of political power through a monolithic party and intelligence services mechanism which they mercilessly used for exploitation of the society. This has been shown in all its nakedness by Alexander Solzhenitsyn in his famous book 'Guland Archipelago'.

Socialism could not even achieve equity and social justice – its apparent strong point in comparison with capitalism. On the other hand Acton's dictum – 'power corrupts and absolute power corrupt absolutely' came true and the sluggish Breznev era saw the worst forms of corruption and misuse of power for personal aggrandizement.

It is obvious that defeat of socialism as a ideology is not temporary; it is complete and final and irreversible. There will be no second chance for the establishment of a socialistic economy. It is gone once and for all. It is to be seen how much time surviving socialistic economies like Cuba and China would take before they also follow the Russian and Eastern European way.

However, it is obvious that the task of going from socialistic economy to capitalistic economy is going to be much more difficult than that of going from capitalistic feudalistic economy to socialistic economy. It will take years before the problems attendant to this transformation could be sorted out. In the meanwhile, these economies would be faced with severe economic problems in providing even the basic necessities of lives to their citizens.

However, the very existence of socialist economies had served a much bigger purpose of focusing attention on the importance of social justice and equity. It is this which inspired the newsly independent developing countries not to go for a unbridled capitalism or lasses faire but for planned socially oriented economy system. Even the Western capitalist countries could not overlook these considerations and had within them parties, groups and intellectuals who stood for policies aimed at these goals. The decisive defeat of socialism might well be detrimental to the very values of equity and social justice.

These values are of great importance even in the capitalistic economies. It is reported that even in the affluent countries like Germany, hundreds of people are houseless and are staying in open parks and abandoned public buildings. Can they be left to the market forces? Perhaps in the market euphoria generated by the eclipse of socialism, this may well happen.

The eclipse of socialism and the triumph of the market has led to the strident and unqualified assertion that only the market can provide the clue to poverty alleviation and 'sustainable' development because the market alone can provide for efficient allocation of resources. Poverty alleviation and environmental preservation can only be the by-product of efficient allocation of resources. All resources invested now on various kinds of public programmes or welfare measures are being interpreted as less than an efficient allocation of resources. The uncompromising admirers of the market like Margaret Thacher would like public services like housing and education and even basic state functions like tax collection to be privatized. At a time when the USA had a fiscal deficit of $250 billions, it is seriously contemplating that it could get out of recession by providing further tax concessions to the affluent classes. It would be great pity if the removal of socialism from the face of the earth were to mean the triumph of crass materialism, total rejection of all human and spiritual values and the denial all together of the moral basis of the economic order.

Chapter - 4

Osama, Obama and India's Foreign Policy

Indian reactions to cold blooded assassination of unarmed Osama Bin Laden by American commandos in a quick 40 minutes operation in a three storied mansion surrounded by a high wall in the garrison town Abotabad not far away from Pakistan's Military Academy, reflected the confusion and pusillanimity of Indian foreign policy and continuous decline in its robust independence and moral stature which characterized the foreign policy in the earlier years of Jawaharlal Nehru and which were maintained to an extent, by his successor Lal Bahadur Shastri and Indira Gandhi. The high point of India's independent foreign policy was reached when Indira Gandhi stood up to the abuses and threats of US President Nixon and his Secretary of State Henry Kisinger and Indian army won the war to liberate East Pakistan from the tyranny of Islamabad and gave birth to a new nation – a several times more spectacular achievement than the US commandos operation in Abotabad.

India did not speak with once voice. The PMO (not PM himself) issued a delayed statement , weak in content, which hardly made any mark and which was followed by even a weaker statement by the Minister of External Affairs. However, Chidambaram, the Home Minister, was quicker and more pointed in his response demanding Pakistan to handover the notorious terrorist leaders like Hafeez Mohammad Saeed, the head of Jamat-ud-Dawa, Maulana Masood, who formed a new terrorist organisation Jaish-e-Mohammad soon after India was forced to release him from prison in exchange of the lives of the passengers of the hi-jacked Indian plane from Khatmandu to Dehli the notorious gangster Daud Ibrahim responsible for the serial bombings in Mumbai and Lakhvi the mastermind of 26/11 horrific carnage in Mumbai which took many innocent lives including foreign tourists. But even more remarkable were statements of Army and Air Force chiefs who asserted that Indian forces were capable of launching a commondo attack of the type made by US commandos. Already deeply embarrassed by the successful US operation carried out without a whisper to the Pakistan authorities, both because it showed eloquently either the deception in hiding the presence of Osama whom US was in search of for several years and whose presence in Pakistan was denied by the Pakistan Civil and military authorities despite doubts expressed by no less a person, than by US Secretary of State Hillary Clinton or sheer incompetence of Pakistan's Security agencies, the ISI and the Army and more importantly the manner in which US trampled upon fact Pakistan's sovereignty as an independent nation, US President rubbed salt in the wounds when it said that, it would not hesitate to conduct a similar operation if and when needed Pakistan gave a prickly response to the statements of Chidambaram and the Army and Air force Chiefs. The Pakistan Foreign Secretary Salman Bashir brazenly characterrised Chidambaram's demand for return of 26/11 carnage plotters, as 'out of date' and warned our Army and Air force chiefs not to indulge in any 'misadventure'. The Army Chief Ashfak Kayani threatened a fitting reply in case India indulged in any misadventure such as America's recent commando operation Prime Ministers convivality with Pakistan Prime Minister Yusuf Raza Gilani at Thimpu and Mohali 'Cricket diplomacy' seemed to have almost been washed out by these acrimonious statements from Pakistan.

That the Pakistan Secretary for foreign affairs and not Chidambaram's counterpart Rehman Malik responded to Chidambaram was itself an affront. But he and the Army and Air Force Chiefs chose to keep quiet, since the Prime Minister had committed India to keep on 'talking' with Pakistan, no matter with what results! On the other hand US leaders were forthright. Both President Obama and CIA Chief Leon Penatta not only justified the commando operation without giving any prior intimation to Pakistan but also added that US would not hesitate to take similar action if need arose. On the other hand, they asserted that what US could do to avenge 9/11 by finishing its chief perpetrator Osama Bin Laden, India could not and should not do to punish the terrorists who plotted 26/11 in Mumbai in which more than 200 innocent people lost lives, many more badly injured and incapacitated and valuable property destroyed. US continued to indulge in double talk of a highly self centered nation which is concerned only about its own interest and has no concern for woes of others however insufferable they may be. To mollify the ruffled feelings of Pakistan, Obama thanked it for 'co-operation' in war against terrorism and promised continued economic and military assistance despite misgivings of US senate members. Obama had also a telephonic conversation with the Indian Prime Minister, what transpired is not known.

But what is becoming more and more apparent is that thanks to Nuclear Treaty and so called 'strategic alliance', India is coming under the US influence and submits to its will, agrees to play the role of a junior partner in US efforts to maintain its supremacy and hegemony and losing its 'independence' which was at the core of Nehru's policy of non-alignment. Our foreign policy is seen more and more as spineless and ineffective and without any sense of direction. This has created empty spaces in the India sub-continent which are filled by the two superpowers – USA and emerging China. Pakistan seeing India's weakness has successful sought the help of both the superpowers to act as a counterweight to India and deal with its on 'equal' terms, spurn India's offers and keep Kashmir 'dispute' alive by keeping on sending infiltrators.

The hope that some of us entertained hopes that bitterness of partition would be forgotten in course of time, the folly of 'two nation' theory would be realised and tied by bonds of lanaugage, culture, music, food and ways of life, the two nations would come closer and live like brothers have been belied. However, brotherly feelings do exist in the ordinary people of Pakistan is reported by many Indian visitors to Pakistan. The ancient university of Takshshila of which we Indians are proud is now in Pakistan. The great Sanskrit grammarian Panini belonged to that region. Both the current Prime Minister Manmohan Singh and the opposition leader L.K. Advani had spent their boyhood days in Pakistan. The author of '*Saare Jahan Se Acchaa*', the song we love, belonged to that region. The author of our both national song and Bangla Deshi national song 'Sonar Bangala' was the great Rabindranath Tagore. Pakistani visit *Ajmer Dargah* which for them is a holy shrine of worship. The Sikh's go for pilgrimage to Nankana Sahib, birth place of the founder of their faith, which is located in Pakistan. The Sri Lankans have their places of pilgrimage, *Bodh Gaya* and *Saarnath* in India. The great Buddha was born and lived in India. When such is our common heritage – indeed we are the same people though politically divided – why should we create spaces for USA and China to interfere? Both of them cannot speak our languages or savour our food. One of the central goals of our foreign policy should be to achieve solidarity amongst all the countries of the sub-continent through cultural exchange and economic co-operation for mutual benefit, share educational and other facilities and emerge as a single entity. If European Union could be formed in spite of greater differences between countries of the union, why cannot SARC achieve the birth of a single entity on the sub-continent?

Chapter - 5

Obama's US Presidency and India's Foreign Policy

Obama's arrival on Jan 20 as the new US President in succession to George Bush has been looked upon in some Indian quarters with certain amount of reservation and even misgivings. According to them, Republicans and not Democrates have been generally friendly to India. Bush was India's best friend. Prime Minister Manmohan Singh went to the extent of telling him that "Indians loved him !".

He sent his Secretary of State Condoleaza Rice with the message that US wants to help India to become a super power ! With this end in view, he took initiatives leading to Indo-US Nuclear Agreement and "strategic" alliance articulated through several agreements including that on military co-operation. He point blank refused Pakistan President Gen. Mushraff's request for a similar nuclear agreement making it clear to him that Pakistan cannot be equated with India, ending once and for all the hyphenated treatment of India and Pakistan. The US Ambassador David Mulford also underlined this in his TV interview. Bush refused to interfere with Kashmir issue expecting the two countries to settle it themselves. In his farewell address at the White House Bush specially mentioned strategic alliance with India as an achievement of his Presidency. This showed the extent of importance he attached to US-India relationship.

Despite all this "goodwill" for India, it should not be forgotten that at no time did Bush support India's longstanding case for membership of the UN Security Council. His "tilt" towards India could well have been a part of America's worldwide strategy aimed at maintaining America's un-questioned supremacy in the world. America (and Bush) looks upon China with her rapidly growing economic and military power, as a threat to its supremacy. It, therefore, needs India to counter balance China. Hence the pursuit of strategic and military alliance with India. America's support to democracy in India is a matter of convenience. When needed, America has never hesitated to support military dictatorship whether in Pakistan or Indonesia.

Will Obama maintain and develop this "cordial relationship" between two democracies- one described as the oldest and the other largest ? The reservations and misgivings about Obama stem from the interpretation of some of his utterances. As a Senator he moved amendments which might have stymied the nuclear agreement. Consistent with the stand of the Democratic party, he is likely to press for India signing the Comprehensive Test Band Treaty and NPT which India has steadfastly refused to do so far. He has linked the Kashmir issue with the war against the Taliban fighters on Pak-Afgan border. It has been hinted that Obama may appoint a special envoy on Kashmir and on Indo-Pak relationship.

It would be a great mistake for India to view's Obama's Presidency in narrow South Asian perspective, more specifically in the context of Indo-Pak relationship. A country like India should view it in a broader perspective or world view as it did to do in early years of Jawaharlal Nehru's leadership of foreign policy.

Obama's arrival as the 44th President of USA marks verily a revolution, a culmination of a long fight of the black (Afro-American) population for equality and human rights. This also has a message to all the oppressed people of the world. Obama has expressed his determination to bring about a qualitative change in internal and external policy which has created an atmosphere of hope and optimism all over the world. That explains the euphonic response in US and elsewhere to Obama's assumption of American Presidency.

The one major departure which Obama is likely to effect from his predecessor foreign policy is in respect of the overwhelming use of military power and war. This was exhibited in full measure in the "shock and awe" attacks on Afganistan and Iraq. Perhaps Bush and his close allies in policy-making Vice President Chenny and the ex. Defence Secretary Rummsfield intended to do the same in case of Iran and Syria. But US was so embroiled in Iraq that perhaps they had no opportunity to actually implement the threats extended to both these countries. Nor is Obama likely to uphold Bush's doctrine of "unilateralism" supported by military might. Obama will rather approach world problems through diplomacy and multilaterarism. He has already expressed his intention to engage in negotiations with Iran. He is likely to use the medium of UN to deal with problems arising in different parts of the world. World Peace rather than war is likely to be goal of his foreign policy.

In his inaugural speech he has eloquently spoken of his ardent desire to unite US bridging different segments of US population and unite humanity transcending national barriers. US he said, will be a friend of every country in the world. These were also the goals of Nehru's foreign policy as a result of which India took a lead in peace missions in different parts of the world.

Obama's support for CTBT and NPT need not cause misgivings to India. India opposed signing these treaties because it felt that they are discriminatory. If the discriminatory approach is given up and abolition of nuclear weapons becomes the goal to be pursued by all nations, big and small, then India should have no hesitation in supporting such an approach. After all this was the keynote of Rajiv Gandhi's proposals made on the forum of UN which were largely ignored by the nuclear powers.

Recession is the biggest economic challenge which Obama will have to face. Even Bush, sworn to capitalist market economy and minimalist state, had to introduce $ 700 billion bail out plan. Obama is likely to follow Keynes rather than Friendmen in dealing with recession. In his inaugural address he has talked of a big infrastructure development plan and welfare plan with emphasis on high quality health services which should encourage similar programme in different countries including the developing ones which under the influence of "Washington Consensus" formed by the Republicans over two decades were perforce required to undertake structural adjustment programmes and so called fiscal discipline with reduced public expenditure with disastrous consequences on the living condition of the poor and the have-nots. This might well pave the way for the reemergence of the concept of New International Economic Order (NIEO) which was rejected under the American influence during the Republican ergime. All in all India should welcome the "regime change" in US.

In this new context India should think of giving up its pusillanimous policy of being a junior partner of the USA and go back to its initial years after independence when India stood for ideals of world peace, equality, freedom and fair play and followed an independent foreign policy based on those ideals.

Index

Q

T